Fly There For Less

Other books by Bob Martin

- *Travel For Less:*
  How to Slash Costs Without Sacrificing Quality

- *Orlando and Disney World:*
  A TravelVenture Guide

Fly There For Less

How to Slash the Cost of Air Travel Worldwide
Third Edition

by **Bob Martin**

TeakWood Press
Kissimmee, Florida

Copyright © 1992 by Bob Martin

Published by:

TeakWood Press, Inc.
160 Fiesta Drive
Kissimmee, Florida 34743
407-348-7330
Order Desk: 800-654-0403

Cover design by Paul LiCalsi, L&L Graphics
Printed in the United States of America

Library of Congress Cataloging-in-Publication Data
Martin, Bob, 1939-
    Fly there for less : how to slash the cost of air travel
worldwide / Bob Martin. -- 3rd ed.
        p.   cm.
    Includes index.
    ISBN 0-937281-08-5 (pbk.) : $16.95
    1. Airlines--Rates. 2. Airlines--Reservation systems. I. Title.
HE9783.5.M37 1992
387.7'12--dc20   91-45532
                                              CIP

Contents

Introduction

To save money on airline tickets, you need to know more than your travel agent's phone number and where you want to go. Since deregulation of the domestic airlines in 1978, air fares have become complicated and constantly changing. So much so that the air-travel marketplace resembles a bazaar.

Early deregulation opened up the airline industry to new carriers. Hundreds of fledgling airlines took off to challenge the older, established lines. The early '80s were tumultuous years that saw heavy, low-fare-generating competition among airlines.

But by 1988 the number of airlines had dropped dramatically. More than 200 carriers had flown into bankruptcy. Additional lines were lost to mergers — Pan Am absorbed National Airlines, Piedmont joined USAir, TWA bought out Ozark, Northwest picked up Republic and Delta took in Western Airlines.

As an air traveler, this consolidation of the airline industry has hurt you. Competition has decreased and fares have risen. Between 1988 and early 1991, promotional fares on the 20 most-traveled routes — routes where a measure of competition still exists — rose an average of 37 percent and full fares jumped 45 percent. Measure those increases against the Consumer Price Index which, during those same years, rose just 13.3 percent.

Unfortunately, that's the good news! The bad news is that travelers flying non-competitive routes — those served by only one or two carriers — have seen fares skyrocket. Air travelers between Chicago and Cincinnati, for example, pay an average FIVE TIMES more than passengers flying about the same distance but on the more-competitive San Diego-Las Vegas route. Chicago-Louisville, Minneapolis-Omaha and Cincinnati-Detroit passengers — just to name a few — have all found themselves paying sharply higher air fares.

Many air travelers, regardless of whether they travel for business or pleasure, now face the significant challenge of keeping the cost of flying from breaking their budget. Air travel costs are taking an increasingly larger bite out of business profits. And leisure travelers are finding themselves making fewer trips or having to stay closer to home, even postponing visits to relatives, friends or destinations they've longed to see.

But, my traveling friend, you haven't seen anything yet. In the not-too-distant future you may very well look back on the level of today's fares with nostalgia for the good old days — for the second phase of airline consolidation is upon us.

The shape of things to come

This second phase is going to leave fewer carriers yet, but these lines will be stronger. They will dominate the routes they fly and the airports they serve. And their domination will allow them to set fares at whatever level they feel is appropriate.

Already the industry has started to undergo significant changes. Carriers whose very names were for decades synonymous with air travel are in bankruptcy or even disappearing completely. Pan American World Airways, one of the earliest globe-spanning carriers, has flown into oblivion. TWA — Trans World Airlines, which traces its roots back to 1928 — is struggling on the brink of bankruptcy and making plans to scale down. And Eastern Airlines, founded by aviation-pioneer Eddie Rickenbacker, has ceased to exist.

You can get a glimpse of what the future holds by looking at the consequences of Eastern going out of business. Upon its demise, fares between cities once served by Eastern mushroomed. Within two weeks one carrier raised its lowest fare between the northeastern United States and Florida from $158 to $430!!! Chicago-Miami fares on American Airlines shot up from $225 to $379!

While Eastern was still flying, it and Delta Air Lines were the dominant carriers serving Atlanta. Delta flew about 450 Atlanta flights daily, Eastern operated about 330. No other independent airline flew more than 20 Atlanta flights a day. With air travel to and from that city tied up between just two carriers, Atlanta fares were traditionally among the industry's highest.

When Eastern went under, that left travelers arriving or departing Atlanta at the mercy of Delta Air Lines. With Delta flying more than 20 times the flights of its closest competition, the airline is unchallenged. Atlanta fares will be what Delta wants them to be.

The airline industry's second consolidation phase will yield a four-tier marketplace dominated by three mega-carriers: American Airlines, Delta Air Lines and United Airlines. Behind these three will be a tier of smaller carriers: Northwest Airlines, TWA, USAir and possibly — unless it merges to get out of bankruptcy — Continental Airlines.

These second-tier carriers will provide some competition where they fly the same routes as the mega-carriers. But their route structures will be substantially smaller than those of the Big

Three. American Airlines, for example, offers passengers twice as many seat miles as USAir.

The third tier will be made up of a handful of small carriers such as: Alaska, Aloha, America West and Southwest. When sharing common routes, these carriers will provide competition for the upper two tiers. But their route structures are small. Southwest flies just 2.6 percent of the air travel industry's available seat miles. Compare that to mega-carrier United's 16.8 percent.

The fourth tier will be made up of small regional airlines with little or no impact on the competitive establishing of fares.

So fares have no where to go but up — dramatically where monopoly and near-monopoly situations exist, somewhat less dramatically where some competition remains.

When you make an international flight, you are no better off. International fares are regulated and not established by competition. They are fixed by agreement between governments and the airlines. Consequently, you will always pay more for your international ticket than if its price were determined by a free market.

Complexity rules the air-travel bazaar

Increasingly higher fares are not the only problem you have to contend with. In the years since Congress deregulated the U.S. airline industry, air travelers have seen an unprecedented era of fare complexity.

Before 1978, if you flew from New York to Los Angeles, the fact that you were flying 2,446 air miles determined the price of your ticket. Today, how much you pay will depend not so much on the number of miles you fly, but upon:

    • your understanding of the air-travel marketplace;

- how flexible you can be;
- the airline you choose;
- where you buy your ticket;
- how savvy a shopper your are.

Before deregulation of the domestic airlines, fares were stable. They were published in bound volumes that changed quarterly. Today, computer systems process and track more than 250,000 fare changes daily. That's a quarter of a million new fares EVERY DAY! And half-a-dozen passengers on the same flight, sitting in the same row, could very likely each pay a different fare — with hundreds of dollars difference between the highest and lowest fares.

Although government-controlled international fares are relatively stable, their volume is staggering. A computer printout of international fares fills some 40,000 pages. And a Miami-Tokyo passenger who paid an airline's lowest promotional fare of $1,325 could very well sit next to a savvy Miami-Tokyo passenger who paid just $698 — a $627 difference!

**You can cut through the high cost and the complexity
to fly there for less**

How did that fare-smart passenger go about saving $627 on his ticket?. Actually, as I'll show you, it's not that difficult if you understand the air-travel marketplace and know the techniques of savvy fare shopping.

"I don't see how anyone can save money on air fare. You have to pay what the airlines tell you," a skeptical woman once said to me. Not being a razor-sharp salesman, I did not immediately reply, "Then, madam, you obviously need to read my book."

Instead, I tried to be helpful. I explained to her a few of the hundreds of ways you can go about lowering the cost of your air fare.

Unfortunately, that lady's outlook is all too typical of many air travelers. They feel calling an airline or travel agent is the best they can do. Even many business travelers who fly frequently and spend substantial sums on air travel feel that just calling their favorite travel agent will get them the lowest fare available.

You CANNOT depend on an airline reservationist or a travel agent to get you the lowest fare. Media and consumer agencies time and again have conducted surveys in which they call a dozen or so airlines and travel agents requesting the lowest fare for a given itinerary. These surveys, several of which I'll cite later, consistently show differences of up to hundreds of dollars between the "lowest" fares quoted by various reservationists — both airline clerks and travel agents.

Studies conducted by travel management firms also show that even travel agents specializing in business travel often fail to come up with the lowest fare for their clients.

I am not putting down travel agents and airline reservationists. These people can be extremely helpful in your efforts to find the lowest fare to your destination. But they operate under handicaps placed upon them by the nature and structure of the airfare marketplace. In addition, they must deal with the day-to-day realities of the business world, which are not always conducive to finding you the lowest fare.

There is only one person you can depend on to see that you get the lowest available fare — that person is YOU! You have to know enough about air fares and the air-travel bazaar to be able to do your own homework.

Just as I divide the airlines into tiers, I also place air travelers into tiers — two of them:

1) those unknowing air travelers who call a travel agent or an airline reservationist and — even if they should ask for the lowest fare available — spend hundreds more of their hard-earned dollars than is necessary because they accept the fare quoted them.

2) those savvy, fare-smart air travelers who know how the airlines establish and market their fares, who know the various types of fares available to them, who know where and how to shop for air fares, and who know how to turn airline marketing strategies into low-fare flying opportunities.

Take heart my friend, I am going to open your eyes to today's world of air travel and turn you into that savvy, fare-smart air traveler.

As long as flights take off with empty seats, you can cut the cost of your air travel. You can take steps, use a variety of techniques and employ certain strategies that will SAVE YOU UP TO HUNDREDS OF DOLLARS each and every time you fly.

If you are a business traveler, you may find these fly-for-less strategies go beyond just saving you money to actually enhancing the prospect of your business survivability. If you don't want the future cost of flying to bust your budget, you will have to know how to fly there for less. Should your competition use these techniques, you had better too just to stay even. And if they don't, you've got the edge on them.

Whether you are preparing for just a single air trip or are a travel-weary frequent flyer, become familiar with the information I am going to reveal to you. Then put it to use when you shop for airline tickets, and you'll save money — I GUARANTEE IT! In fact, THIS BOOK WILL RANK AMONG THE BEST INVESTMENTS YOU HAVE EVER MADE — and the more you fly, the more you will value it.

What you'll find in this book

I'll start at the beginning, with the basics, and move through progressively more sophisticated money-saving techniques and strategies. The material is not difficult — some have called it easy, others well-ordered and logical. And even before you've completed the book, you can start using the information to cut the cost of your air fare.

Applying the information is easy as well. I've packed these pages with the names, addresses, and telephone numbers — many toll-free — of the contacts you need.

Here's an overview of what you'll get:

• Chapter 1. Every traveler needs to know the basics, and that's what I cover in this first chapter. You'll find out how to put money-saving flexibility into your travels and how to select flights that offer low fares. You'll get a complete look at how promotional fares work and how you can obtain maximum benefit from them. Neglect these simple, easily applied techniques, and you'll wind up paying more for your air fare than you have to. Use them and you'll save.

• Chapter 2. This chapter is the only one that does not show you how to save money. Instead it shows you how to hold on to the savings you make by avoiding the costly pitfalls awaiting the unwary in today's air-travel bazaar. I'll show you how to cope and deal with airline bankruptcies, nonrefundable and lost tickets, excess and overweight baggage as well as airline bumping policies that can strand you and destroy the schedule you've planned for your destination.

• Chapter 3. You cannot buy a low-cost ticket unless you first find a low fare. Properly using just three simple tools found around every home and office, you can come up with the lowest fare to your destination, anywhere in the world. This chapter shows you how.

• Chapter 4. Airlines offer a variety of not-so-well-known fares that will cut your air travel costs. Finish this chapter and you will know your way around money-saving status fares, stopovers, travel packages, standby fares, round-the-world fares and those incredible air passes that let you fly more for less — much less.

• Chapter 5. Here I'll show you that all airlines are not the same. Knowing the differences in their operating philosophies and objectives will allow you to pick the airline that can get you to your destination for the least amount of money.

• Chapter 6. Most travelers buy their tickets from an airline or a standard travel agency. You'll be amazed, however, at the different types of outlets offering airline tickets. You'll be even more amazed at the savings Chapter 6 shows you how to get using these ticket sources. Your discoveries will include no-frills travel agencies, discount ticket brokers, a ticket auction and even air courier brokers.

• Chapter 7. A variety of cost-cutting clubs and programs are available to you, the low-fare shopper. Some are free, others charge a membership fee, but they'll all help you fly there for less. In this chapter I'll show you how to use to advantage these clubs and programs — including frequent-flyer plans, last-minute travel clubs and bartered-travel organizations.

• Chapter 8. Circumstances and situations, both within the airline industry and external to it, can offer you opportunities to slash your air fare. Here you'll find what to watch for and how to take money-saving advantage of such things as fare wars, strikes, international currency fluctuations, economic slowdowns and more.

• Chapter 9. I'll reveal to you in this final chapter how to turn the shape of today's air-travel marketplace — its complexity, its competitiveness — into cost-cutting, low-fare opportunities. You can employ these imaginative strategies to top the airlines at their own game.

A bit about who I am

I am a traveler. I have been traveling all my life. My fortunes at any one time have determined whether I would journey frugally or go first class. But, regardless of the size of my travel budget, I have always tried to get good value for the money I've spent. I don't enjoy paying more than I have to for a given product or service. And when someone else pays less than I do, I want to know what that person knows that I don't.

Not spending more than I have to when traveling is important to me. Being a savvy shopper lets me upgrade and even extend my travels. If I can shave thirty bucks off an airline ticket, it can go toward a fine meal in a special restaurant. Better to put it into my belly than an airline's corporate coffers. If I can save several hundred dollars, I may be able to take a trip when I otherwise could not.

I must admit, though, that when it comes to getting maximum value from my travel dollars, I have an edge over most travelers. I know how the travel industry works! As a writer with a love for travel, I was fortunate enough to obtain jobs writing and editing training lessons and textbooks — including college-level texts — for the travel industry. This gave me an insider's knowledge of the entire industry, from airlines to cruise lines, from tour operators to hotels.

Later, as editor of a consumer-travel newsletter, I was able to put my knowledge of the industry to work helping other travelers obtain maximum value for their travel dollars.

Then, as the head of a publishing business, I had to take a different view toward saving money on travel — especially air fares. No longer was cutting travel costs a matter of wanting to get the best value for my money. Now it became essential to the continued operation of my business. Facing the sky-high airline fares of the short-notice business traveler forced me to expand my travel-shopping horizons. I had to learn and develop techniques and strategies that would allow me to obtain the absolutely lowest air fares possible. And I did — survivability is a powerful motivator.

Like all who journey widely, I have developed a travel philosophy. Among my convictions is the idea that the benefits of travel far outweigh any drawbacks. Therefore, I encourage travel. All too often, however, among the reasons people find for not traveling is cost. *Fly There For Less* — and its companion book, *Travel For Less* — are my contributions to helping overcome that obstacle.

Some ground rules

Before I move on to the ground rules of shopping for low air fares, let's go over some ground rules covering my approach in this book.

I do not tell you that the lowest fare between points x and y is on airline z, information that could very well be outdated five minutes after I write it. Instead, I'll show you how the airline industry establishes its fares and markets its flights. And I'll reveal to you a multitude of timeless tips, tactics and strategies that take advantage of these marketing patterns to let you consistently pay the lowest possible air fare.

These strategies range from the basics — selecting the right days and times for the least expensive flights — to creative techniques such as buying two round-trip tickets instead of one to save money. And these strategies work. Everyday, travelers in the know — both leisure and business travelers — use them to cut the cost of their air fare.

To illustrate just how much a particular strategy can save you, I've used examples that include actual fares. Of course, these fares are no longer valid. But they are representative of the savings involved.

When I compare two or more fares, the fares will be for the same ticket class and will have been valid at the same time. The examples show the actual dollar spread available to any air traveler at one time in the past. When you use the strategy, you may pay more — or perhaps less — for your ticket, but the savings over the alternative will still be about the same.

Do not take my mentioning an airline, a travel agency, a travel supplier or any other firm in this book as a recommendation. Providing contact information is simply an aid to help you explore your options. Neither I nor TeakWood Press vouch for any of the companies listed or mentioned. To play it safe when dealing with a company unknown to you, check with the better business bureau in the firm's hometown.

Okay, let's get started saving you money.

1

Your first steps to air-fare savings

Every traveler needs to know the basic strategies for obtaining the lowest air fares. These are the ground rules. If you don't use them, you're paying more than you should for air travel. Apply them to your travels, and you'll fly there for less.

Flexibility — you need it, but it's not as difficult to get as you think

Here's the primary rule for obtaining low air fares: be flexible! The more flexible you can be, the greater your potential savings. Being flexible can sometimes involve nothing more than putting yourself into the proper mental outlook. Think flexibility — to yourself and in your planning. Be willing to modify every aspect of your trip — your airport, your airline, your departure time, your return date. Be willing to make a stop en route instead of flying nonstop. And if you're a leisure traveler, even be willing to reconsider your destination. The pages that follow will show these ideas are not as startling as they may at first sound.

Flexibility for leisure travelers

Many leisure travelers plan a trip by first deciding when and where they want to go. Then they start looking for the lowest fare. That's the expensive way. They've already locked themselves into a destination and a set of departure-return dates.

Take a flexible approach when planning your trip and you'll save money. Give yourself flexibility by initially keeping your options wide open. At first, choose a geographical area rather than a specific city. Germany rather than Munich. Just Europe would be better still. Next decide on a general time frame for your visit. Don't be too specific. Plan in terms of seasons rather than months — fall instead of October, late spring and early summer instead of June. Then, using the strategies that follow, you'll be able to compile a list of fares for various destinations in your geographical area for different dates within your time frame. Once you've gathered the information, zero in on the specific city and pair of departure-return dates that will give you the lowest fare.

Flexibility for business travelers

Business travel has an image of inflexibility. As a business traveler you may not have the leisure traveler's range of flexibility, but you do have available numerous flexibility options that will cut the cost of business travel. As you go through the techniques and strategies that follow, you, too, must think flexibility. For example, you're planning a major sales meeting that has the sales force flying in from distant points. Schedule the meeting for a travel off-season. Aim for the lower fares of spring and fall rather than the higher fares of summer.

Although business needs dictate your geographic destinations, don't stop thinking flexibility. Before setting up appointments and meetings for a multiple-city itinerary, for example, determine the lowest air fares between the cities you'll be visiting. Domestic fares are not always based on distance. On highly competitive routes, distance is often not even a consideration. Therefore, your fare on a multiple-city domestic itinerary can vary with the order in which you visit each city.

International fares, on the other hand, tend to based upon mileage flown. Therefore, you want to arrange your multiple-city international itinerary so that you continuously move forward as though along a loop. Avoid backtracking which will increase your mileage and thus your costs.

The sequence of stops along your loop, however, will likely be vulnerable to fare differences. At one time you would have saved about $300 if you were flexible enough to fly a loop from Los Angeles to Tokyo to Hong Kong and back to Los Angeles rather than flying a Los Angeles-Hong Kong-Tokyo-Los Angeles loop.

When fare shopping, your itinerary should be flexible enough so you can arrange stopovers in the order that will yield the cheapest fare. Start your air-fare hunt equipped only with the cities you need to visit and a general time frame for visiting them. After determining a routing that will give you the lowest fare, schedule your contacts to fit your low-fare itinerary.

The strategies that follow will show how flexibility can pay off in big savings for both the leisure and the business traveler. Even a minimum of flexibility, such as being able to change a departure time by an hour or two, will let you arrive with more of your money in *your* wallet.

Off-peak flights — an easy step to savings

Shift your departure time just a couple of hours and you could save significantly. Most travelers, particularly business travelers, want flights that depart and arrive between about 7 a.m. and 9 p.m. These are the peak hours for air travel. To tempt flexible-thinking travelers to switch their departures to late-evening or early-morning flights, airlines cut their fares during these off-peak hours.

Delta Air Lines, for example, once wanted $260 for a 7:35 a.m. peak flight from Nashville to Houston. If you left at 6 a.m. instead, you would have been on a $208 off-peak flight with an extra $52 to spend in Houston. Another airline sold one-way tickets between Indianapolis and Orlando, Florida, for $99 peak. If you shifted your departure time to off-peak, however, you would have gotten the ticket for $79. And still another carrier priced seats on a 7:30 a.m. flight at half the price of its more-popular 9:30 a.m. flight.

Many airline timetables indicate which flights are off-peak. If you regularly fly a few particular airlines, pick up a copy of their timetables at the airport. And on your next flight, fly off-peak and save.

Weekday or weekend — what a difference a day makes

The day of the week on which you fly can make a difference in the fare you'll pay. Airlines charge higher fares when demand for air travel is high. But demand can vary according to the day of the week.

On an international flight, avoid weekends. Because of work and vacation schedules, travelers tend to fly to and from overseas destinations on weekends. To shift some of those passengers, airlines offer lower fares on weekday international flights. TWA once sold weekend tickets on its New York-Copenhagen route for $785 round trip. If you flew on a weekday, however, you could have gotten that ticket for $735 and saved $50. And if your spouse was flying with you, your savings jumped to a $100.

USAir charged passengers on its Orlando-Frankfurt route $458 to fly on a Friday, Saturday or Sunday. For travelers flying

Monday through Thursday USAir's fare dropped $60 to $398.

Flying within the United States the situation is less clear cut. Some airlines offer cheaper fares for weekend flights. One airline charged $52 for its Monday flights between Houston and San Antonio. But on a Sunday flight the cost was $36.

Because fewer business travelers fly during the middle of the week, most airlines also offer lower fares on their midweek flights — Tuesday through Thursday. When shopping for air fares, be flexible about your departure day and ask the reservationist if fares are cheaper on certain days of the week.

Travel seasons — they greatly affect the cost of your ticket

In addition to varied demand throughout the week, demand for airline seats varies throughout the year. And as you just saw when selecting the day of the week for your flight, when demand is high you can count on fares being high. However, if you fly when demand is down, fares will also be down. And you'll reap the savings.

European travel seasons

Flights between the United States and Europe have three distinct travel seasons. Demand for European flights is highest in summer. From about June 15 to September 1 is the peak or high season, and you'll pay peak dollar. But if you fly on June 14 instead, this one-day change will put you into the shoulder season, a season of lower fares. Usually — but not always — the date you start your round trip determines the travel season into which your flight falls.

April to mid-June and September through October generally fall into the shoulder season. But you'll get the greatest savings from November through March, the off-season (also called basic season, low season and off-peak season).

At one time, KLM Royal Dutch Airlines would have flown you off-season between Chicago and Amsterdam for $739 round trip. KLM's shoulder season flights on that Chicago-Amsterdam route jumped to $819. High season flights leapt to $938. By flying off-season instead of peak, you would have saved $199.

Other international travel seasons

Flights to other areas of the world also have peak and off-peak seasons that vary with demand for air travel. When searching for the lowest fare, keep in mind that peak and off-peak seasons can vary depending on the destination. While the summer vacation months are Europe's peak season, the wintery December through April months have North American travelers packing for the sunny warmth of the Caribbean, causing a peak-demand season.

If you're bound for the Far East, Japan Air Lines says their flights are full during August, their busiest month. But demand is down during January and February when about 40 percent of Japan Air Lines' seats fly empty.

When heading down under to Australia, you'll pay low season fares from April through August. Since Australia is south of the equator, their summer and winter months are the reverse of those in countries north of the equator. And on such a long-distance flight, seasonal fare differences are substantial. Qantas Airways, the Australian airline, once set its Los Angeles-Melbourne peak-season fare at $1,395. The fare dropped to $1,195 during the shoulder season and $995 off season. That's a $400 difference between peak and off-peak fares.

For planning, here's a range of travel seasons over some broad geographical areas. Seasons can vary, though, for different destinations within these broad areas. When checking fares with a reservationist, verify the travel seasons for your specific destination.

- Asia - High season: June through December, shoulder season: April and May, low season: January through March.

- Caribbean - High season: mid-December through mid-April plus July and August, low season: September through mid-December and mid-April through June.

- Europe - High season: mid-June through August, shoulder season: September through October and April through mid-June, low season: November through March.

- South America - High season: December through March, low season: April through November.

- South Pacific - High season: December through March, shoulder season: September through November, low season: April through August.

U. S. travel seasons

For flights within the United States, deregulation has blurred the distinction between airline travel seasons. The rule, however, still applies: when demand is up, fares will be up.

More people fly in summer than winter, and you'll pay more for a summer flight. While fares tend to be lower for winter travel — January and February are especially low-demand months — demand will be higher during holiday periods and for flights to popular winter destinations such as Colorado's ski slopes.

When planning travel, call a travel agent or an airline reservationist to determine the low- and peak-demand travel seasons for your destination. Then schedule your trip for a low-demand season and save. And if you are completely flexible, remember, it's always off- or shoulder season somewhere.

Promotional fares — your all-around money savers

Most airlines offer three classes of fares: first, business and coach or economy. *Coach* is the term used for domestic flights, *economy* applies to international flights. First and business class offer amenities such as roomy seats and upgraded meal service. Consequently, these classes are more expensive.

To fly first class on American Airlines from New Orleans to Acapulco, Mexico, once cost $524 round trip. Business-class tickets sold for $480, while economy class cost $422. Obviously, the savings are significant for travelers who fly economy. All three of these fares, however, are full fares.

As a low-fare traveler, you'll want to avoid full fares. Think of them as being similar to the sticker price on a new car. You know you shouldn't pay the sticker price because the auto dealer will likely offer you a discount. And so it is with airline tickets. You shouldn't pay the full fare because the airlines will offer you a discount.

The airlines know from experience they will not always sell all seats on all flights. Each empty seat, however, represents lost revenue that can never be recouped. If an airline can fill some of those seats that would otherwise remain empty, they gain additional revenue. So the airlines offer a portion of each flight's seats at discounted prices known as promotional fares. The airlines also know that these lower, promotional fares will do their job and will attract more passengers to their flights, particularly leisure travelers who would otherwise not be flying.

These reduced-price promotional fares offer substantial savings over full fares. In the case of the round-trip flight between New Orleans and Acapulco, American Airlines offered some seats at a $319 Advance Purchase Excursion fare — an Apex fare. The Apex promotional fare saved travelers $103 over the lowest full fare.

Apex is the name for these promotional fares on international flights. On domestic flights, where deregulation has spurred competition, Apex has given way to a variety of names created by the airlines' marketing people. Look for names such as: Super Saver, Easy Saver, Ultra Saver, Ultimate Super Saver or MaxSaver. If you stick with the term *promotional fare,* though, you'll get your point across.

There is no difference between the seating and service provided travelers on a full-fare coach or economy ticket and those on a promotional-fare ticket. Yet promotional fares are set between 20 and 80 percent lower than coach or economy fares.

Obviously, any New Orleans-Acapulco passenger would want to pay American's lower-priced Apex fare instead of the full economy fare. After all, the passenger would be sitting in the same seat and eating the same meal as if he or she had paid the full economy fare. But if every passenger bought promotional-fare tickets, the airline would not sell any of its higher-priced economy tickets. And remember that American only wanted to offer promotional fares on seats expected to otherwise go unsold. To prevent selling all its seats at promotional fares, American and all the other airlines limit the availability of these fares.

Capacity control and yield management limit your use of promotional fares

The airlines set aside only a certain number of seats on each flight to be sold at promotional fares. After those seats are sold, passengers will have to pay full coach fare. In airline jargon, promotional fares are capacity controlled.

To determine how many seats will be offered at promotional fares, the airlines rely on a process known as yield management. Each airline employs a sophisticated computer program that uses past and present ticket sales to track the demand for each of its flights. Based on the projected demand, the computer divides each flight's seats between full and promotional fares with the goal of selling all seats on a flight while maximizing the number sold at full fares and minimizing the number sold at promotional fares. In effect, the yield management strategy enables an airline to sell the same product at a variety of prices.

Yield management is an on-going, continual process. It begins as much as a year before a flight's departure and continues right up to the day the plane takes off. As the computer updates its estimates based on the latest ticket sales, the airline will modify the flight's promotional and full-fare allocations. If a flight begins to fill up quicker than expected, the computer cuts the number of promotional-fare seats, assigning them to full fare. Conversely, when a flight sells slower than expected, the number of promotional-fare seats is increased.

Just how many seats each airline allocates for promotional fares is a closely guarded secret. On the average, about 20 to 40 percent of an airline's total seats may be assigned to these fares. That percentage can vary widely, however, depending on the demand for air travel and the degree of competition among the airlines. And that 20 to 40 percent does not apply evenly to every flight. On a peak-season, peak-hours flight which the airline feels will sell out, there may be no promotional-fare seats at all. Other flights may have only a mere handful, less than 10 percent. Still others, particularly off-peak flights, may offer most of their seats at promotional fares.

Restrictions also hamper your use of promotional fares

Most business travelers have to travel, often on short notice, and will take a flight regardless of whether they can get a promotional fare. Therefore, to keep business travelers from using promotional fares, the airlines put varied restrictions on them. (If you travel on business, subsequent chapters will show you techniques that will let you obtain promotional-fare tickets.)

Here's a look at some typical promotional-fare restrictions. If a flight has empty seats, an airline will sell you a full coach or economy ticket right up to boarding time. But promotional fares carry a restriction that says you must buy your ticket in advance of your flight date, anywhere from two to 30 days in advance. Usually, the further ahead you buy the more you'll save.

In addition to requiring an advance purchase, promotional fares have other restrictions. They may carry a cancelation penalty. If you have to alter your flight plans or even turn the ticket in for a refund, you will pay a substantial percentage of its cost as a penalty. These tickets may also be completely nonrefundable and nonchangeable, which means you cannot get a refund nor change your flight plans, regardless of the reason.

In addition, promotional fares are generally available only for a round trip. They also stipulate a minimum and maximum number of days you must spend at your destination. Typically, the minimum is set at seven days, or the airline may simply require that your stay include a Saturday night, there again trying to prevent business travelers from using promotional fares.

These lower-cost promotional fares are what you want to aim for, but to fly at these fares you need to plan ahead. Not only to meet the advance-purchase requirement, but also to buy your ticket before the airline sells the limited number of low-fare seats allocated to your flight. And you'll still need a measure of flexibility to avoid peak flights with few if any promotional-fare seats.

Early bookings get greater savings

Buying your ticket up to 30 days in advance to get a promotional fare may seem like firming up your plans early. But if you can even go beyond that and fix your travel dates three or more months ahead of time, you may be able to fly to Europe for less. Some U.S. and European airlines occasionally set a special early booker promotional fare for European-bound passengers flying between May and September. To be eligible for the early booker fare, though, you have to make your reservation no later than the last day of February.

One year, the lowest promotional fare for a peak-season New York-Copenhagen flight on SAS, the Scandinavian airline, was $875. But passengers who booked their flight no later than February paid $815 and saved $60. If there are several passengers in your party, that $60 saving quickly adds up.

Waitlisting — a tactic to use when you can't get a promotional fare

If the flight you want has only full-fare seats left, and you don't have the flexibility to try for another flight, ask the airline or travel agent to "waitlist" you. The reservations computer will list your name as waiting for a promotional fare. Additional seats may be allocated to promotional fares as the airline shifts the flight's seat inventory in response to the yield-management computers. Canceled reservations can also make more low-fare seats available. These additional promotional-fare seats are then assigned to passengers on the waitlist before being offered to the public.

Here's an important point. Computers give priority to the order in which names are added to the waitlist. But order is not the only consideration; the computer also looks at the size of the party. If a single promotional-fare seat opens up, the computer will skip over parties of two or more. To increase your chances of getting off the waitlist and picking up a low fare, list each member of your party separately.

You'll also want to play it safe and reserve a full-fare coach seat as a back up. If waitlisting pays off and you get a promotional fare, be sure to cancel your full-fare reservation. That's important! Don't keep somebody else from getting a seat on that flight because you're holding two reservations, only one of which you'll be using. Let me emphasize that again. If you get your promotional fare, CANCEL THAT EXTRA RESERVATION!

Blackouts — they keep you from flying on low-cost tickets during high-demand periods

Demand for air travel is exceptionally strong for flights to special events such as Carnival in Rio de Janeiro or during certain holiday periods — especially Thanksgiving and Christmas. Since the airlines will have little trouble filling their planes during these strong-demand periods, they will severely cut back on the number of promotional-fare seats. They may even blackout, or suspend, all or most promotional fares.

Even though winter is generally a low-demand season, travelers will have to pay top dollar to fly from about December 18 through January 2. To save money on your air fare and still get where you want to go for Christmas, or any other blacked-out holiday or special event, you may have to fly around the blackout. Call the airlines to determine on which dates they will implement and lift their blackouts. Then make your reservations to fly the day before the blackout starts and to return the day after it ends.

Low Thanksgiving and Christmas fares are available to savvy shoppers

Airlines have found some blackouts to be self-defeating. Take Thanksgiving for example. Tens of thousands of travelers fly in time to reach their destination before Thanksgiving Day. So many, in fact, that the Wednesday before Thanksgiving is one of the busiest air travel days in any given year. Of course, promotional fares are usually blacked out.

But on Thanksgiving Day itself, practically everybody who wanted to fly somewhere for the holiday has already arrived, and it's one of the slowest days for air travel. The airlines find themselves with a promotional-fare blackout on at a time when few people want to fly.

To attract passengers to fill those Thanksgiving Day seats that otherwise would remain empty, some airlines lift their blackout and slash fares for flights originating on Thanksgiving and the Friday after. Return flights for these low-fare specials originate not later than the Saturday following Thanksgiving. The blackout closes in again on Sunday, a peak-demand day when the bulk of Thanksgiving travelers use the return portion of their tickets. If you're flexible enough to catch a flight early on Thanksgiving Day, you can be where you want for Thanksgiving dinner at great savings over flights originating the day before.

Over a recent Thanksgiving, USAir lifted its blackout and gave air travelers discounts ranging between 60 and 70 percent off the full fare on seven-day advance-purchase tickets. That put USAir's Thanksgiving fares as low as just about any promotional fare you could get. To qualify for the fare, travelers had to depart on either the Sunday or Monday before Thanksgiving, on Thanksgiving day itself or on the Friday after. Return flights had to be made on the Friday or Saturday following Thanksgiving.

At Christmas, airlines generally lift their blackouts in similar fashion over Christmas Day and the days immediately following.

You may, however, have to be persistent in coming up with low Thanksgiving and Christmas fares. An informal survey conducted by a Massachusetts consumer affairs office found that lower fares on Christmas Day were frequently not offered unless the surveyor pressed the airline reservationist.

2

Avoiding unexpected budget-busting costs

Okay, you're on your way to air-travel savings. But, if you're not watchful, you may encounter a variety of air-travel pitfalls that could cost you much more than the savings gained by using low-fare strategies and techniques. Here's what to watch for and how to avoid monetary loss.

Excess baggage — it means excess costs

When you make a U.S. domestic flight or an international flight to or from the United States, you can generally check up to two bags, each of which must not exceed 70 pounds. Each bag must also not measure more than 62 inches when its length, height and width are added together.

You can also carry on board the plane either one or two bags which will have to fit under your seat or in an overhead compartment. If you take no carry-on luggage, some airlines will let you check a third bag.

Exceed your baggage allowance on a domestic flight, and the airline will charge you a per-piece rate in the range of $30 to $55, depending on the carrier. On an international flight to or from the United States, the excess-baggage charge will vary with the airline and the route.

Between New York and London, for example, British Airways has charged $85 per bag while Air India wanted $66. American Airlines between New York and Tokyo has levied an $86 per bag charge.

Some carriers use weight to determine your luggage allowance

So far the excess-baggage situation is fairly clear cut. You can pretty well tell before you leave home if you are going to be hit for excess bags. But you need to be aware that in some parts of the world, your luggage allowance is based upon its total weight, not how many individual pieces you have.

If you fly most anywhere OTHER than within, to or from the United States or Canada, the piece rule disappears in favor of a weight-based baggage system. Weight-based systems allow you to check luggage weighing a total of 44 pounds (20 kilograms) on economy-class flights. Business- and first-class travelers usually get a higher weight limit — 66 pounds (30 kilograms). If you exceed your limit, you'll be hit with an expensive — no, make that OUTRAGEOUS — excess-baggage charge.

One traveler checking in for an economy Tokyo-London fight was overweight by about 13 pounds. The airline assessed the passenger a $293 excess-baggage charge.

Other than keeping close tabs on the weight of your bags, or trying to shift any excess weight to your carry-on luggage, there's not much you can do. That's the rule for most foreign domestic flights and international flights not flying to or from the United States or Canada. You may try to haggle with the clerk to get the charge reduced, but —unless the overage is very minor — you won't get it eliminated. That Tokyo-London passenger argued the charge down to $53.

When your bags are packed, a tape measure and the bathroom scale can give you a good idea if you will fall within your baggage allowance. But if you think you are pushing the limits in either weight or size, you would be smart to call your airline to determine exactly what their limit is and what you'll have to pay should you go over it.

A mid-trip system switch can catch you unawares

Alright, there's two luggage-allowance systems in use around the world. Each system's rules are clear enough, however, so you would think you'll encounter no difficulties as long as you abide by the limits of the system you will encounter. In one particular situation, though, you — as many an unwary traveler has — can get hit with an unexpected excess-baggage charge.

The problem comes when you fly from the United States or Canada and then, somewhere in your journey, make a foreign domestic flight or an international flight between two non-U.S. or non-Canadian cities.

When you leave the United States, you are able to check one or two bags, each weighing up to 70 pounds — that's a maximum of 140 pounds of luggage. When you board your foreign domestic flight or your international flight between two non-U.S. or non-Canadian cities, you will switch to the weight-based system. And YOU WILL ONLY BE ALLOWED TO CHECK 44 POUNDS!!!

That's right! On your international departure from the United States you could check up to 140 pounds of luggage. But switching to a flight that will fall within a weight-based system limits you to just 44 pounds. It makes no difference that you made a flight on a piece system that allowed you to take up to 140 pounds. When you switch to the weight-based system, your allowance automatically and unequivocally drops to 44 pounds.

If you are unaware of this small quirk in international air travel, you could be standing at a check-in counter in a foreign country with as much as 95 pounds of excess baggage. Being alert to this pitfall and adjusting your luggage accordingly is far preferable to holding up a check-in line while your banker arranges a second mortgage to cover you excess-baggage charge.

To avoid excess-baggage charges when switching from a piece-based flight to a weight-based flight, you will have to limit yourself to 44 pounds of luggage throughout your entire journey.

Bankrupt airlines — they can offer low fares, but you need to protect yourself

Given the financial instability of some carriers in today's air-travel marketplace, you may find yourself asking, "Should I buy a ticket on a bankrupt airline?"

While a Chapter 11 bankruptcy allows a carrier to continue flying, it is clearly an airline whose financial difficulties have put it at the brink. Buy a ticket on a bankrupt airline and you risk the line going completely under and ceasing operations before you can use it.

But, as a low-fare shopper, you need to be interested in bankrupt airlines. These carriers, looking for quick cash, tend to come out with some very attractive fare deals.

You can take advantage of these low-fare opportunities and still give yourself some protection by paying for your ticket with a credit card. Do not pay for tickets on a bankrupt airline with cash or a check. If you do and the line stops flying, the only way to get any of your money back is get in line with the other creditors at the bankruptcy court.

But if you pay with a credit card and you can't use your ticket because the airline stops flying, you can have the charge removed from your credit card account. If you've already paid the credit card company, you can get a refund. Federal law requires credit card companies to remove a charge from your account and issue full credit if the service you purchased — air transportation in this case — is not provided.

It does not matter that the card company may not be able to get its money from the airline. You did not receive what you paid for, so you are entitled to a "chargeback" — removal of the charge and, if appropriate, a refund.

You can also consider buying trip-cancellation insurance, which can cost 5 percent or more of the ticket price. The insurance, though, will not help if you pay by credit card. The insurance company will require you to request a chargeback before they would pay your claim. But if you cannot avoid paying with cash or a check, then the insurance is a good idea.

Neither of these two options, however, will be of any use to you in obtaining a new ticket to your destination on another airline. You may, if you can't meet advance-purchase requirements, then be looking at paying a full fare costing hundreds of dollars more to reach your destination. As you progress through this book, though, I'll show you techniques to avoid paying that full fare.

If, on the other hand, the airline goes under while you are on your trip, other airlines will most likely honor your return ticket on a standby basis.

Bumping — it can cost you more than the inconvenience

Too many travelers holding a flight reservation fail to cancel when their plans change. Consequently, airlines overbook their flights, accepting more reservations than the aircraft has seats. Through overbooking they try to keep flights from taking off with "no-show" empty seats — a particularly aggravating and money-losing situation when the airline has turned passengers away from a flight because it was completely booked.

Each airline has its own formula to determine which flights will be overbooked and by how many seats. And they do a good job at predicting the seemingly unpredictable. Most flights take off with no overbooking problems.

Occasionally, however, the worst happens and more passengers than the plane can hold show up at the gate. Obviously, some of those passengers are not going to get on that flight. And if you happen to be one of those passengers, the impact on you can range from minor inconvenience to major expense incurred through missed meetings or appointments.

To determine who gets "bumped" from the flight, the airline will follow both federal regulations and their own procedures. Here's what you can expect to happen.

First, the airline will ask passengers to volunteer to be bumped from the flight. The U.S. Department of Transportation requires this. The DOT does not specify what compensation the airlines must offer voluntarily bumped passengers. That's left as a negotiable item between the airline and the volunteers. (See Chapter 9 to learn how to turn voluntary bumps to your advantage.)

Failing to get enough volunteers, airline personnel will select those passengers to be bumped. Most carriers operate under a policy of "last at the gate, first to be bumped."

If you are bumped involuntarily, the airline MUST put you on its next available flight to your destination. That's a DOT regulation. The DOT also says that if the airline can get you to your destination within an hour of your original arrival time, the carrier owes you nothing in the way of compensation.

On the other hand, if the airline gets you to your destination later than one hour but within two hours of your original arrival time — within four hours on international flights — the airline must pay you an amount equal to the one-way coach fare on your oversold flight, up to $200,

If you arrive at your destination more than two hours late — more than four hours on international flights — the airline must double the compensation. The carrier would then have to pay you double the one-way fare of your original flight, up to $400.

Beyond that, the airline owes you nothing. But you do have one option if you feel the compensation is not appropriate to the expenses or other injury you may incur. The DOT's regulations allow you to refuse the airline's compensation and sue for damages in a state court.

While you have the right to litigate, from what I can determine, you will probably make out better accepting the airline's compensation.

European Community bumping rules

Flights that begin in a country belonging to the European Community — Belgium, Denmark, France, Germany, Greece, Holland, Ireland, Italy, Luxembourg, Portugal, Spain and the United Kingdom — also provide some relief to passengers involuntarily bumped from an overbooked flight.

• If the airline gets you to your destination within two hours of your original arrival time for a flight of up to 2,100 miles (3,500 kilometers), the carrier will pay you approximately $95.

• If you arrive at your destination more than two hours late on a flight of up to 2,100 miles, you are entitled to receive about $190.

• When an airline fails to get you to your destination within four hours on a flight of more than 2,100 miles, you're entitled to receive abut $190.

• Your compensation jumps to approximately $380 for the longer flights should you arrive more than four hours late.

The airline will pay you in the currency of the country where the bumping occurs. The carrier must also pay for both a telephone call to your destination and meals eaten during your layover. If you can't get to your destination until the next day, the airline must provide you with a hotel room as well.

Bumps on other international flights

On international flights departing from the United States, you are protected by U.S. law and entitled to the compensation established by the DOT should you be involuntarily bumped. But on international flights originating outside the United States or a European Community country you are on your own, not protected by law.

In most cases, however, airlines are sensitive to the ill-will bumping can cause. Typically, the carrier will hand you a free round-trip ticket, and you shouldn't have much difficulty talking them into reimbursing reasonable expenses.

How to avoid the hassles and potential expense

To avoid the inconvenience and potential expense of an involuntary bump, you need follow only one rule — CHECK IN EARLY! And the more catastrophic an involuntary bump would be, the earlier you should arrive at the airport.

Airlines require that you arrive at the BOARDING GATE — not the terminal check-in counter — at least 10 minutes before departure of a domestic flight. If the flight is overbooked, at 10 minutes before departure carriers start bumping the passengers who have not yet arrived. I recommend you plan on being at the boarding gate a MINIMUM of 30 minutes before scheduled departure. That should allow time for the unexpected, such as heavy traffic en route to the airport or a long, slow-moving check-in line.

Let me emphasize that again. Those times are for you to be at the BOARDING GATE with baggage already checked.

On an international flight check-in lines tend to be longer and slower moving. The airlines want you to be at the boarding gate at least 20 minutes before departure and at the terminal check-in counter anywhere from 30 minutes to two hours before departure, depending on the airline and the destination. But if you want to avoid the possibility of an involuntary bump, which can be even more inconvenient on an international flight, arrive at least TWO HOURS early.

One final word on involuntary bumping. An advance boarding pass with seat assignment, furnished either by the airline or a travel agent, does NOT make you immune to being bumped. When you reach the gate and there are no seats left on your flight, your paid-in-full ticket and advance boarding pass will count for nothing.

What does guarantee that you'll get on the flight is to have a "boarding assignment." This is not the same as a boarding pass. The way to get a boarding assignment is to check in within the appropriate time frame.

Always take the precaution of presenting your boarding pass to the airline's departure-gate personnel to be sure you do have a boarding assignment. If the flight is not expected to be full, the clerk may just hand your ticket/boarding pass back and say you are all set. But if the flight could be overbooked, the clerk can check his or her computer to verify that you have a boarding assignment and are thus guaranteed to board the flight.

Nonrefundable tickets — perhaps you can get your money back

As a low-fare shopper, nonrefundable and nonchangeable pro-motional-fare tickets are the type you are going to be using — they carry the lowest price tags. But are those nonrefundable-nonchangeable rules chiseled in stone? Or will the airline bend its rules when the unexpected happens? That depends — upon your reason, upon the airline and upon who you talk to.

The rules state that you can't get your money back on a nonre-fundable ticket and that you can't change a nonchangeable ticket. In reality, however, some airlines maintain policies that tend to be more flexible than their rules. But you'll find little consistency among the carriers or even among employees of the same airline. Some airlines give their personnel much individual discretion in this area, others do not. And among those person-nel exercising that discretion, some will be more lenient than others.

If illness, injury or death, either your own or an immediate family member's, keeps you from using a nonrefundable ticket, most airlines will issue a refund. Immediate family is usually considered to be spouse, children, siblings, grandparents, grandchildren and in-laws. The problem will, however, have to be documented with a letter from a physician or a copy of a death certificate.

There are also less-serious circumstances such as jury duty, a court summons or military orders that can also keep you from flying on your nonrefundable ticket. Here you're moving into a gray area. But many airlines will bend their rules if you can show them that the situation was unforeseeable and beyond your control. You will still need some type of written documen-tation, however.

Jury duty offers a good example of the inconsistencies you could run into. United Airlines will refund your money when you can't use a nonrefundable ticket because of jury duty, but

American Airlines usually does not. An official with American, however, said that when requesting a jury-duty refund you could be talking to an American agent who had recently been called to jury duty and who might, therefore, be inclined to grant the refund.

When the worst happens, contact the airline's customer relations department (get the number from the Airline contacts appendix). If at all possible, try to postpone and reschedule your flight instead of cancelling and asking for a refund. You'll find airlines more receptive to arranging a new flight than to returning your money.

If you know there's a likelihood of something occurring that could keep you from making a flight, you may want to avoid the least-expensive promotional fares, which are normally nonrefundable. Instead, see if you can pay a bit more for your ticket to get one that allows changes or cancellation upon payment of a small penalty fee.

What to do when you miss your flight

There's another not uncommon situation you could run into — literally. Picture yourself running down an airport concourse after having spent an extra 30 minutes tied up in traffic on your way to the airport. Just as you reach the departure gate, you glance at the window and see your flight slowly taxing to the runway.

After you get rid of the sick feeling in your stomach, walk up to the gate agent and utter your humblest apologies for missing your flight. You are now at the mercy of that agent. If it soothes you, explain why you were late. But make it brief. The agent has heard the story before — many times.

Typically, the agent will put you on standby for the next flight with available seats to your destination. If the next flight is not until the next day, however, you will have to arrange for your own overnight accommodations.

If you are really in dire straits because you missed your flight, you can ask the agent to endorse your ticket for use on another airline. But it's very unlikely the agent will do so. That would involve transferring the payment for your ticket to the new carrier, and your airline will not want to give up its revenue for a situation which you created. I know...the traffic. But the airline will feel that you should have anticipated potential delays and left for the airport earlier.

Lost tickets — they can cost you a bundle

Guard your ticket — it's almost the same as cash. No, actually, it may be worth more than the cash you paid for it. If you have a $350 promotional-fare ticket and lose it shortly before your flight date, most airlines will make you buy a replacement at the fare valid on the day you purchase the new ticket. That could very well be a full fare. Say the full fare costs you $900. You've now spent a total of $1,250 to get on that plane!

American Airlines, however, will sell you a replacement at the same fare you paid for the missing ticket.

You can apply to the airline for a refund on a lost or stolen ticket. Processing your refund, however, may take up to four months, and you will have to pay a $50 or $70 processing fee. And should your ticket be used by another person, you will not receive a refund at all.

To make your job of filling out the forms easier should your ticket be lost or stolen, make TWO photocopies of it. Be sure to copy each flight coupon. Keep one copy in a safe place at home, at your business or in a safe deposit box.

Carry the other copy with you BUT SEPARATELY FROM YOUR TICKET. If you lose your ticket, contact your airline's customer service people or an airport counter supervisor. Ask to have your ticket reissued based upon your photocopy. This tactic does not always work, but you have nothing to lose by asking.

3

How to find and buy the lowest fares

Regardless of where in the world you want to fly, you need only three tools to scout out low air fares — a telephone, a pencil and a pad. With these tools and the information in the strategies that follow, you'll be able to search out the lowest fare to your destination.

Advertising — it alerts you to the latest bargains

Start your low-fare search with airline advertisements. Scan your local newspaper. If you normally read a small-town paper, you may miss the best bargains. The airlines will place their ads where the largest numbers of people will read them. Start buying a copy of the leading newspaper of the nearest major city with a large airport, at least for the duration of your fare search. Watch especially the ads in Sunday newspaper travel sections. When listening to the radio or watching television, be alert for airline advertising.

Media ads will give you an idea which airlines fly to your destination and the fares they charge. Jot down airline names as well as their advertised fares. If the ad lists a special name or designator for the fare, make note of that also. It will help you identify that exact fare when talking with an airline reservationist or a travel agent. Be sure to note any restrictions attached to the advertised fares. You'll find them in the fine print.

Let me mention here that among my *Traveler's Reports* you'll find a handy, multi-page aid called THE AIR TRAVELER'S EASY LOW-FARE FINDER. This form will simplify and organize your task of recording the information you obtain while ferreting out low fares. THE AIR TRAVELER'S EASY LOW-FARE FINDER's specific references to pages in this book also make it an excellent guide and reminder for applying the tips, tactics and techniques in *Fly There For Less*. See the catalog at the back of the book for ordering information.

Checking airline ads will also keep you on top of any low-priced, short-term specials that pop up. The airlines maintain full-time marketing departments whose job is to keep track of the number of passengers flying their routes and to devise long-term plans to increase those numbers. They also have a short-term concern. If the numbers show the airline losing passengers on a route, perhaps because of low off-season demand, or if passengers could be lost because a competing airline implements a new marketing strategy, alarm bells go off and the marketing people scramble into action.

An airline will not tolerate losing its share of any given route or market. Faced with a potential loss of market share, an airline will strike with its most readily available tool — fare cuts. To get the word out on these fare cuts, and to get it out fast, the marketing people will use media ads.

Shopping the ads for an international flight

When shopping for an international flight, obtain copies of the newspapers from your gateway city — the city from which the international portion of your flight will start. For distant gateway cities, you should be able to obtain newspapers from a large newsstand. Many libraries also have newspaper collections. Just as you did with your local newspaper, scour the ads, particularly those in the Sunday travel section. Note the airlines flying to your international destination and the fares they're advertising.

Watch the fine print in matching-fare ads

When airline competition heats up, the air fare market can become particularly turbulent. Fares may be especially short-lived as airlines jostle to meet or beat the competition. Airlines may then switch to advertising that says they'll match any fare. That's fine. But you need to read and understand the fine print.

The ad will state that the advertising airline will match fares carrying similar restrictions. Say you bought a 30-day advance-purchase ticket for an American Airlines flight to Oklahoma City. You normally prefer to fly Delta, but American had the lowest fare so you took it. Two weeks before you have to be in Oklahoma City you spot a newspaper ad saying Delta will match any fare with the same travel restrictions. Don't call American to cancel your reservation, because Delta is not going to give you the same price. The key words are "with the same travel restrictions." Delta will match American's price but will also require you to meet the same 30-day advance purchase that American imposed. And if you have to be in Oklahoma in two weeks, Delta's match offer won't do you any good.

Be alert to wording that indicates a limit on the number of seats available at matching fares. If the ad reads, "as long as the supply of discount seats lasts," the airline will not match fares once it sells its allocation of capacity-controlled promotional fares.

Also, watch for wording whose exact meaning may be ambiguous, such as when an airline will match only those fares which are "published," or fares only on "comparable flights," or only the fares of "major airlines." Call the airline and ask them to explain any phrases whose meaning is not perfectly clear.

Matching ads can help you get the best low fare to fit your needs. But they also call for close scrutiny and further investigation to clarify terms and conditions.

More advertising fine print

The airlines consider ticket price to be the key element in their ads. And the ads will display prices so they will readily catch your eye. The price you see, however, may be 50 percent less than the actual cost of your ticket. That eye-catching price in the ad may represent only half the round-trip fare.

Some states now require the airlines to list the full round-trip fare if the fare is valid only on a round-trip ticket. But the airlines can still use the one-way fare in an ad if you can actually buy a one-way ticket at that price. You'll have to read the fine print to determine if the advertised price is a one-way or round-trip fare.

Now you need to go beyond the ads

Don't assume advertised fares are the lowest you can buy. Consider advertised fares only as a starting point in your fare search.

An airline may be heavily promoting its seven-day advance-purchase tickets, but the carrier may also offer a lower-priced, 30-day advance-purchase fare which it is not advertising.

Also, keep in mind that another airline, which may not be advertising as heavily, could offer a still lower fare.

Airline reservationists — how to get the lowest fare from one

After your excursion through the advertisements, telephone not only the airline promoting the lowest fare, but also the other airlines you've written down. Use the Airline contacts appendix to find the reservations telephone numbers, many of which are toll-free.

Also use the Airline contacts appendix to add carriers to your shopping list. It's unlikely that you will have found all airlines serving your destination just by checking the ads. If you are not sure whether a carrier serves your destination, call and ask.

When calling for fare information, ask the reservationist for the airline's lowest fare to your destination. If you've seen a lower fare in the ads than the reservationist quotes you, ask about the availability of that fare. Mention the fare's special name or designator if it was listed in the ad.

When a reservationist quotes what you feel to be an appealing low fare, ask to make a 24-hour "courtesy reservation." That is, you want to reserve your seat or seats, but not pay for them for 24 hours. Just tell the reservationist your plans are not yet entirely firm — and they are not. You are still not sure you have found the lowest fare. Until you do, your flight plans are in a state of flux.

Note on your shopping list next to the airline's name that you have made a courtesy reservation. If you are using THE AIR TRAVELER'S EASY LOW-FARE FINDER, make your notation in the courtesy-reservation column. Continue calling the remaining airlines. Should you find a still lower fare, again make a courtesy reservation.

Now, this is important, and I don't want you to let me down here. I am revealing to you extremely valuable inside information that has the potential in the long term to save you thousands and thousands of dollars. So I feel I can be a bit demanding. Therefore, I insist that you call back each airline with which you have made a courtesy reservation that you are not going to use, and CANCEL THAT RESERVATION. Don't wait! As soon as you you hang up after having made a courtesy reservation for a lower fare, IMMEDIATELY call back the carrier holding your previous reservation and cancel it.

Don't adopt the attitude that the airline will cancel the reservation when you do not pay for the ticket within the allotted time. That's not good enough. Around the country countless thousands of other shoppers are trying to get a low fare, and one of them could wind up paying substantially more because you did not cancel a reservation you do not intend to use.

Okay, you've now telephoned all the airlines serving your destination. You have one courtesy reservation outstanding and have cancelled all other reservations. Now, call the airlines again. And again ask for the lowest fare to your destination. This redundancy is absolutely essential. Survey after survey has shown that it's not unusual for different reservationists at the same airline to come up with different "lowest" fares.

If your itinerary calls for more than a simple point-to-point flight, your chances are increased that you'll receive different fare quotations. One shopper looking for the lowest fare for a trip from New York to Louisville to Denver and back to New York made five calls to three different airlines. The airline reservationists quoted fares ranging from $277 to $673. You can see it's imperative to call more than one airline — and then call back again.

Airline reservationists have a high-pressure job. They must process calls as quickly as possible yet provide potential passengers with as much information as they need. The reservationist will guide the conversation to achieve, from the airline's point of view, maximum efficiency.

Your best approach is to be open, honest and friendly. But you must stress that the lowest fare is all important to you. Also be sure to let the reservationist know your degree of flexibility. As you've already seen, the more flexible you are, the greater the likelihood you'll save money on your air fare.

To improve your chances of getting a reservationist who can take the time to thoroughly search out the lowest fare — which is not always an easy task despite the fares being listed in computers — avoid calling during weekday business hours. If, when you call, all reservationists are busy and you get put on hold, hang up and telephone again at a different time.

Many airline reservation centers are staffed 16 to 24 hours a day, seven days a week. Call late in the evening or on a weekend. One slow Sunday morning an airline reservationist was able to take more than 20 minutes to dig out a fare and routing that saved me almost $200 over a previous "lowest" fare.

Travel agents — how to get the lowest fare from one

Once upon a time a GOOD travel agent was a valuable asset. Today, however, if you want an agent to help you fly there for less, you will have to have an OUTSTANDING travel agent.

A travel agent receives input from a variety of travel suppliers and has computer access to the fares of most airlines. Often, a travel agent will be in the know about the latest low-fare deals. Since travel agents make their money from commissions paid by the airlines, you can expect to pay the same price whether you buy your ticket from the airline or from a travel agency.

But the complex structure of airline fares means you'll again need to make several phone calls. Select two or three travel agencies from among those who advertise in your Sunday newspaper's travel section. Also turn to the yellow pages of your telephone book and choose a couple from the *Travel Agencies* listings. Add their names and phone numbers to your shopping list or enter them in the appropriate section of THE AIR TRAVELER'S EASY LOW-FARE FINDER.

When you telephone a travel agency, you will probably not know whether you are talking to a good travel agent or an outstanding one. The difference, however, is crucial.

That low-fare shopper with the New York-Louisville-Denver-New York itinerary fared no better with travel agencies than with the airlines. Three agencies quoted fares of $327, $407 and $603. And several agencies responded erroneously that the shopper did not qualify for a low promotional fare because the itinerary was not a point-to-point round trip.

The problem, however, does not always center on the travel agent — or the airline reservationist. Much blame must also be placed on the complicated, continually changing morass of air fares and the rules that govern those fares. That's why you need an outstanding agent, not just a good one.

So until you've lined up one or two outstanding travel agents, you'll have to survey at least five or six travel agencies to be sure of being quoted the lowest fare.

As a low-fare shopper, though, you could run into problems. Before deregulation, when airlines charged the same fares for the same routes, a travel agent could quickly process your reservation and receive a 10 percent commission. Today, however, it takes a travel agent longer to search out the lowest fare. And when the agent does come up with a low fare, he or she will receive fewer commission dollars. In effect, the travel agent works harder for less money.

As a result some travel agents may balk at working with you to find the lowest fare if they feel you are merely shopping. This became clear in a telephone survey conducted by the New York City Consumer Affairs Department. The consumer office shopped 49 travel agencies seeking the "lowest possible weekend direct round-trip fare" to several popular destinations.

The survey came up with fares for identical trips that varied by as much as 115 percent. For a New York-New Orleans flight agents came up with "lowest" fares ranging between $198 and $400. For New York-Berlin the range was $649 to $1,029. And New York-London $416 to $898.

The head of the Consumer Affairs Department, Mark Green, cited travel agents as the main reason for the variation in the fares quoted.

"Apparently, large numbers of travel agents won't spend the time necessary to search out the best deal for inquiring consumers or don't know how to access the airline's mainframe computers," Green said.

Of course, there was an immediate outcry from the travel agent community and its professional organizations. Their response focused blame on several areas, including the airlines' complicated fare structure. But it also brought out how travel agents respond to "cold calls."

Richard Copeland, a travel agent and president of the New York chapter of the American Society of Travel Agents, replied that a travel agency is not a telephone-shopping business. Copeland said travel agents believe they get little or no business through phone calls from strangers and that only one out of a 100 telephone shoppers will buy a ticket. Therefore, Copeland added, no reasonable or prudent business person would think that a travel agent should spend "a half-hour or more" to find the lowest fare for a cold caller.

Philip Davidoff, national president of the ASTA, had similar feelings. He said travel agents would go out of business if they spent "half an hour" on every cold caller asking for the lowest fare. Davidoff went on to say that agents are even encouraged to spend less time on cold calls than on calls from known customers.

That's absolutely incredible!

Businesses around the country spend huge sums of money trying to generate sales leads. And here many travel agencies are apparently throwing away a golden opportunity to expand their customer base. Potential clients are crying out, "I need your help. I need your expertise. Help me get a low fare, and I'll be your customer." And their cries are apparently falling on un-hearing ears.

The travel agent community is being extremely short-sighted. Instead of looking at a cold call as an intrusion that will not generate revenue, travel agents need to view the caller as a prospective customer. They need to see the caller as someone who they can help and who will gratefully turn again to that agent's expertise for their next trip. And the one after that. The cold-caller-turned-customer will be so delighted to have found a knowledgeable, service-providing travel agent that he or she will shout the good news to friends. And, of course, those friends too will turn to that travel agent for help.

Why don't travel agencies turn shoppers into loyal customers by displaying their expertise? Perhaps not all of them have the expertise to display.

That's not a snide remark. This problem, too, was brought to light by the response to the consumer department's survey. ASTA-president Davidoff acknowledged there's some truth to the consumer department's claim that "large numbers" of travel agents do not know how to use the full capabilities of their computer systems.

Davidoff said that even though he is a spokesman for the travel agency industry, he had to admit that not all travel agents are as qualified or as well trained as they should be.

Where does all this leave you, the low-fare shopper — that dreaded cold caller? You will just have to be persistent in your cold calling. All travel agents do not subscribe to the theory that fare shoppers need to be shunned like the plague. One travel agent stated the philosophy of the more-enlightened agents when he pointed out that their business is to provide service. He added that if he can find the lowest fare for a cold caller, that person may come back and book a trip to Europe.

That's the type of travel agent you want. They are out there. You just have to keep looking and telephoning.

Remember, too, that the travel agencies in the survey were big-city agencies, perhaps used to viewing their customers in a somewhat impersonal manner.

Try telephoning a variety of travel agencies. Try a mix of urban and suburban, even rural travel agents. In my area — Orlando, Florida — I can easily reach out by telephone, even if I do have to go beyond my calling area, to contact not-too-distant travel agents located downtown in a city, in the suburbs and in rural small towns. Try also to contact a mix of large chain travel agencies and smaller independent shops. Your telephone book's yellow pages will provide you with the contact information you need.

Regardless of where you live, you should be able to find a couple of travel agencies willing to search out low fares for you. As an incentive, let the agent know that should he or she come up with the lowest fare, you will certainly buy your ticket through that agency.

Here's what to consider when estimating an agent's capabilities and expertise:

• Does the agent appear willing to give your needs his or her personal attention?

• Does the agent show a willingness to consistently go above and beyond the call of duty?

• Is the agent friendly and outgoing and enthusiastic about

his or her job? Does the agent appear to genuinely like and enjoy his or her work?

• How do you feel about the agent. Are you compatible? Can you talk comfortably with the agent? Does he or she listen attentively? Does the agent understand you easily — not just your words but your wants and needs as well?

• What kind of training has the agent undergone? Does the agent have formal schooling designed for travel agents or merely much-less-desirable on the job training. Also ask about recent training. The travel industry is continually changing. A top travel agent will keep up to date by attending industry seminars and conferences.

If a particular airline tends to get most of your business, then you need a travel agent that uses that airline's computer system. While a travel agent can get most airlines' fares out of any system, using a computer system owned, wholly or partially, by a particular airline will give the agent a better, more fruitful, relationship with that carrier. And as you progress through this book, you'll see there are times when that relationship may be able to save you money on your air fare. If you fly Continental, the agent should subscribe to "System One." For TWA, Delta or Northwest look for an agent with a "PARS" computer system. And American Airlines flyers need an agent who uses "Sabre."

When you have found an outstanding travel agent, establish a working relationship. In addition to your airline reservations, let that agent book all your travel services, including hotel reservations and car rentals. If you make yourself a regular customer, you'll get a better reception, even when shopping for the lowest fare.

A caution when buying tickets through a travel agent

When you telephone a travel agent to book your flight, but for whatever reason have your ticket issued at the airport, you will incur a hidden charge. When you check in and pick up your ticket, the airline will tack on a "prepay charge" — usually $25 on a domestic ticket, $30 for an international flight.

The airlines see it this way. The travel agent is doing the work of making the reservation, and thus the airline pays the agent a commission. But the transaction has not yet been completed, and the airline must issue the ticket at the airport. The airlines say the cost of bookkeeping and writing the ticket then falls on the airline. While this is a normal cost of doing business, the airline has already paid that cost in the form of the travel agent's commission. So they slap on a prepay charge to recover the additional cost from you.

You can avoid prepay charges by not splitting the booking-ticket issuing between a travel agent and an airline. If you can't pick up the ticket at the agency, have the travel agent send it to you by overnight express. Even if you have to pay the express charge, it will be less expensive than the prepay charge.

If you have no other option but to book with a travel agent but have the ticket issued at the airport, see if you can talk the travel agent into absorbing the charge. If you are doing a fair volume of business with the agent, he or she just may agree to pick up the cost of the prepay charge.

Another alternative is to forsake the travel agent completely for this transaction and telephone the airline directly to see if you can get the same fare. When the airline handles the entire transaction, even though you pick the ticket up at the airport, they will not impose a prepay charge.

Questions to ask — these will help you get the lowest fare

Even though you ask an airline reservationist or a travel agent for the lowest fare, it should now be clear that the fare quoted will not always be the least expensive. It would be ungracious, however, to ask in response, "Are you sure that's the cheapest fare?" Whether it is or not, you may still get an affirmative reply.

You can test the fare and perhaps prompt additional searching by asking questions based on the strategies you now know:

• Could I get a still lower fare if I buy my ticket further in advance?

• Would it be less expensive to fly off-peak?

• Would it be cheaper to fly on a different day of the week?

• If I changed my departure date by a few days (or weeks, or months) would my ticket cost less?

• Do you know of any special fares that could save me more?

When dealing with a travel agent, you can also ask, "Would another airline have a less expensive fare?"

These types of questions can keep the subject open for discussion and encourage the reservationist or agent to explore further. They also signal that you know something about air fares and are determined to get the lowest price.

Personal computers — they offer low-fare shopping advantages

If you own a modem-equipped personal computer, you can hook up to a telephone line and have available several sources of air fares.

While numerous data bases offer a variety of travel services, not all are of interest to you, the low-fare shopper. You'll want to investigate those that contain airline fares.

Computerized data bases filled with air fares offer several advantages. Since the fares in these data bases are updated frequently, usually daily, you know you are looking at the latest fares available. You also know that the person looking for the lowest fare — YOU — is concerned only with your interest and will take the time and effort to seek out the lowest fare.

Most travel data bases are also available 24 hours a day. You can low-fare hunt on a weekend or during the evening when a travel agency would be closed. And when you find a fare you like, you can make a reservation, buy your ticket and have it mailed to you. Or, if you prefer, you can give the flight information you come up with to your travel agent or the airline.

One traveler had to attend a meeting in New Orleans and used his home computer to search out a low fare for the trip. While examining his options, he discovered that if he stayed in New Orleans an additional night, he could use a fare that was $180 less than if he returned right after the meeting. Subtract the cost of an additional night at his hotel and the traveler still saved well over $100.

Would an airline or a travel agent have come up with this fare? Possibly, if the reservationist were carrying out a thorough search for the lowest fare. But if the reservationist merely checked fares for the day the meeting ended, he or she would have missed the substantially cheaper fare.

How air-fare data bases work

Let me run through the procedures necessary to find fares in these data bases. Since they are similar to what a travel agent or airline reservationist uses in coming up with a fare for you, you can get an idea of just what is involved — and why they sometimes miss coming up with the actual lowest fare.

After going through the introductory menus, you type in your departure city, destination, flight dates and the flight times you're interested in. The computer then retrieves the information and displays available flights on the screen.

The screen, however, can only display a given amount of data. Frequently, the flight information meeting your criteria will require scrolling through several screen displays to view it all. If you — or a reservationist — should select your flight from the first screen display only, the flight with the lowest fare might be missed.

As you can tell from the criteria you entered into the computer, these data bases — as are those used by travel agents and airline reservationists — are schedule driven. If the lowest fare to your destination is on a flight that departs 30 minutes later than the time frame you entered, the least expensive flight to your destination will not be displayed.

Finding the lowest fare requires you to rummage around through the data. You have to examine all possible options. And you will need to shift back and forth among displays containing schedules, fares and the restrictions and rules that apply to the flights. While this is not overly difficult, it does require some time and effort — time and effort that a reservationist may not always be willing or able to give you.

Contacts

Here's a run down on home-computer data bases that contain air fares and the networks through which they are available.

• Official Airline Guides (OAG) Electronic Edition - The OAG Electronic Edition lists more than 600,000 fares for the flights of some 750 airlines worldwide. North American flight listings show fares for both direct and connecting flights and are updated daily. On international flights, however, the data base lists fares only for direct flights between most of the world's major cities. The international fares are updated weekly. The OAG Electronic Edition will let you check restrictions, make reservations and arrange for ticketing. Among your ticketing options are airport pick up, city ticket office pick up and tickets by mail.

The OAG Electronic Edition is available from:

• CompuServe, 5000 Arlington Center Blvd., P.O. Box 20212, Columbus, OH 43220, telephone 800-848-8199.

• Delphi, 3 Blackstone St., Cambridge, MA 02139, telephone 800-544-4005.

• Genie (the General Electric Network for Information Exchange), 401 N. Washington St., Rockville, MD 20850, telephone 800-638-9636.

• The Source, 1616 Anderson Rd., McLean, VA 22102, telephone 800-336-3366.

To receive complete information on the OAG Electronic Edition, write or call: Official Airline Guides, 2000 Clearwater Dr., Oak Brook, IL 60521, telephone 800-323-4000.

• Eaasy Sabre - The Eaasy Sabre data base is operated by American Airlines, but its data is not confined to American's flights. American says Eaasy Sabre lists 13,000,000 fares for more than 650 airlines worldwide. The data base incorporates a feature called "bargain-finder" which helps you find any short-term promotional fares. Eaasy Sabre also lets you make reservations and arrange ticketing.

Eaasy Sabre is available through CompuServe, Genie, Delphi and:

• Prodigy, 445 Hamilton Ave., White Plains, NY 10601 telephone 800-822-6922, extension 888.

Note that with the Prodigy system, Eaasy Sabre uses menus,

displays and screen sequences that are quite different than those used on CompuServe, Genie and Delphi. Prodigy's Eaasy Sabre is, consequently, easier to understand and use but much slower. In addition, the Prodigy software only allows a few specified screens to be printed or copied to a disk.

This is not necessarily a serious drawback though. Since Prodigy does not charge an hourly usage fee as do the other three systems, you are not running up charges because the system is slow or because you can't download the information you want. Many Prodigy users, depending on their location, also do not incur long distance telephone charges.

• Travelshopper - This data base lets you look at the fares of about 750 airlines worldwide using the PARS data base operated by Northwest Airlines and Trans World Airlines. Features are similar to the other two data bases. Travelshopper is available through CompuServe and Delphi.

Drawbacks

The biggest drawback to using a personal computer to find low air fares is, as I indicated above, that it costs you money. You'll encounter one-time enrollment fees, telephone charges, computer service charges and data base charges. Total costs could approach $1 or more per minute of on-line computer time.

For an uncomplicated low-fare search between two cities, you could probably come up with the lowest fare for about $2 to $4.

A complicated search, however, one in which you are examining trade-offs, checking other than a point-to-point itinerary or using the creative techniques shown in later strategies, would take longer and cost more.

Since studying data on line costs money, you can cut costs by using on-line time only to find the appropriate information. Then download it to inexpensively study at your leisure. You can also cut costs by avoiding computer searches during weekday business hours. Instead, use evenings and weekends when fees and charges are lower.

Fees vary among the data bases and among the computer services. So before choosing a service, contact each to find out what they offer and what they charge. Then decide which can serve your needs at the lowest cost.

When to buy — your timing is important

You'll have to carefully consider when to buy your ticket. Most promotional fares are nonrefundable or carry a cancellation penalty. A nonrefundable fare means you won't get any of your money back should you not be able to use the ticket. With a cancellation penalty, the airline will charge you a fee for canceling, even if it's just to switch flights on the same airline.

To get the lowest promotional fare, however, you must purchase your ticket well in advance of your flight date. Obviously, you'll want to buy one of these tickets only when your plans are absolutely firm. If you book 30 days in advance but your plans change and you cannot use your ticket, or get your money back, your low-cost promotional fare becomes expensive.

Should the fare you've come up with be unrestricted, buy it early to lock in your price. If the fare increases before you fly, the airline will not ask you to pay the increase. If the fare goes down, or if another airline comes out with a still lower fare, the airline will let you turn in your ticket for a refund.

Buying a ticket early on a foreign airline, though, generally does not lock in your fare. Most foreign carriers charge the price in effect on the day you start your flight. If the fare increases after you've bought your ticket, you'll have to pay the increase when you check in.

Once you've started your itinerary, though, your foreign-airline fare is locked in. International and foreign-domestic fares, however, are much more stable than U.S. domestic fares. So post-purchase fare increases will seldom be a problem.

Extraordinary bargains — you have to move fast on these

Being alert to the airlines' media advertising may occasionally put you in touch with an extraordinary bargain. But you may have to move fast to pick up a bargain fare. The more extraordinary the bargain, the faster you will have to make your buying decision.

Early one November, the airlines announced greatly reduced fares for travelers who booked a flight on Thanksgiving Day. By flying on Thanksgiving Day, travelers could save as much as 70 percent compared to the cost of a flight the day before.

The response to this well-advertised promotion was tremendous. Within the first eight hours of announcing the low fares, American Airlines, for example, sold one-third of its available low-fare seats. In the days that followed, many would-be travelers around the country were disappointed to find these low-fare seats to their destinations already sold out.

Continental Airlines once announced an extraordinary New York-Honolulu fare of $99 one way. Continental had at least 1,596 seats for sale at the $99 price. Within 12 hours of announcing the promotion, however, all seats had been sold.

Virgin Atlantic Airways offered an incredible $99 New York-London round trip and sold out its allotted 222 seats in just nine minutes. The combination of extraordinarily low fares and capacity-controlled promotional seats makes it imperative that you move fast on this type of promotion.

Act quickly but be wary of travel scams

There's danger in moving quickly to pick up a bargain. You'll need to be sure you're not getting into a travel scam. The travel marketplace seems to attract more than its share of fraudulent operators and firms employing deceptive selling practices. A few guidelines can help you avoid problems.

• If the price seems too good to be true, it probably is. An unrealistic price calls for investigation before parting with your money. One scam promoted a $29 round-trip air fare to Hawaii. The catch was that you had to buy a hotel package to get the $29 fare. Of course, the hotel package carried an inflated price that included the real cost of the air fare.

Those $99 fares offered by Continental and Virgin Atlantic should have seemed too good to be true, and they should have raised suspicions. Since the fares were offered by well-established, reputable airlines, however, interested shoppers could easily telephone to verify that there were no strings attached and then feel confident in the truthfulness of the answer they received.

• Shun telephone solicitations for travel. And NEVER NEVER NEVER give your credit card number to an UNSOLICITED telephone caller.

• Be leery of bargains available only to a selected few "lucky" individuals. If it's a valid travel bargain, it will be open to all.

• Don't be pressured to make a decision immediately or lose the opportunity. That kind of pressure is a scam tip-off, and you're better off losing the "opportunity."

• Watch out when you come across what appears to be a bargain but then learn the price is only for one component of a travel package. To get that bargain-priced component, you'll have to buy the entire package at a much higher price. That's deceptive advertising, and your total price probably represents no bargain at all. Remember the example above of the $29 Hawaiian air fare.

• Take time to investigate a bargain. Determine the details. Add up the cost of any extras to come up with your actual cost. Even with Continental's 12-hour sell out of its $99 Hawaii-New York fare, you would have had time to question Continental. If you don't have time to investigate, it's probably best to avoid the bargain. Should you have doubts after getting all the facts, err on the side of caution and don't part with your money.

Post-purchase searching — you may find a still-lower fare

The airlines' yield-management techniques keep fares under constant reevaluation and practically in a state of flux. Most fares are short lived. In fact, the average airline fare is said to survive only two weeks. Therefore, you must continue to be alert to radio and newspaper advertising. Also continue to periodically call the travel agents and the airlines on your shopping list or THE AIR TRAVELER'S EASY LOW-FARE FINDER to check for a still lower fare.

You need to carry out post-purchase searches regardless of whether you hold a refundable or nonrefundable ticket. Of course, with a refundable ticket you will have no problem taking advantage of any less-expensive fares your airline — or any airline — comes out with.

If you have a nonrefundable ticket and discover a lower fare offered by your airline, you may be entitled to a refund for the difference between the two. The rules vary with each carrier.

Variations in airline policies run from TWA's refunding the difference only if seats — not counting yours — are still available in that fare category to United's liberal policy of refunding even if the fare appears on the day of your flight. Practically all airlines, however, will refund the difference in fares if your ticket and the new, lower fare are for the same fare class and you meet all the restrictions — including the advance-purchase time frame.

If your ticket carries a cancellation penalty, a greatly-reduced fare could come along on another airline that would let you buy the new fare, pay the cancellation penalty and still save money.

At one particular time, you could have bought Delta Air Lines' Orlando-Los Angeles 14-day Super Saver for $300 round trip. The fare carried a 25 percent cancellation penalty. Before your flight date, however, another airline would have came out with an unrestricted $79 one-way fare between Orlando and Los Angeles.

If you had kept up your post-purchase fare search and learned of the lower fare, you would have flown to Los Angeles for less. All you had to do was turn in your Delta ticket and pay a $75 cancellation fee. Then buy the competition's $158 round-trip ticket and put the extra $67 in your wallet.

Computerized searches for still-lower fares

If you obtain your ticket through a travel agency, ask if the agency uses a computerized fare-check system. Many travel agencies, particularly the larger firms, employ computer programs that make a daily scan of the fares in a reservation system to see if a lower fare has become available for booked tickets.

Some of the larger agencies develop their own fare-check systems. Others may subscribe to a computer reservations system that incorporates a fare check. Agent's using the System One reservations computer, for example, can have the system's Fare Assurance program carry out a post-purchase search for a lower fare.

One authority on these systems says that travel agencies using a fare-check program for post-purchase searches find about 95 percent of any new, lower fares available to their ticketed clients. On the other hand, agencies depending solely on an agent to conduct a post-purchase search dig out only about 50 percent of any new, lower fares for their booked customers.

Despite your travel agent's ability to check for lower fares, DO NOT depend entirely on the agent. You must continue to rely only on yourself.

One traveler flying between Washington, DC, and California purchased a promotional fare more than 30 days in advance for $527. But he didn't stop checking the ads, and the week before departure he found the airline advertising that route for $400. Although he had bought his ticket through a travel agency, he never heard a word about the lower fare from the travel agent. However, because he was a savvy air-fare shopper who continued to check the ads, he as able to point out the new, lower fare and get a $127 refund.

4

Using lesser-known fares to reap air-travel savings

Full and promotional fares are not the only ones airlines offer. They're just the most common. You need to go beyond these standard fares to check out a variety of lesser-known fares that are at you your disposal to help you fly there for less.

Status fares — savings just for the asking

Airlines offer some travelers special low fares because they have a certain status. There's a good chance you may qualify for one or more of these status fares. If you're an active-duty member of the military, a dependent of an active-duty military member, a student age 26 or younger, a youth, a child, a member of a family flying together or a senior citizen, you've got clout. Most airlines will discount fares, in some cases up to 75 percent, for passengers who fit into one of these status groups.

Both eligibility for status fares and the size of the discount vary among the airlines, among the status groups and even among destinations. If an airline confirms you are eligible for a status fare, don't automatically assume that fare will be the lowest you could obtain. Should the status fare represent a discount only off a full fare, a promotional fare could very well be cheaper.

Military

Most airlines offer active duty military discounts on both domestic and international flights. Discounts for military dependents, although not as common, are also available.

At a time when New York-Frankfurt, Germany, Apex fares sold for $599 round trip, military passengers and their dependents paid just $458. That's a substantial $141 savings.

Students

To be eligible for student fares, you'll need proof of student status. These fares are available at varying times of the year, under varying conditions. Age is the condition that varies most. Minimum ages range between 12 and 17, maximum between 22 and 26. Airlines may offer student fares only during summer. They may also restrict the fares to certain days of the week or to off-peak flights.

A couple of airlines have established discount programs aimed at traveling students. Continental Airlines offers a 10 percent discount to college students who join its "Collegiate FlightBank" program. Although the program requires a $15 membership fee, students who enroll will receive a certificate good for an additional $25 off any fare.

With TWA's Getaway Student Discount Card program, full-time students 16 to 26 years old receive 10 percent off most fares. The card, which is valid for one year, costs $15 and is good for discounts on both domestic and international flights.

Youth Fares

Young people aged 12 to 22, occasionally up to 25, can sometimes pick up a youth discount. Youth fares differ from student fares in that eligibility depends on age rather than enrollment in a school.

Youth fares were once common on international routes, but around the mid-1970s most disappeared.

These fares, however, have made a comeback. During spring and summer 1986, fear of terrorism caused thousands of Americans to cancel plans for European flights. Counting on the adventurous spirit of youth to fill those empty seats, several airlines revived youth fares. They offered discounts ranging from 20 to 55 percent off Apex fares on their European and Middle Eastern flights.

In spring 1986, for example, TWA was charging $425 one way for its lowest promotional fare between Washington, D.C., and Paris. To boost sagging sales, the airline brought out a Washington-Paris one-way youth fare of $198 — that's a discount of some 53 percent off the Apex fare and a saving of $227.

It looks as though youth fares will be around for a while for the airlines have continued to offer them, especially the European airlines which have deeply discounted their youth fares. Some recent examples:

• Iberia, the Spanish airline, set a New York-Madrid high-season youth fare at $476. Iberia's cheapest high-season Apex fare sold for $652. Purchasing the youth fare represented a $176 savings.

• Scandinavia's SAS airlines priced a high-season Chicago-Copenhagen youth fare at $656. The airline's least-expensive, high-season Apex fare went for $985. Youth fare buyers saved a substantial $329.

• Greece's Olympic Airways once sold its New York-Athens

high-season youth fare for $512. Olympic's least expensive Apex fare at the time cost $997, or a hefty $485 more.

Many youth fares are available year round. But they do carry restrictions, so you'll need to be flexible. In the examples I used above, the airlines would not confirm your seat until 72 hours before flight time.

Children

When a child aged 2 to 11, occasionally up to 17, is accompanied by a fare-paying adult, most airlines will discount the child's ticket between 25 and 50 percent.

Australia's Qantas Airways has been especially generous with children, knocking 70 percent off their fares.

Families

Under a typical family fare, one adult would pay full fare. The spouse then receives a 25 to 50 percent discount. Children's tickets would be discounted in the area of 50 to 85 percent

Family fares can vary, though. One airline came out with a "Family Plan" that offered discounts for all members of the family. The head of the household received a 40 percent discount, the second traveler 70 percent and each additional traveler 85 percent.

Senior Citizens

Over the years, airline discounts for senior citizens have been quite fickle — here today but often gone tomorrow. Sometimes the discount applied only to full coach fares rather than to less-expensive promotional fares. But the airlines have now turned serious about courting senior citizens.

Many offer seniors age 62 and over discounts which fall into four categories: clubs, coupon booklets, straight discounts and passes.

When the airlines first started courting seniors, they used a variety of clubs. Most of the clubs, however, have disappeared in favor of more attractive discount programs. One that's still around, though, is United Airlines' "Silver Wings Plus."

Silver Wings Plus membership makes seniors age 62 and over eligible for a 10 percent discount on most fares, including promotional fares. There are no restrictions on the discount. But if the fare to be discounted is a promotional fare, the usual restrictions will apply to it.

Silver Wings Plus also offers its members a variety of hotel discounts. United's club charges an annual membership fee of $25 which is offset by a $25 discount certificate good on any United flight.

One club-like program drops the age for discounts to 50. American Airlines cuts its fares 10 percent for members of the American Association of Retired People (AARP) and a spouse of any age. American's AARP fares apply to the airline's domestic routes — except Alaska — and to its flights to the Caribbean and Mexico.

Most airlines have come out with another, more-valuable innovation for senior fares. America West, American, Continental, Delta, Northwest, United and USAir offer seniors 62 and over booklets containing four or eight coupons, each coupon being good for a one-way trip on any of their domestic flights. For an eight-coupon booklet (four round trips) Delta Air Lines charges $896, four-coupon booklets go for $516. Coupons are valid for one year.

These coupon booklets offer senior citizens one of the best fare deals going. With an eight-coupon booklet a one-way flight costs only $112. You could fly Delta round trip between Miami and Seattle, for example, for just $224. Seniors in the market for fares that really offer super savings should contact America West, American, Continental, Delta, Northwest, United or USAir for the latest details.

Another airline offers coupon booklets but puts a partial high-season cap on their use. The booklets sold by TWA limit each coupon to a maximum of 2,000 miles during the month of August.

Obviously, TWA's coupons are not as good a deal if you plan to travel during August. Instead of using two coupons to make a round-trip transcontinental flight on TWA, you would have to use four coupons. But if you live in the Midwest where you can reach any part of the country on a 2,000-mile coupon, TWA's more limited mileage would not really be of concern to you.

Before buying a coupon booklet, check with all the airlines serving your hometown to determine the cost of their booklets and restrictions on using the coupons. You'll find variations in prices, advance-reservation requirements, blacked-out holiday periods and authorized travel days. Some also allow discounts for a senior's traveling companion. Compare the variations, and then make your decision.

When ordering a set of coupons for yourself and another for your spouse, be sure the airline knows to put your name on one and your spouse's name on the other. If you order the coupons under one name only, the other person will not be able to use them.

If you don't think you'll be doing enough flying with any one airline to justify the cash outlay to join a club or buy coupons, you can still pick up a discount. Just about all major airlines give seniors a 10 percent discount off any of their fares, including promotional fares. There's no club to join or coupons to buy. Just ask for the discount and show proof of age — typically 62. Most carriers also grant the discount to a companion of any age who accompanies the senior.

On the other hand, if you are a frequent traveler, look into the senior pass offered by Continental. The airline offers a "Freedom Passport" that lets seniors 62 and over fly the airlines' routes in the United States, Canada and the Caribbean — more than 140 destinations in all — for one year for a single price of $1,799. If you renew the pass for a second year, the price drops $300. You can also buy attractively priced add-ons to fly to a particular part of the world, including Mexico, the Caribbean, Central America, Hawaii, Europe and the South Pacific.

A "Global" version of the pass sells for $2999 and combines the domestic pass with a flight to each of the add-on areas. Continental also sells a "Companion Passport" that allows a spouse, friend or relative under 62 to accompany the holder of the Freedom Passport.

The Freedom Passport allows up to three trips to any one city but can be used no oftener than once a week. Restrictions include blackout periods and travel only on certain days.

While the Freedom Passport represents a good buy, you will need to consider Continental's financial condition before you enter into a year-long contract with the airline. As I write this, Continental is in Chapter 11 bankruptcy. Although the airline appears to be holding its own, with no collapse imminent, that could change. Check with a travel agent or a stockbroker to see if you can get an idea of the airline's stability.

Consider also when you will be using your Freedom Passport. If the bulk of your travel will come well into the life of the pass, thus extending the point in time at which you will break even on its purchase compared to purchasing individual promotional fares, your risk in buying the pass is greater.

But if you will be doing a substantial amount of flying early on, you will be minimizing your risk by reaching your break-even point sooner.

Senior discounts from international airlines

Several international airlines establish deeply discounted special fares for seniors. When Sabena, Belgium's airline, was selling its New York-Brussels Apex tickets for $496, the airline offered that ticket to seniors for $338, a 32 percent discount and a $158 saving. Among other international airlines that have set special fares for seniors are Alitalia, Finnair, JAT (Yugoslav Airlines), LOT Polish Airlines, SAS (Scandinavian Airlines System) and TAP Air Portugal.

British Airways looks after seniors by offering discounts to those 60 and over through a no-cost "Privileged Traveler" program. Once enrolled, the traveler is then eligible for special senior Apex fares or a 10 percent discount off the airline's other fares. A companion traveler aged 50 and over is also eligible for the discounts.

Meeting fares — a break for the business traveler

If you are planning to attend a large meeting or convention, you may be able to use a meeting fare. Organizers of such events can prearrange these discounted fares with an individual airline.

Most meeting fares offer a discount of about 40 or 45 percent off the airline's full fare or a 5 percent discount off any promotional fare. Generally, an airline will want at least 100 people to be attending before they will provide a meeting fare.

Discounted meeting fares are available on the dates of the event plus a few days before and after, which allows you to attend and also add on a few days for sightseeing or additional business.

To obtain a meeting fare, you normally have to tell the airline reservationist the special identifying code which has been assigned to the meeting. The code is available from the meeting organizer and is also generally printed in the literature promoting the event. In some cases, reservations for meeting fares may have to be made through a particular travel agency.

Family members and friends accompanying the attendee, even though they may not be participating in the event, can generally use these fares as well. And if your company is providing a service for a meeting or exhibiting at a convention, your employees can also use the event's meeting fare.

Emergency-travel fares — discounts on short-notice travel

If you have to make a short-notice emergency flight, the good news is that most airlines will give you a reduced fare. The alternative would be a full coach fare costing two to three times as much.

The bad news is that each airline has its own emergency-travel policy that determines under what circumstances they will provide a reduced fare, which family members must be involved in the emergency, the size of the reduction and the procedures for obtaining the fare. So, at a time when you least feel like running into hassles, you'll have to shop around and keep track of the variations if you want the best deal.

These fares, which are called bereavement or compassion fares, typically amount to a waiver of the advance purchase requirement on promotional fares when a sudden illness or death in the immediate family forces you to take an unexpected flight. You probably will not get the carrier's least-expensive promotional fare, but you'll get one that cuts the full fare by about 45 or 50 percent.

To give you an idea of the variations you can run into:

• Some airlines have published, reduced-rate bereavement

fares that either provide a discount off the full fare or waive advance purchase restrictions. Others allow reservationists and supervisors to handle emergency travel on a case-by-case basis. Still others require you to pay the full fare and apply for a refund upon your return. And with at least one airline — TWA — that refund comes in the form of a voucher good for future transportation.

• Some airlines waive all restrictions. Others do not waive the Saturday-night stay over requirement. That could be a serious drawback. Depending on the day of the week you fly, you may have to extend your stay several days to get the bereavement fare.

• Some U.S. airlines waive restrictions for both domestic and international passengers. Others do so only for domestic travelers. Some foreign airlines provide reduced fares for emergency travel. Others, — such as Lufthansa, the German airline, do not.

• Some airlines require that the illness be life threatening. Others evaluate the seriousness of an illness case by case.

• Some airlines define immediate family as spouse, children, parents, grandparents, grandchildren, brothers, sisters and in-laws. Others expand the definition to include great grandparents/children, aunts, uncles, nephews, nieces and cousins.

The only consistency you'll find among the airlines is their requirement that you prove your claim of an emergency. You'll have to provide documentation from a physician, a hospital or a mortician. The airlines will not issue a bereavement-fare ticket just on your say so.

How to get a bereavement fare

Should an emergency-travel situation come up, follow these procedures:

• First thing you need to do is get the information and documentation that will substantiate your emergency and convince the airline the crisis is real. At a minimum, obtain the names, addresses and telephone numbers of all the service providers involved in the emergency — doctor, hospital, funeral home, mortician as appropriate.

Try to have someone fax you the documentation — a letter written on letterhead, a published obituary or a copy of a death certificate. Have them follow up by mailing you the original. If you don't have ready access to a fax machine, perhaps at the office, call a neighborhood print shop or mail center and get their fax number. These establishments will receive your fax at a nominal charge.

• Now you have to start shopping. If you have a travel agent with whom you do business regularly, turn the whole affair over to the agent. You probably will not be in a mental state that's up to enduring the haggles and hassles necessary to obtain a reasonably priced fare, anyway. A travel agent will have more pull than you and will be more likely to know which airlines tend to put more compassion into their compassion fares. A travel agent who has some real clout may be able to get you a bereavement fare based on their word without the need to supply immediate documentation.

However, at least one airline — Northwest — will not let travel agents handle its bereavement fares. Other airlines will let travel agents obtain and reserve the fare, but you'll have to pick your ticket up at the airport.

• If you call the airline yourself, explain your situation and request a bereavement or compassion fare that waives any restrictions. Even though you may be upset and in a hurry, be patient with the questions. It's not in your interest to alienate the person working to get you a lower fare.

You will need to convince the airline that the crisis is real. Have names and telephone numbers ready to give the reservationist, so the airline can verify the emergency itself. If the reservationist seems hesitant, he or she may not be sure of either the airline's policies or their own authority to grant compassion fares. Ask to speak with the reservations supervisor or call instead the airline's customer service department. Get the number from the Airline contact appendix at the back of this book.

Once convinced an actual crisis exists, airline personnel may be willing and able to stretch the definition of immediate family, perhaps to include the family of a significant other. Or, they may grant a compassion fare for a serious accident or sudden illness even if not life threatening.

• If several family members will be flying, stress just how many in your conversation with the airline. The more business you offer, the more inclined an airline may be to give you a better deal to get that business.

• If you don't like what one airline offers, call other carriers to see what they can do for you. During a crisis, however, you may not be up to shopping around for a rock-bottom deal. If so, just take the first halfway reasonable fare you can get. But should financial conditions force you to get the absolutely best deal, you will have to keep slugging away.

Emergencies and circumstances beyond your control after you've bought a ticket

An emergency could also force you to postpone or cancel a trip for which you have already purchased tickets. Or, you could have to cut short a journey and return home early. In addition, non-emergency situations beyond your control, a court summons for example, could also affect your air-travel plans. Even though your ticket may be nonrefundable, the airlines tend to show compassion in these situations as well. If you are seeking a change of dates rather than a refund, you may find a higher level of compassion.

Contact the airline and explain your circumstances. But you will still need to provide the airline written, authoritative documentation confirming your situation.

Air transportation to medical facilities

If you — or someone you know — needs transportation to a distant city because that town has specialized medical facilities, but cannot afford the cost of transportation, contact AirLifeLine, 1116 - 24th St., Sacramento, CA 95816, telephone 916-446-0995. This organization can help arrange air transportation in these cases.

Another charitable group, Corporate Angel Network, specializes in arranging free air transportation on corporate jets for cancer patients. Financial need is not a necessity. With the aid of hundreds of corporations that provide space on their aircraft, this nonprofit organization seeks to help spare patients the stresses of commercial air travel.

Among the rules Corporate Angel Network operates under:

• Patients must be going to or returning from a treatment, consultation or checkup at a recognized facility.

• Patients must be able to board the aircraft unassisted. They cannot be on a stretcher or require life-support systems or other special services during the flight.

• If space permits, another passenger may accompany the patient. Both parents may accompany a child.

• An appropriate corporate flight may not always be found, so patients must arrange a commercial-flight backup.

To arrange a flight, contact Corporate Angel Network, Westchester County Airport, Building One, White Plains, NY 10604, telephone 914-328-1313, fax 800-328-4226.

Standby fares — discounts for the truly flexible

To fly standby, you arrive at the airport several hours prior to departure of the flight you want. If the flight has empty seats, you get one. A few airlines make standby a bit easier by selling you a confirmed-seat ticket at one of their city ticket offices on the day of your flight.

Standby can be risky. But if you are flexible as to when you arrive at your destination — and will not incur major expenses should you miss a flight or two — you can save big with some standby fares, as much as 50 percent less than the lowest promotional fares.

Some airlines modify the traditional last-minute standby fare by turning it into a late-booking fare. Typically, you get a deep discount for buying your ticket between one and three days before flight time. Virgin Atlantic Airways, for example, once offered passengers purchasing New York-London round trips either the day before or on the day of departure a fare of $398. At the time, with New York-London promotional fares selling for around $588, travelers saved $190.

Icelandair once implemented a late-booker standby fare on its Baltimore-London flights. You had to reserve your flight no more than one day before departure.

Standby fares come and go in popularity. When they are offered you may find them restricted to youthful travelers under age 25. You're also more likely to find standby fares on international flights, primarily to Europe and particularly to London.

Compare costs to see if standby is worthwhile

Before investigating standby fares be sure to determine the lowest Apex fare to your destination. The dollar difference between a standby fare and an Apex fare may not always be enough to make standby worthwhile. Here's some examples of standby fares with widely varying savings:

• Air Canada has offered standby fares on its routes between the United States and Canada that allowed passengers to cut their cost in half.

• To fly standby from Pittsburgh to London and back once cost $518. The cheapest Pittsburgh-London round-trip Apex fare at the time ran $699. Standby savings: $181 round trip.

• Round-trip standby New York-London on British Airways once cost $578. The airline's least-expensive Apex fare was $688. Standby savings: $110.

• Icelandair's New York-Luxembourg one-way standby fare was once set at $149. Icelandair's lowest Apex fare cost $179. Standby savings: $30 one way.

Standby offers tremendous savings over full-fare alternatives

Standby fares offer advantages that go beyond their obvious savings. Typically, they are available as one-way fares. Since most promotional fares require a round trip, a one-way standby ticket can save you big bucks over the alternative — an expensive full-fare ticket.

Standby fares also do not carry the restrictions of a promotional fare. If you need to make a short-notice trip that won't let you meet the advance-purchase requirement of an Apex fare, a last-minute standby ticket can again give you tremendous savings over the full-fare alternative.

When British Airways was offering their $578 New York-London standby fare, their full-fare round trip sold for $1,462. That round-trip standby ticket would save you $884 over the full fare.

Two one-way tickets might cost less than a round trip

Whether you should buy your standby fare as a round trip or

two one-way tickets depends on the strength of the dollar in relation to the currency of your destination country. If the dollar is stronger, you would probably save with two one-way tickets. If the dollar is weaker, you would probably be better off buying a round-trip. To determine which will save you money, ask the reservationist for the cost of your flight priced as a round trip and as two one-way tickets.

Stopovers — squeezing extra destinations from your fare

A stopover is a break in your flight of 24 hours or more in a city other than your ultimate destination. Some airline routes allow free stopovers that will let you extend your travels at no cost beyond the price of the ticket to your destination. While you can find occasional stopovers on domestic flights, they are most common on international routes. When talking with a reservationist, ask about the possibility of free stopovers.

At one time, for example, if you flew Mexicana Airlines from Los Angeles to Acapulco, you could stopover in Mexico City for several days at no extra charge. On New York-San José, Costa Rica, flights the Costa Rican airline Lacsa has given one free stopover in each direction at any of several cities that serve as gateways to Mexican and Central American Mayan ruins.

Stopovers do not have to be on a direct line to your destination, some fairly wide swings may be permitted. American Airlines and South African Airways once teamed up to offer passengers flying Dallas-Johannesburg, South Africa, a free stopover in London.

And stopovers are not always confined to just one city. You may be able to make multiple stopovers before reaching your ultimate destination, still without paying an additional charge.

Many South Pacific flights allow multiple stopovers. United Airlines' flights between Australia and the United States have offered stopovers in Fiji and Auckland, New Zealand.

Thai Airways has allowed travelers on its New York-Bangkok route a free stopover in each direction. For example, you could tack onto your New York-Bangkok flight stopovers in Tokyo and Hong Kong.

Continental's U.S.-Australia flights have offered up to four stopovers: Honolulu, Tahiti, Fiji and Auckland. And Australia's Qantas Airways has given its passengers unlimited free stopovers both in the South Pacific and within Australia.

Stopovers may also be available for a small additional charge. AeroPerú has offered Lima-bound international passengers one free stopover in any Peruvian city plus as many additional stopovers as desired for $25 each.

Aer Lingus, Ireland's airline, once offered Apex ticket holders en route London a stopover in Dublin for an additional $25.

One domestic airline, America West, has offered its promotional-fare passengers connecting in Las Vegas or Phoenix a stopover in either of those cities for $10.

A drawback

Some stopovers have a drawback — they may be available only when you pay the full excursion fare. If you're flying on a lower-priced Apex fare, you may not have stopover privileges. Therefore, you'll have to weigh the costs and benefits of a full fare plus stopovers against the Apex fare with no stopovers.

There are many exceptions though. Most South Pacific stopovers, for example, are available to Apex passengers.

Stopovers for a package deal

Airlines may also offer Apex ticket holders a stopover if the passenger purchases, for use in the stopover city, a prepaid package (air fare, hotel accommodations, sometimes meals all sold for a single price).

Tower Air once allowed travelers on its New York-Tel Aviv route a stopover in one of several European cities, provided the passenger bought a package for use in the stopover city.

Air Korea has offered one-night stopovers in many cities along its routes when the passenger buys a land package which includes accommodations, breakfast, a city tour and airport-hotel transfers. Among the carrier's stopover cities: Bangkok, Hong Kong, Jakarta, Kuala Lumpur, Manila, Singapore, Taipei and Tokyo.

Business travel stopovers

If you are a business traveler, look into stopovers anytime you need to fly a multiple-destination international itinerary. Free or low-cost stopovers on an Apex ticket would be ideal. But even a full-fare ticket with stopover privileges could cost less than multiple Apex tickets for your itinerary. Have the reservationist price your flights both ways to see which will let you fly there for less.

You can also use free stopovers to squeeze in some rest and relaxation. After concluding your business, fly to a stopover city before returning home to the job. You can spend a few days vacationing with no additional cost to your company.

Use maximum permitted mileage to extend your travels

On international flights, a fare-calculation method known as maximum permitted mileage can add stopovers to your route. As long as you continue to fly in the same general direction, maximum permitted mileage allows you to vary your route, change airlines and make stopovers before reaching your destination. You may be able to add as much as 25 percent to the direct mileage between your departure city and destination.

Talk to a travel agent about maximum permitted mileage rather than an airline. Since you are allowed to change airlines, you'll probably get a better itinerary from a travel agent who can book you on any airline.

Look for an agent who's been around for a while and knows the ins and outs of the airline tariff guides — the primary source of airline fares in pre-computer days. A knowledgeable agent skilled in using these guides, and in applying the airlines' rules and formulas to calculate fares, can probably save you money on all but the simplest international itineraries.

These veteran agents, whose creativity can't be programmed into a computer, know which cities and which obscure routings will increase your maximum permitted mileage to give you the most stopovers.

Air passes — extend your travels but cut your costs

Many travelers know foreign railroads sell passes that let you crisscross a country, even a continent, at bargain prices. Not so well known, however, is the variety of airline passes that will also let you crisscross a country, even a continent, at bargain prices.

With an air pass you can visit widespread cities in such popular destinations as Western Europe, Australia and New Zealand. Air passes will also take you to far-flung destinations off-the-beaten path in Asia, Africa, South America and the South Seas.

Restrictions and rules for use vary among the airlines and their passes. But there are a few general rules applicable to most.

• Air passes usually have to be bought in the United States in conjunction with an international flight.

• Some passes require your international flight be on the flag carrier of the country of destination.

• An occasional pass may require you to set your itinerary when you purchase your ticket. Altering that itinerary may then involve an additional charge.

• Passes may allow only one stopover in each city, although you may return to a city to make a connection.

• Passes generally confine you to a single airline, sometimes a group of airlines. If your flight is delayed, you will not be able to switch carriers.

• An occasional pass may be available only during certain times of the year.

• All air passes require that travel be completed within a given time period.

An air pass can represent a good bargain, but not for every traveler. Have an idea of where you will be flying with the pass, and then contact the appropriate airline (use the toll-free numbers listed in the Airline contacts appendix) or a travel agent to determine the cost of covering that itinerary with individual tickets to each destination. If the pass costs less than the individual tickets, as it generally will if your itinerary covers extensive distances and involves quite a few stops, then go ahead and buy the pass.

The following is a rundown of air passes and pass-like fares offered by airlines serving destinations worldwide. I've included fares with the pass information, and sometimes a non-pass fare that may help you decide whether the pass represents a good buy for your travels. But, as you well know by now, fares change. So use these fares only to give you an idea of what your costs could run.

Europe

• France - The French domestic airline Air Inter sells a $250 *"La France"* pass. This pass gives you unlimited air travel on Air Inter's 30-city route system on any seven days within a month.

Another domestic carrier, Air Littoral sells a $229 pass good for seven consecutive days of unlimited travel to any of the line's 23 French cities. A 10-day pass costs $279.

These passes can save you substantially — a round trip between Paris and Avignon costs $351. You can obtain passes on these French domestic carriers in the United States by contacting France's international airlines: Air France and UTA.

• Iceland - Traveler's within Iceland can choose from two Icelandair passes. An "Air Rover" ticket provides travel from Reykjavik to Isafjordur, Egilsstadir, Akureyri, Hofn and back to Reykjavik. The Air Rover ticket costs $210 and is valid for 30 days after the first flight. An Icelandair "Air Pass," priced at $165, allows you to choose any four flights within Iceland.

• Scandinavia - Scandinavia-bound passengers on SAS can buy a "Visit Scandinavia" ticket good for flights within or between Norway, Sweden and Denmark. A ticket for one flight costs $80, two flights $160, three flights $230, four flights $300 and six flights $420. The pass is valid for three months from first use on flights operated by SAS, Danair, Linjeflyg and Norving. The Visit Scandinavia ticket is generally only available during the summer months. It represents a real good buy — an Oslo-Stockholm round trip would cost $229.

Finnair sells a "Holiday Ticket" good for 15 days' unlimited travel in Finland on Finnair, Finnaviation and Karair. Cost is $300.

Braathens SAFE, a Norwegian airline, sells a "Visit Norway" pass from May through September. Valid for one month, the pass allows flights between 14 cities for $15 plus a charge based on distance — $57 for "short" flights and $114 for "long" flights.

• Spain - A "Visit Spain Airpass" costs $249 and allows unlimited travel for up to 60 days to any of 25 destinations in Spain, including the Balearic Islands. An additional $50 extends the pass to include Spain's Canary Islands. You must fly to Spain on Iberia, the country's national airline. Flights within Spain will be on either Iberia or Aviaco, a Spanish domestic carrier.

With a Madrid-Balearic Islands flight costing $240, this pass is a great buy. And $50 for a flight to the Canary Islands? Get out your atlas and see just how fare you would be flying. (In case your neighbor borrowed your atlas, it's about the same distance as from Miami to Washington, DC.)

• United Kingdom - A Dan-Air "Visit UK" ticket will let you visit cities in England, Scotland, Wales and Northern Ireland. The flight to your first city costs $99. Each city thereafter costs $89. Tickets are valid for 60 days. An independent British airline, Dan-Air will take you to cities such as London, Newcastle, Bristol, Jersey, Leeds, Aberdeen, Inverness, Cardiff, and Belfast as well as numerous smaller cities.

British Airways has a similar pass. The airline's "UK Air Pass" offers you from three to 12 flights priced at $85 for a flight to or from London and $65 for each additional flight. You must make at least three flights but no more than 12. British Airways also sells a "Highland Rover" pass good for eight flights within Scotland during a 14-day period. This pass costs $254.

Africa

• South Africa - South African Airways has a "Visit South

Africa" fare that permits visits to four South African cities for about $234. Travel must be completed within a month.

North America

• Canada - An "Atlantic Canadapass" provides travel among 16 cities in Canada's four Atlantic provinces — Newfoundland, Nova Scotia, Prince Edward Island and New Brunswick. Cities include Blanc Sablon, Charlottetown, Deer Lake, Fredericton, Goose Bay, Halifax, Saint John, St. John's, Stephenville, Sydney and Yarmouth. The pass costs $233 for three destinations, $271 for four, $316 for five and $358 for six. Flights are available on Air Canada and Air Nova. Travel must be completed within 30 days.

A four-flight, non-pass itinerary covering Halifax-St. John's-Charlottetown-Fredericton-Halifax would cost you $487. With an Atlantic Canadapass that itinerary would drop to $271.

• Mexico - Mexicana Airlines' "Vimex" program provides a 15 percent reduction on domestic flights made during a 45-day period.

• Mexico and Central America - Two Central American airlines sell 21-day "Mayan World Fares" that allow you to visit the sites of significant Mayan ruins located in southeast Mexico, Belize, Guatemala, Honduras and El Salvador. Aviateca, Guatemala's airline, and Tan Sasha, the national carrier of Honduras, both offer visits to four cities adjacent to Mayan sites for $399, including air fare from U. S. gateways. Among the stops available: Mérida, Mexico; Flores and Guatemala City, Guatemala (Mayan sites at Tikal and Quirigua); Belize City, Belize (ruins of Zunantunich, Altun Ha and Lamani); San Pedro Sula (Mayan city of Copán) and Tegucigalpa, Honduras.

Caribbean

The Antigua-based LIAT airline sells two air passes. A "Super

Caribbean Explorer Pass" provides 30 days of unlimited travel among 21 islands, including Puerto Rico, The U.S. and British Virgin Islands, St. Martin, St. Kitts, Guadeloupe, Martinique, Barbados and Trinidad. The pass, which costs $357, also includes stopovers in Venezuela and Guyana on the South American mainland. The line's "Caribbean Explorer Fare" allows up to six island stopovers within 21 days for $199 peak season, $167 off season.

LIAT's passes will give you good value for your money. A San Juan, Puerto Rico, to Trinidad fare sells for $311 while a Guadeloupe-Barbados ticket sells for $167.

South America

Three airlines, AeroPerú, Air Paraquay and Avianca offer some good deals that let you cover the main cities on the sprawling South American continent. Note, though, that each of the three airlines requires backtracking to its domestic hub to make the international connections.

AeroPerú's "Visit South America" pass gives you 45 days of international travel to visit, via the airline's hub in Lima, any six of the South American cities it serves. Destinations include La Paz, Santiago, Buenos Aires, Rio de Janeiro, São Paulo, Bogotá and Caracas as well as cities within Peru. Cost including air fare from Miami is $813 in low season, $963 high season. You can tack on additional cities outside of Peru for $100 each. Peruvian cities are available for $40 per flight.

Passengers flying Air Paraguay (Lineas Aéreas Paraguayas — LAP) from Miami can make up to six free stopovers in cities the airline serves, including Buenos Aires, Rio de Janeiro, São Paulo, Montevideo, La Paz, Santiago and Lima. Connections between these cities must be made via Asunción, Paraguay's capital, and travel must be completed within 30 days. Air Paraguay's "Visit South America" fare costs $899, including air fare from Miami. You can purchase additional stopovers for $100 each.

The Colombian airline, Avianca, offers a Miami-Bogotá round trip plus flights to any five South American cities for $899. The fare must, however, be purchased in conjunction with a land package costing at least $380. Cities served by Avianca include Lima, Quito, Buenos Aires, Santiago, Montevideo and Rio de Janeiro. All your flights have to be made within 21 days and must connect through Bogotá.

• Argentina - Argentine airlines Austral Lineas Aéreas, Aerolíneas Argentinas and LADE (Lineas Aéreas del Estado) offer a "Visit Argentina" pass good for 30 days. The pass costs $359 for four flights, $409 for six flights, $459 for eight flights.

Argentina is a big country, about as long as the United States is wide. A Visit Argentina pass will go along way in keeping your expenses down when traveling among the country's distant cities. A Buenos Aires-Iguazú round trip, for example costs $326.

• Bolivia - Bolivian airline Lloyd Aéreo Boliviano sells a "Visit Bolivia Pass" for $150. The pass allows visits to any six Bolivian destinations within 28 days.

• Brazil - Brazilian airlines Varig, VASP and Transbrasil offer a $440 "Brazil Airpass" that permits travel to five domestic cities within 21 days on any one of the three airlines. You may purchase up to four additional flights for $100 each.

You'll find the Brazil Airpass a tremendous value in covering the long distances in this massive country.

• Chile - LanChile offers a "Visit Chile Fare" for $450. The fare permits 21 days of air travel to nine cities including Antofagasta, Calama, Iquique, Arica, Santiago, Puerto Montt and Punta Arenas. Adding a round trip to Easter Island pushes the cost to $750. The airline also offers two other options priced at $250 that allow travel only from Santiago south or only from Santiago north.

Another Chilean airline, Ladeco, also offers the 21-day Visit Chile Fare and options at the same prices.

Although an extremely narrow country just a couple of hundred miles wide, Chile is more than three thousand miles long. And Easter Island sits more than 2,500 miles off its coast The Chilean passes are a great buy if you are going to be covering these distances.

• Colombia - A 30-day "Discover Colombia" fare on Avianca Airlines provides up to 10 Colombian stopovers within 30 days for $224. To include Leticia (on the Amazon River in southern Colombia) and San Andrés (a Caribbean island) the cost goes to $325. You can also buy a "Discover Colombia 5" ticket allowing five stopovers in 14 days for $112. To include Leticia and San Andrés Island, the cost rises to $190.

• Peru - A "Visit Peru" pass on either AeroPerú or Faucett permits visits to 12 cities within 30 days. The pass costs $180 if your international flight is on AeroPerú or Faucett, $250 if on another airline.

• Venezuela - Avensa Airlines offers an "Avensa Airpass" which covers its 23-city route system within Venezuela. Fourteen days of unlimited travel costs $400.

Asia

• India - With Indian Airlines' 21-day "Discover India" pass, you get unlimited travel on the airline's 64-city network for $400. The airline also sells an "India Wonderfare" pass that costs $200 and offers seven days of unlimited travel within one of four regions. Unlike most other passes, you can by these after you arrive in India. You must, however, pay for the pass in foreign currency.

Indian Airlines' passes are good values for widespread travel in India. A New Delhi-Bombay one-way fare sells for $115. Between New Delhi and Srinagar the fare runs $174.

• Indonesia - Garuda Indonesian airlines offers three "Visit Indonesia Air Pass" options: $350 for up to four cities within 20 days, $500 for a maximum of 8 cities within 30 days and $600 for as many as 12 cities within 60 days. The passes are also valid on the Indonesian domestic carrier Merpati Nusantara.

• Malaysia - With a Malaysia Airlines pass you can visit four cities within any one of the country's three regions. This "Discover Malaysia" pass sells for $99 and gives you 21 days to complete your travels. Pass holders can also get 50 percent off the fares for travel between the three regions up to a maximum of five trips. You can buy the Discover Malaysia air pass after arriving in Malaysia.

• Thailand - Thai Airways sells a $219 "Discover Thailand" pass good for four domestic flights. You can purchase up to four additional flights for $45 each. The pass gives 60 days to complete your travels.

If you plan to travel extensively throughout Thailand, you'll probably save money buying the pass. A flight from Bangkok to Chiang Mai costs $65.

Australia and New Zealand

Airlines in both Australia and New Zealand offer a wide variety of air passes and discounted pass-like fares. The passes of both countries offer good values for extensive itineraries. Australia's passes are especially attractive in view of the vast distances they cover. Although the passes seem to undergo fairly frequent modifications and name changes, this rundown will give you a good idea of what's available.

One pass, offered by the Ansett group of airlines (Ansett Australia Airlines, Ansett Express, Ansett New Zealand and Ansett W.A.), allows you to travel in and between both Australia and New Zealand. Carrying a name that seems as lengthy as the distances it covers, the "Down Under Discount Deals — an

Australia & New Zealand Airpass" will let you reach just about any city in those two countries that has commercial airline service.

The pass assigns values ranging from one to five "units" for one-way travel between various cities. Each unit costs approximately $48. After constructing your itinerary, you add up the units and multiply by $48 to determine your fare, which will save you up to 60 percent off the regular economy fare for the routes you've selected.

An itinerary, say, calling for travel from Sydney to Melbourne (2 units), Melbourne to Ayers Rock (4 units), Ayers Rock to Alice Springs (2 units), Alice Springs to Brisbane (5 units), Brisbane to Christchurch in New Zealand (5 units), Christchurch to Wellington (2 units) and Wellington to Auckland (2 units) adds up to 22 units. Multiplying the 22 units by $48 gives you a fare for this extensive international itinerary of $1,056.

For travel on the Down Under Discount Deals pass you can select from nine airlines: Aeropelican, Ansett Australia Airlines, Ansett Express, Ansett New Zealand, Ansett W.A., Eastwest, Flight West Airlines, Kendell Airlines and Qantas. Travel within Australia, however, is not permitted on Qantas.

• Australia - Eastwest Airlines, an Australian carrier, offers a variety of air pass options at fares ranging from about $368 to $640. The carrier's 14-day "East Side Air Pass" covers 18 cities in eastern Australia plus a flight to Ayers Rock. The East Side Air Pass allows backtracking, so you can visit each city more than once.

Eastwest also offers two air passes that allow only one stopover in each city. The "Trans-Continental" pass allows flights to Cairns, Brisbane, Surfer's Paradise, Sydney, Ayers Rock and Perth, in that order or the reverse order. With the carrier's "Coastal Air Pass" you can visit, in order, Cairns, Brisbane, Surfer's Paradise, Sydney, Melbourne, Hobart (Tasmania) and back to Melbourne. You can also reverse the order. Both the Trans-Continental and the Coastal Air Pass give you 60 days to complete your travel.

Australian Airlines sells an "Experience Australia" air pass that offers eight different preset itineraries at a price about 30 percent lower than the line's standard economy fare. Prices range from $260 to $620. Five of the itineraries are loops starting and terminating in Sydney, with travel allowed in either direction: Sydney-Canberra-Melbourne-Sydney ($260), Sydney-Canberra-Melbourne-Hobart-Sydney ($390). Sydney-Canberra-Melbourne-Adelaide-Sydney ($409), Sydney-Canberra-Melbourne-Coolangatta-Sydney ($433) and Sydney-Cairns-Alice Springs-Sydney ($626). The other three itineraries: Sydney-Alice Springs-Cairns ($390), Cairns-Darwin-Alice Springs-Perth ($579), and Sydney-Cairns-Alice Springs-Perth ($626). Travel on these Experience Australia fares must be for at least seven days but no longer than 90 days.

• New Zealand - With a "Kiwi Air Pass" from New Zealand's Mount Cook Airline, travelers have 30 days to travel the airline's route system. Destinations served by Mount Cook Airline include Auckland, Bay of Islands, Christchurch, Dunedin, Manapouri, Mount Cook, Nelson, Queenstown, Rotorua, Te Anau and Wellington. The Kiwi Air Pass costs $559. But if your transpacific flight is on United airlines, you can pick up the Kiwi Air Pass for just $395. United's pass, however, does not include flights to the Chatham Islands, Kerikeri and Milford Sound.

Ansett New Zealand offers its passengers a "See New Zealand" ticket book good for three domestic one-way flights for $223 or eight flights for $526. Air New Zealand sells a similar pass called "Explore New Zealand."

Another ticket book, called "Freedom Pass," is available for use on the domestic flights of Air New Zealand or Mount Cook Airlines. Books permitting four one-way flights cost $232, six one-way flights sell for $324.

Pacific Rim

Multi-stop fares called "Circle Pacific fares" will let you visit such countries as Japan, Korea, Taiwan, Hong Kong, the Philippines, Thailand, Malaysia, Singapore, Indonesia, Australia, New Zealand, Fiji and French Polynesia. Using a combination of two or more airlines, you can construct your own itinerary for making a circular trip around the Pacific. The number of stops is limited only by the routes served by the airlines you select. Your travel, however, must continue in the same direction without backtracking.

Circle Pacific fares range from about $2,229 to $2,500 for the first four stops. Additional cities usually cost $50 each. Your travel must be competed within six months.

Here's some of the airline combinations you can use to build your Circle Pacific itinerary:

- Air New Zealand, Japan Air Lines and Qantas

- Air New Zealand and Korean Air Lines

- Canadian Airlines International and your choice of one of these carriers: Air New Zealand, Cathay Pacific, Garuda Indonesia, Malaysia Airlines, Qantas or Singapore Airlines

- Continental and Garuda

- Continental and Thai Airways International

- Northwest, Fiji Air, Qantas and Singapore Airlines

- United and Qantas

South Pacific

A 30-day "Pacific Air Pass" from Air Pacific permits round-trip travel between Fiji, Tonga, Vanuatu and Western Samoa for

$449. For another $59 travelers can also visit the Solomon Islands.

Polynesian Airlines of Western Samoa features a "Polypass" that allows 30 days to visit Pago Pago, American Samoa; Apia and Savaii in Western Samoa; Nadi and Suva in Fiji; Rarotonga in the Cook Islands; Nukualofa, Tonga; Auckland, New Zealand; and Sydney, Australia. The Polypass costs $999. For an additional $100 Polynesian Airlines will extend the pass seven days and add a stop in Tahiti.

The Polypass is a real bargain. A round-trip flight between Sydney and Apia costs $692.

Solomon Airlines, based in the Solomon Islands, and Air Caledonie International, which flies out of New Caledonia, sell a "Discover Pacific Pass" that lets you cover large areas of the South Pacific for 30 days. The pass consists of three flight coupons selling for $499. You can purchase one additional coupon for $100. Travel to Australia or New Zealand carries a $100 surcharge, Tahiti a $200 surcharge.

• Fiji Islands - Fiji Air's 30-day "Discover Fiji" pass offers travel to 15 destinations for $99. You must purchase the Discover Fiji pass after arriving in Fiji.

• French Polynesia - Air Tahiti sells a 28-day air pass good for travel to selected islands in French Polynesia. A $250 pass offers air travel to Papeete, Moorea, Huahine, Raiatea and Bora Bora. Rangiroa and Manihi or Rurutu and Tubuai can be added for an additional $182.

• Papua New Guinea - A "Visit Papua New Guinea" pass on Air Niugini allows four flights for $299. Additional flights cost $50 each. Travel must be completed in 30 days. In this rugged country, air travel is the only practical means of transportation. With a Port Moresby-Mt. Hagen round trip selling for $171, the pass is not only essential but a good buy.

• Solomon Islands - You can island hop through the Solomons with a "Discover Solomon" pass. Four pass flights within 30 days on Solomon Airlines costs $199.

Whenever planning travel within a foreign country, check with a travel agent or that country's international and domestic airlines to see if the airlines offer an air pass or multiple-stopover fare that will help you fly there for less.

U. S. air passes for all travelers

A few U.S. airline have come out with air passes. These passes, though, vary somewhat from those offering extended domestic travel to foreign passengers. TWA, Hawaiian Airlines and Aloha Airlines offer passes good for extended U.S. domestic travel to anyone — including U.S. residents.

TWA will sell any traveler a pass valid for at least a year and good for a given number of flights to specific geographic areas. The airline's "TWA Takeoff Pass" provides one round trip to Europe, one to Hawaii and three within the continental United States. The pass costs $1,995 and is valid for a year. TWA will extend it to eighteen months for an additional $150. The pass also carries restrictions, including limited seat availability and blackout dates.

Hawaiian Airlines offers anyone purchasing a ticket to Hawaii a pass good for unlimited interisland travel. A five-day "Hawaiian AirPass" sells for $129, seven days of interisland travel goes for $149, 10 days costs $199 and two weeks runs $239. The carrier's non-pass interisland fares cost between $50 and $75.

Hawaiian has not forgotten island residents. The carrier offers a resident interisland unlimited-travel pass good only on weekends — Friday through Sunday — for $119.

Another carrier serving Hawaii, Aloha Airlines, also offers an interisland pass. Aloha's "Island Hopper" provides five days of unlimited interisland travel for $129. Unlike the Hawaiian Airlines pass, Aloha does not offer additional time periods.

Aloha does, however, offer the $119 resident pass, calling it a "Kama'aina Island Hopper," which is good for unlimited interisland travel from Friday through Sunday.

U. S. air passes for foreign visitors

Most U.S. airlines that fly international routes offer discounted "Visit USA" fares. These fares are equivalent to an air pass and offer foreign visitors attractive, low-cost, extended-travel opportunities throughout the United States.

The Visit USA fares, which come in the form of coupon books, carry restrictions similar to other air passes:

• Visit USA coupons must be bought before the traveler arrives in the United States.

• Some passes require the first U.S. domestic flight to be reserved before arrival in the United States. Subsequent flights can be reserved anytime. Other Visit USA passes require that the traveler's entire itinerary be booked before arrival.

• Most passes require the traveler's international flight to be on the same carrier that issues the pass.

• Each pass coupon is good for one nonstop flight. A connection requires an additional coupon.

• Coupons usually have to be used within 60 days of first use or within 120 days after arriving in the United States, whichever comes first.

Here's an example of what two carriers, Northwest and American, offer foreign visitors to the United States.

Northwest has a variety of pass options. A two-coupon pass

sells for about $186 in most countries. A four-coupon pass costs $379 and allows additional coupons to be purchased for $35 each. Both passes require the itinerary be booked before arrival.

Northwest's passes allow travelers to make some extensive journeys at bargain prices. For example, a trip from New York to Chicago, to Seattle, to San Francisco, to Denver and then back to New York would cost $414 — $379 for a four-coupon book plus one additional coupon at $35. Extending the itinerary with additional $35 coupons would make the pass even more of a bargain.

For travelers wanting to keep their itinerary flexible, Northwest sells a four-coupon "Open Pass" for $439. Flights can be reserved at anytime, and additional four-coupon passes may be purchased for $140.

Still another Northwest option is a "Standby Pass" which allows overseas travelers 30 days of unlimited flights within the United States and Canada. As the name indicates, however, the traveler must fly standby on these domestic flights. This pass costs $399.

American Airlines' Visit USA pass offers a minimum of three coupons or a maximum of eight for $100 each. American will also sell the pass coupons for $130 to travelers who do not fly American to the United States. American requires the first flight to be reserved before arrival, but subsequent flights can be booked at anytime.

U.S. air passes for business travelers

If you're a business traveler who feels you spend most of your life on an airplane, the U.S. airlines have a pass for you. These air passes allow you to lock in the cost of flying at today's prices.

Typically, the programs offer two-year, five-year and lifetime passes. American Airlines' "Air Pass Program," for example, sells a five-year pass for $35,000. The pass allows up to 25,000 flight miles per year. American's lifetime pass costs $350,000 for travelers under 40. Those over 40 get a discount on the price. A companion can fly with the pass purchaser and have his or her miles deducted from the pass's allotment.

If you use the entire 25,000-mile allotment of a five-year pass, your cost breaks down to about $.28 per mile. Any of those 25,000 miles you leave unused, however, would raise your per-mile cost.

The least expensive promotional fares will let you fly for around $.09 to $.15 a mile. But if you do much of your flying at higher-cost promotional fares or full fares, you may want to explore the pass's possibilities. Remember, too, that you are locking in that $.28 a mile for the next five years, and air fares will rise over those years.

Figuring your air-travel costs over the next two or five years — never mind over a lifetime! — can be difficult, and working your way through the rules that govern these passes can be complicated. But the airlines offering them will work with you to help determine if your travel patterns justify buying a pass.

You also need to give strong consideration to the financial condition of the airline from which you buy a pass. Will that carrier be around for two years, five years, a lifetime? These passes represent a substantial dollar commitment. And with a financially weak carrier, you could wind up losing a large chunk of change.

Today's climate of consolidation and bankruptcy in the airline industry should cast serious doubts on the desirability of entering into a long-term agreement with any but the strongest of today's airlines. If these long-term passes appear to be a worthwhile deal for you, stick with such airlines as American, Delta or United.

Travel packages — getting more for less

Purchasing the right travel package can help you fly there for less. A package combines your air fare, hotel and possibly some miscellaneous arrangements such as airport-to-hotel transportation, certain meals, a visit to an attraction or a short guided tour at your destination. A package, however, is not a tour. You travel independently on a scheduled airline and are merely pre-purchasing your land arrangements.

Packages can be put together by travel operators, travel agencies or even an airline. And package deals are available for just about every area of the world, including destinations within the United States.

Package operators deal in tremendous volume, delivering a steady flow of travelers. They therefore receive substantial discounts on the components they buy and put together.

Sometimes the package price will be less than if you went out and separately bought each individual component, but not always. With many packages you'll find the price adds up to more than the price of its components. To find out if a package represents a good deal, you'll have to telephone airlines, travel agents and hotels to determine what it would cost you to buy each component separately.

To find packages, check the ads in your Sunday newspaper's travel section. Travel agents are also a good source of package deals. In addition to reading the ads and visiting a travel agency, call an airline or two to see what package deals they may be offering.

A few packages cost less than the lowest promotional air fares

Here's the real beauty of package deals for the traveler who wants to fly there for less — you can occasionally come up with a package priced CHEAPER THAN THE LOWEST AVAILABLE

AIR FARE. You read right. Paying a single price for a flight to your destination, a hotel room and a ride between the airport and your hotel sometimes costs less than if you bought the lowest-priced promotional fare to your destination.

Look at this example. You could once fly a major airline between Los Angeles and Papeete, Tahiti, on a round-trip Apex ticket for $1,029. But if you had purchased a package to Tahiti, which included your round-trip air fare from Los Angeles, an economy hotel room and airport-hotel transportation, you would have paid just $649 AND SAVED $380!

Don't want to stay in an "economy" hotel room? Don't. Stay anywhere you want and throw away the hotel portion of the package. You'll still be $380 ahead on your air fare.

Here's a few more packages worldwide that have had price tags lower than promotional air fares:

• One week in Copenhagen, Oslo or Stockholm, including round-trip air transportation on SAS, airport transfers, hotel accommodations for six nights, full breakfast each day and a $50 refund on the first $100 spent shopping. Price from New York: $495. Apex fare: $740. Savings: $245.

• Athens with hotel for seven nights, breakfast, airport transfer and a round-trip flight on KLM. Price from New York: $549. Apex fare: $799. Savings: $250.

• A week in Rio de Janeiro, including hotel, continental breakfast, airport transfer and round-trip air. Price from Los Angeles: $799. Apex fare: $1,027. Savings: $228.

• A hotel for five nights in Hong Kong, round-trip flight on Korean Air from San Francisco or Los Angeles, airport-hotel transfers. Price: $824. Apex fare: $900. Savings: $76.

• Three nights in a Bermuda hotel and round-trip air from the U.S. East Coast. Price: $283. Apex fare: $372. Savings: $89.

That's just a sampling. Recent packages priced lower than the lowest promotional fare would also have let you travel to Amsterdam, London, Austria, Florida, Jamaica, Argentina, Venezuela, Ecuador and Peru.

Drawbacks

Don't look for these packages if you're traveling during the peak season. Packages priced lower than air fare pop up during the off season to fill empty airline seats and vacant hotel rooms. If you're planning an off-season trip, thoroughly check out package opportunities.

When investigating package prices, note that the price will be listed as per person, double occupancy. If you are traveling alone, you'll have to add a single supplement to the price. All prices used in the above examples are per person for two people traveling together.

When buying a package because you want a less-expensive air fare and plan to throw away the ground features, keep in mind that your return air reservation will let you stay at your destination for only as long as the package calls for. Most are sold for one-week stays, but you can also find three-, four- and five-day packages.

Additional money-saving opportunities with low-cost packages

The rules that govern international fares do not allow airlines to easily and quickly adjust their fares like they can on domestic routes. Consequently, to boost demand, airlines may implement a short-term promotion that gives passengers flying a particular route an extraordinary bargain or even a freebie.

To encourage travelers to fly its Dallas-Madrid route, American Airlines once offered six free nights at certain hotels in Madrid. Iberia, Spain's national airline, has offered its U.S.-Spain Apex passengers a Hertz rental car for just $1 a week. Other airlines, including Belgium's Sabena and Germany's Lufthansa, have offered free rental cars for a week.

Air Fare to Your Cruise

Another type of package combines a cruise and round-trip air fare to and from the port of embarkation. Despite their bulk-buying power, using a cruise line's "free" air fare to get to your port of embarkation may not always be the cheapest way to go.

Of course, the air fare is not free. It is included in the cruise line's cost when establishing their own fares.

Before booking a cruise, especially if you will be flying to a foreign port to catch the ship, contact the cruise line to determine how much they will deduct from the cost of the cruise if you make your own way to the port of embarkation. Then shop around on your own for the best air fare. It's not unusual for cruise passengers to save several hundred dollars each by arranging their own flight.

Round-the-world fares — taking the long way home could cost less

If your international journey involves flights to several widely separated cities, you may be able to fly there for less by taking the long way home and flying completely around the world. In fact, you may want to take the long way home if circling the globe appeals to your spirit of adventure.

International carriers have worked out joint agreements that allow them to offer round-the-world fares. These fares call for you to use two or three different airlines to make a series of stopovers as you fly completely around the world.

To plan your journey, you can select from more than 50 round-the-world itineraries, making unlimited stopovers in the cities served by the airlines writing your ticket. But you can only stop once in each city. And travel on a round-the-world ticket has to be either continuously eastward or continuously westward. Once you start you can't backtrack, but you can zigzag north and south.

Whether you fly eastbound or westbound is your choice. Westbound travel will mean fewer nights spent on a plane. Eastbound travel will mean more nights spent on a plane, which could cut your hotel costs. Some tickets give you six months to complete your trip, others allow a year.

Round-the-world fares range from about $2200 to $2,600. An itinerary that crosses the Pacific in the southern hemisphere will cost hundreds more than a northern hemisphere Pacific transit.

You'll find round-the-world fares cost about the same regardless of the airlines involved. But the cities available for you to visit will depend upon the combination of airlines you select. So you'll have to comparison shop and choose your airlines based upon the cities they serve and the cities you want to visit.

You should also comparison shop to be sure the round-the-world ticket will be cheaper than buying individual tickets to your destinations. If you are planning to visit only a few cities, you may find buying individual tickets will save you money. But if you are planning an extensive itinerary, the round-the-world ticket could come out on top.

Here's a sampling of U.S. and Canadian airlines and the foreign airlines with which they have round-the-world joint agreements.

• Air Canada - All Nippon Airways, Cathay Pacific, Japan Air Lines, Kenya Airways, Qantas Airways, Singapore Airlines.

• American Airlines - Cathay Pacific, China Airlines, Japan

Air Lines, Korean Air, Qantas Airways, Royal Jordanian, Sabena, Thai Airways International.

• Canadian International - Cathay Pacific, KLM, Philippine Airlines, Singapore Airlines, Swissair, Thai Airways International.

• Continental - Air India, Alitalia, Cathay Pacific, JAT Yugoslav Airlines, KLM, Malaysia Airlines, Singapore Airlines, Thai Airways International.

• Delta - Cathay Pacific, Japan Air Lines, Philippine Airlines, Qantas Airways, Singapore Airlines, South African Airways, Thai Airways International.

• Northwest Airlines - Air France, Air India, Alitalia, Cathay Pacific, Garuda, Gulf Air, KLM, Malaysia Airlines, Pakistan International Airlines, Qantas Airways, Sabena, Saudi Arabian Airlines, Singapore Airlines, South African Airways, Swissair, Thai Airways International.

• Trans World Airlines - Cathay Pacific, China Airlines, Japan Air Lines, Korean Air, Malaysia Airlines, Qantas Airways, Singapore Airlines.

• United Airlines - Air France, Air New Zealand, Alitalia, British Airways, Finnair, KLM, Korean Air Lines, Lufthansa, Qantas Airways, SAS, Swissair, Thai Airways International, Varig Brazilian Airlines.

• USAir - Air New Zealand, British Airways, Cathay Pacific, Qantas Airways.

Notice that Northwest and United have more round-the-world fare agreements than the other airlines, so you'll get plenty of options from Northwest and United. But you'll still want to check out what cities the other airline combinations can offer. Contact the U.S. and Canadian airlines in the listing to come up with a routing you like. Here's some potential itineraries to stimulate your thinking:

• With TWA and Singapore Airlines: New York, San Francisco, Honolulu, Tokyo, Tapei, Hong Kong, Singapore, Bangkok, Bombay, Karachi, Tel Aviv, Cairo, Istanbul, Athens, Vienna, Copenhagen, Rome, Zurich, Amsterdam, Brussels, Paris, London, New York.

• With Northwest and KLM: Chicago, Toronto, New York, London, Amsterdam, Frankfurt, Copenhagen, Stockholm, Athens, Delhi, Bangkok, Hong Kong, Manila, Taipei, Seoul, Osaka, Tokyo, Guam, Honolulu, Seattle, Chicago.

• With Delta and Qantas: Boston, London, Frankfurt, Bombay, Bangkok, Singapore, Hong Kong, Perth, Melbourne, Sydney, Brisbane, Auckland, Nadi (Fiji), Papeete (Tahiti), Honolulu, San Francisco, Boston.

• With United, British Airways and Qantas: Los Angeles, Papeete (Tahiti), Nadi (Fiji), Auckland, Brisbane, Sydney, Melbourne, Tokyo, Manila, Perth, Hong Kong, Djakarta, Singapore, Kuala Lumpur, Bangkok, Delhi, Bombay, Athens, Berlin, Oslo, Amsterdam, London, Boston, Toronto, Los Angeles.

5

Choose the right airline and cut your costs

The airline you choose can help determine if you'll fly there for less. Some airlines set themselves apart from other carriers by stressing low fares. Others forsake flying a scheduled route in favor of chartering their aircraft over a few highly popular routes. These charter airlines will also offer you low fares. And still others provide air taxi services that in some situations may be able to get you to your destination at the lowest cost. Let's look first at the low-fare carriers.

Low-fare airlines — a dwindling breed that offers air-travel savings

Airline deregulation opened the U.S. skies to a new breed of air carrier. And this new breed met the older, established airlines head on by offering lower fares. Employing a variety of methods to keep their operating costs down, these low-fare carriers are able to charge less for their flights. Some, for example, keep

105

costs down with their food and beverage service. Rather than a complete hot meal, they may serve sandwiches or only a snack.

Some low-fare carriers maintain a simplified fare structure. Instead of a standard coach fare supplemented by a variety of advance-purchase promotional fares, low-fare airlines typically offer just two fare types — peak and off-peak, with few if any restrictions. And with an unrestricted fare, you don't have to worry about meeting advance-purchase requirements. The business and leisure traveler can make a last-minute reservation and still fly there for less.

But the low-fare concept hasn't held up as expected. Such low-fare lines as People Express, TranStar Airlines, New York Air, Presidential Airways, Midway Airlines and Sir Freddie Laker's Skytrain are no longer flying. If they didn't go bankrupt, they were bought out and absorbed by a larger carrier. Of the handful of low-fare airlines still around, a couple are struggling even as I write this to get out of Chapter 11 bankruptcy.

What went wrong?

The major airlines were just too powerful, and the low-fare carriers could not compete over the long haul.

Using yield-management techniques to identify seats likely to remain unsold, the majors were able to minimize the edge of the low-fare carriers. They put those potentially unsold seats on sale at fares matching those of the low-fare airlines. In some cases, they were even able to undercut the cut-rate carriers.

A major airline once charged $784 for an unrestricted round-trip coach ticket between New York and Los Angeles. A low-fare airline at the time charged $298 for its unrestricted New York-Los Angeles ticket. But if you planned a month ahead, the major would have sold you a 30-day advance-purchase fare for $278, beating the low-fare carrier by $20.

The major airlines also have the financial clout to outlast the low-fare airlines. While the majors' cut-rate fares might cause them to lose money on routes where they were they were competing with the low-fare carriers, the major airlines could survive on revenue received from less-competitive routes where fares are higher.

A new airline offers hope for the low-fare concept

A newly created airline may be joining the ranks of the low-priced carriers. Perhaps, the low-fare concept, although still an endangered species, may not yet be headed the way of the dinosaur.

Reno Air, based in Reno, Nevada, has applied to the Department of Transportation to begin offering low-fare transcontinental service.

Run by a former Midway Airlines president, Reno air says it has studied and analyzed the operations of low-fare carriers and feels it knows where most of the defunct lines went wrong. Low-fare carriers that started out serving a niche not filled by the major airlines proved to be successful. But as they grew, the low-fare carriers tried to expand out of their niche. That's when they would meet their fate in head-on competition with the big guys.

Reno Air plans not to make that mistake. While undercutting the fares of the major airlines, it will avoid being a direct threat to them by establishing its hub at Reno. That city tends to be at the end of the spokes of the major hubs. So to get to Reno, passengers must travel through hubs such as Chicago, Denver or Minneapolis. Reno Air, however, will offer nonstop service to Reno from Boston, Newark, Los Angeles and San Francisco and one-stop transcontinental service between those cities through its Reno hub.

Low-fare airlines keep all fares down

Don't disregard low-fare airlines in your quest to fly there for less. Even though the majors do their best to keep the low-fare carriers from offering a price advantage on important routes, the cut-rate lines are extremely advantageous in helping you to save money. Keep these points in mind:

• The fare you pay on any route over which a low-fare carrier flies, is substantially less than what you would pay if that low-price line were not flying. For example, when Southwest Airlines, a low-fare carrier, began flying a Los Angeles/Ontario-San Francisco/Oakland route, Los Angeles-San Francisco fares plunged by more than 50 percent.

In an even more dramatic example, the major airlines set the lowest-available fare to cover the 500 miles between Kansas City and St. Louis at $218 round trip. When Southwest started flying between those two cities, the lowest fare dropped 73 percent to $58 round trip — a $160 difference because a low-fare airline was flying the route.

• Low-fare airlines allocate a substantially higher percentage of their seats to low fares than do the major airlines. While both types of carriers may advertise and promote a similar low fare for a particular route, your chances of actually getting that low fare are much greater with the low-fare carrier than with the major airline.

• Low-fare airlines tend to offer their lowest fares with fewer restrictions than the lowest fares of a major carrier. The low-fare lines also have more lenient cancellation policies and penalties. If you had to make a short-notice one-way flight from New Orleans to Phoenix, a major airline once would have charged you $420 for its cheapest unrestricted one-way fare. But low-fare Southwest Airlines would have sold you that ticket, unrestricted, for just $99. THAT'S A SIZEABLE SAVINGS OF $321.

Okay, give me your full attention now. What I'm going to say here is extremely important. You want to fly there for less, but, as the number of airlines decreases and the majors grow and thrive in the less-competitive atmosphere of the '90s, you are going to find yourself paying increasingly higher air-travel costs.

Yes, you can use the strategies I'm imparting to you. They will help you get the lowest-available fare. But that lowest-available fare in the future will cost you more than it does now.

You can, however, help to keep the overall level of fares from rising by thinking long term and helping promote the survival of the remaining low-fare carriers. It's in your own self-interest to see that they survive.

If your fare search boils down to a choice between a low-fare and a major carrier, ALWAYS give your business to the low-fare airline. If that low-fare carrier were not flying that route, you would be paying the major airline much more for your ticket. It's just a matter of sound economic sense.

Let's take a look at Southwest Airlines in this regard. Some travelers complain that the carrier's seating seems to be more cramped. Some complain that Southwest doesn't assigns seats, so there's a scramble at boarding time. These travelers, even though they may want the lowest fares possible, will neglect Southwest and choose a major when there's little difference in the fares.

That's short-sighted. Should the low-fare lines disappear, these travelers, and every other air traveler, will regret that passing every time they buy an airline ticket. If you're interested in saving money on your air travels, fly the airlines that help make lower fares possible.

Here's the mini-shopping list of low-fare carriers:

• America West Airlines - From its hubs in Phoenix and Las Vegas, the carrier started out servings cities in the West, the Midwest and Western Canada. America West has expanded its route system to include Atlanta, Baltimore, Boston, Honolulu, New York, Orlando and Washington, DC.

• Braniff International - Serves Islip — about 30 miles east of New York's JFK Airport — Chicago, Dallas/Ft. Worth, Newark and Orlando.

• Continental - An extensive route system that covers the United States, extends into the Pacific (including Australia) and touches Europe.

• Mark Air - Flies within Alaska.

• Reno Air - A brand-new low-fare airline still getting ready for its first takeoff as I write. The carrier will offer transcontinental flights through its hub in Reno, Nevada. From Reno, the airline plans to serve Boston, Los Angeles, Newark and San Francisco.

• Southwest Airlines - A Sun Belt carrier with a route system serving cities in the Midwest, the South and the West.

International low-fare airlines

Most international airlines belong to the International Air Transport Association — IATA. When you fly the regulated international skies, IATA is the organization that determines how much you'll pay for your ticket. IATA and the airlines establish international fares, and the governments involved in the flight routes approve them. Competition, which generates air-fare bargains on U.S. domestic routes, plays little or no part in setting international fares.

A handful of international airlines, however, have not joined IATA. Or if they are IATA members, they refuse to participate in the organization's price fixing. Be sure to put on your international low-fare shopping list any of the following airlines:

• Air Jamaica - Flies between Jamaica and Miami, Atlanta,

Baltimore, Philadelphia, New York, Toronto, Los Angeles, Grand Cayman and Port au Prince.

• British Midland Airways - Serves cities in Britain and on the continent.

• Cathay Pacific Airways - Flies between Hong Kong and the U.S. West Coast. From its hub in Hong Kong, Cathay has an extensive route system serving Asia, Australia and Europe.

• Continental Airlines - From U.S. cities, flies to Europe and to Pacific destinations including Tokyo, Manila, Australia and New Zealand.

• Icelandair - Connects several U.S. cities, including New York, Chicago, Detroit and Orlando, with Iceland and Luxembourg on the European continent.

• Korean Air - Flies between destinations in the United States, the Pacific and Asia.

• Malaysia Airlines - Offers a worldwide route system serving cities in the Far East (including Bangkok, Beijing, Kuala Lumpur, Ho Chi Minh City, Hong Kong, Jakarta, Manila, Seoul, Singapore, Taipei and Tokyo), India, Pakistan, Sri Lanka, Australia, New Zealand, the Middle East (including Amman, Jiddah and Tehran), Europe and the United States (Los Angeles and Honolulu).

• Ryanair - An Irish airline serving cities in Ireland and Britain, including London. The airline also flies between London and Brussels and has plans to extend its service to Frankfurt and Paris.

• Singapore Airlines - Flies between destinations in Asia, the Pacific, Europe and the United States.

• Thai Airways International - From Seattle and Dallas flies to Tokyo, Hong Kong and Bangkok.

• Tower Air - Serves Los Angeles, New York, Paris and Tel Aviv.

• Virgin Atlantic Airways - Flies between London's Heathrow Airport and Boston, New York, Miami, Orlando and Los Angeles. The carrier's future plans call for expanding its service by adding flights between London and San Francisco, Chicago, and Washington.

Eastern European airlines — more low-fare savings opportunities

Before the Iron Curtain came tumbling down, the airlines of the Eastern European countries offered an opportunity to fly there for less. Several were not adverse to undercutting the fares of other airlines, and at times you could pick up some real bargains. An airline official once quipped that if you ask an employee of Russia's Aeroflot airline how much it costs to fly from London to Singapore, you'll be asked how much you have on you. One traveler flew Aeroflot from London to Nairobi, Kenya, via Moscow, for just $230. That's roughly the same distance as flying from New York to Rio de Janeiro.

Now Eastern European countries have started to experiment with free-market economies. Will the airlines of these countries still provide an opportunity to fly there for less?

I believe they will.

Let's look at one Eastern European carrier to see how it plans to adapt to the new world it faces.

LOT Polish Airlines intends to jump right into the international air-travel marketplace as a strong competitor. The airline has reshuffled its top management, bringing in people who want to inject some privatization into LOT — probably along the lines of 51 percent government controlled and 49 percent investor controlled.

A LOT executive has said the carrier wants to use money brought in by investors to upgrade its fleet. LOT has 31 aircraft, 28 of which are Russian made. The other three planes are Boeing 767s which the carrier uses on its transatlantic routes. LOT plans to dispose of its Russian planes in favor of a fleet of all Western aircraft.

According to the executive, "The new management desires to unify the fleet with all Western planes. They are more economical and more in line with Western styles of service, enabling us to better compete with U.S. and European carriers."

He added that the new LOT could also go head to head with its European competitors on flights and connections within Europe.

Obviously the airline is going after a share of the market and will be competing not only with upgraded service and equipment but with attractive fares as well. While all Eastern European carriers may not keep up with Poland's LOT, you can count on them to continue their policies of using low fares to attract hard-currency-paying passengers.

From the United States, Eastern European airlines — including JAT, the Yugoslavian airline, Tarom, the Romanian airline and LOT — offer low fares to Eastern Europe, parts of the Middle East, the Far East and Australia. When using the Eastern European airlines, the trend has been that you'll get the lowest fares when flying to cities other than those in the airline's home country.

Eastern European airlines fly into most Western European gateways where you can book them for low-fare flights within Europe. Travelers flying one Eastern European airline to such destinations as Amsterdam, the Greek Isles and even North Africa have saved up to 70 percent on their fares.

Note, though, that when using an Eastern European airline your flight will normally involve at least one stop and possibly a change of planes in Belgrade, Bucharest, Budapest, Moscow, Prague or Sofia.

Charter flights — an old standby for low-cost air travel

When Air France wanted $689 for a round-trip Apex ticket between New York and Paris, you could have taken a charter flight for $399 and arrived in Paris with extra $290 to spend. A typical charter is a flight on an aircraft that a wholesaler has leased from an airline. The airline provides the plane, but the charter operator — the wholesaler — sells the seats. And your travel arrangements form a contract between you and the charter operator, not the airline operating the flight.

Occasionally, the major airlines will lease aircraft to charter operators. More frequently, the plane will belong to a company that specializes in chartering — Condor, Tower Air, Martinair, American Trans Air, Balair, Spantax or LTU International Airways among others.

Charter operators put their sales efforts into a limited number of flights, which fly to popular destinations such as Europe, the Caribbean and Hawaii. Charter flights also tend to be seasonal, flying primarily during peak and shoulder travel periods. While peak-season flights to the most popular destinations may have daily departures, other flights may operate only several days a week, possibly even once a week.

Generally, charter operators can count on selling practically all seats on their flights. So you'll find charters offering attractive fares, savings of up to several hundred dollars compared to flights on scheduled airlines are not unusual.

During a recent peak-season, a round-trip charter flight between New York and Munich would have saved you $232 compared with a scheduled airline's lowest peak-season Apex fare. If your destination had been Amsterdam, your savings would have been $249, Zurich $278, and Rome $301. And if you had wanted to fly down to Rio, a $579 New York-Rio de Janeiro charter flight would have saved you $539 over a scheduled airline's $1,118 lowest promotional fare.

Tickets on charter flights do not carry the advance-purchase restrictions found on promotional fares. You can buy a last-minute charter ticket at the same price you would have paid a month or two earlier. In fact, if the flight has many unsold seats, the operator may start to offer last-minute discounts. But you can't always count on last-minute seats being available. Charter flights can sell out fast, especially during peak season.

Charters also offer one-way fares that are priced only slightly higher than round trip fares — perhaps $20 to $50 per person. If faced with making a one-way flight on a scheduled airline's full-fare economy ticket, a one-way charter could save you a substantial amount of money.

Drawbacks

There are trade-offs you need to consider. Charter flights have drawbacks that range from the inconvenient to the potentially serious. When looking into a charter, consider also the type of traveler you are. If you're not completely flexible, easy-going and adaptable, you may find the monetary savings not sufficient compensation for the potential rise in your blood pressure.

On the other hand, if you're a grin-and-bear-it type, you'll delight in the money saved — money that can let you travel farther or even allow a trip that otherwise would not be possible.

Here's what you need to consider.

• Charter operators may not have the financial stability of a major airline. Occasionally, the news carries stories of travelers stranded because their charter operator went under. In an effort to prevent stranding or monetary loss, the law requires that revenue from each charter flight be deposited in an escrow account until the flight is completed.

• When paying for your charter, do not make your check out to the charter operator but to the charter operator's bank escrow account. Be sure also to write your flight number and flight dates on the check. The escrow account system helps protect you, but it is not foolproof. Things can go wrong if all funds are not put into the account or if the bank mismanages the account, allowing funds to be withdrawn before completion of the flight.

• Charter flights are more prone to delays than flights on scheduled airlines. In fact, your charter flight can be delayed up to 48 hours before you're allowed to back out and get a refund.

• Charter flights usually carry a cancellation penalty. You may, however, be able to pay a nominal additional charge to receive a completely refundable ticket. However, most promotional-fare tickets offered by the scheduled airlines also carry cancellation penalties.

• Up to 10 days before departure date, charter operators can cancel a flight that is not selling well.

• After you buy your ticket, charter operators have the right up to 10 days before departure to raise your fare by as much as 10 percent without your being able to cancel. If the fare increases more than 10 percent, you have 14 days in which to cancel and get a refund.

• Charter operations tend to be inefficient. You'll have to arrive at the airport as much as four hours before flight time. And you'll probably spend much time standing in line to check in for your flight.

Shopping For a Charter

Obviously, you'll want to weigh the low-fare advantage with the drawbacks to determine if charter flights are for you. And before you start your shopping, determine the cost of a ticket on a scheduled airline to your destination. While you can normally count on saving money with a charter, there are exceptions to that rule.

You can arrange your flight directly with some charter operators. Others sell only through travel agents. You may, however, have to shop around to find a travel agent who works with charter operators.

Most charter flights do not appear in travel agent computer reservations systems. So the travel agent has to research the flights and make phone calls. Because booking low-fare charters requires more work for a lower commission, some travel agencies are reluctant to handle them.

Contacts

To help you shop the charter market, here's a list of a few of the major players who sell directly to the public.

• American Trans Air, 7337 W. Washington St., Indianapolis, IN 46251, telephone 800-225-9920 or 317-247-4000.

• Balair Air Charter of Switzerland, 608 Fifth Ave., New York, NY 10020, telephone 800-322-5247 or 212-581-3411.

• Condor, 875 N. Michigan Ave., Suite 3222, Chicago, IL 60611, telephone 312-951-0005.

• Meier Tours, 3900 N.W. 79th Ave., Suite 431, Miami, FL 33166, telephone 305-591-1566 or in Florida 800-472-8208.

• Martinair Holland, 1165 Northern Blvd., Manhasset, NY 11030, telephone 800-366-4655 or 516-627-8711.

• Spantax, 10 Rockefeller Plaza, New York, NY 10020, telephone 212-582-8267.

• SunTrips, 2350 Paragon Dr., San Jose, CA 95131, telephone 408-432-0700.

• Tower Air, Hangar 8, JFK International Airport, Jamaica, NY 11430, telephone 800-221-2500 or 718-917-8500.

Save with Non-Regulated Intra-European Charters

Although competition is beginning to creep into the European air transportation system, the European airways are still very much regulated. Without the spur of wide-spread competition, European air fares tend to be expensive compared to American fares.

But one area of European air travel is not regulated — the price of a seat on a charter flight. Consequently, one of the cheapest ways to fly within Europe is on charter aircraft.

Intra-European charters are required, however, to be sold with a land package. But some of these packages carry minimum accommodations which are intended be thrown away. Tacking on minimum, throw-away accommodations allows the charter operator to meet the land-package requirement yet still keep the charter cost well below the least-expensive fares on scheduled flights.

Restrictions and drawbacks on European charters are similar to those associated with U.S. charters. One rule, however, requires that you wait until you arrive in Europe to book an intra-European charter. Once over there, you can visit a travel agency to see what's available to your next destination.

Although you face the inconvenience and uncertainty of having to wait until you arrive in Europe before booking, you will save money. When the lowest Amsterdam-Stockholm round trip cost

$394, a round-trip charter out of Amsterdam would have put you in Stockholm for $163, a $231 savings.

Air taxis — a potential money-saver for small groups

In some situations it may pay you to forget about flying on an airline — scheduled or charter — and consider hiring a private airplane instead. If three or four people are facing full-fare on a scheduled carrier — business travelers or even family members — you may find an air taxi will get you there cheaper and maybe even faster.

The U.S. air taxi industry is made up of some 3,000 operators coast to coast flying about 6,500 aircraft. Not only is the industry itself federally regulated, but its pilots must be federally licensed and undergo periodic performance and health tests. And air-taxi aircraft must meet federal standards as well.

These planes can range from four-passenger single-engine craft to a variety of jet aircraft. The most common air taxi, however, is a twin-engine plane holding up to four passengers plus baggage. Rates for a twin-engine taxi can range from about $250 to $500 an hour.

And just like an automobile taxi, you don't have to worry about schedules. Just call and an air taxi can be ready to take off in as little as an hour.

To get a rough idea of your air taxi-costs, figure about a $1 per mile round trip — you'll have to pay for a round trip even if you travel only one way. Compare that figure with the cost of scheduled airline tickets, and you'll know whether you should check further into hiring an air taxi.

To locate these carriers, check your yellow pages. Try looking under *Aircraft Charter* or *Aircraft Rental*. And of course, just as you would any other time you are shopping for fares, you will need to call several companies to compare costs.

You may try contacting a firm through a travel agent. But — here again — many travel agents are reluctant to book an air taxi. It's the same old story — they are not listed in the agent's computer system. In addition, no procedures have been established for agents to collect a commission from an air taxi.

6

Save big using little-known ticket sources

Before deregulation travelers bought their air tickets from an airline or a nearby travel agency. There was no need to go farther than the travel agency around the corner, or over on Main Street. You would just inconvenience yourself and would still wind up with the same ticket at the same price.

But that was yesterday. Today, if you want to fly there for less, it could pay to use a travel agency across town or even across the country.

The travel agency industry has become segmented. And some travel agencies now tailor their services to clients who are seeking lower fares. Regardless of where these travel agencies are located, your telephone, a credit card and the mail or overnight express will let you shop at the one offering the best fare.

Deregulation has also spawned other nontraditional sources of airline tickets. Some are the creations of enterprising entrepreneurs. Others are spin-offs of airline marketing strategies. But these ticket sources will also help slash the cost of your air travel.

Creative travel agencies — limited service but unlimited savings

The typical travel agency offers a complete range of travel services. They are staffed with experts who can help travelers plan their dream vacations.

But a number of agencies have moved away from the full-service concept. These agencies specialize in serving travelers who know where they are going and want to pay the least amount of money to get there. Many of this new breed of travel agency guarantee their clients will get the lowest fare. Often they establish their own computer systems. They study fares. They examine routings. They keep alert to bargains. And they creatively combine the variables to come up with low fares.

Creative travel agencies represent only a small segment of the travel agent community. That means you'll have to search them out. Start with the ads in the yellow pages of your local telephone book. Check also the ads in your Sunday newspaper's travel section and the travel sections of major metropolitan newspapers. Look for ads saying "low-fare specialists" or those indicating you're guaranteed to get the lowest fare.

Just how creative a creative travel agency can be depends on the skill of its personnel. So you'll still want to compare fares.

Contacts

If you can't find a creative agency in your area, try one of these:

- Farefinders in Beverly Hills, California, at 213-652-6303.

This agency serves clients nationwide using the mail or overnight express companies to deliver tickets.

• Traveltron, 121 E. Dyer Rd., Santa Ana, CA 92705 telephone 714-545-3335. If you take advantage of Traveltron's expertise in searching out the lowest possible fare for your route. the firm will deduct the cost of the telephone call when you pay for your ticket.

Rate Desks

If you're in the market for an extended or multi-stop international itinerary, the travel agency does not have to have its creativity in-house. Coming up with fares for these itineraries can be an art — a time-consuming art. So some travel agencies depend on the creative services of a "rate desk."

Travel agents contract for rate-desk service with firms such as ABC Corporate Services and Stevens Travel Management. These organizations staff their rate desks with international-fare experts whose only job is to track and manipulate international routings, fares and currencies. They maintain extensive computer networks. One has ten different computer systems, allowing it to delve into multiple information sources. And the rate desks can even reach out beyond their own expertise to touch their fare-knowledgeable contacts inside the airlines.

While the international airlines maintain their own rate desks, you'll be better off with a travel agency that uses an independent service. That way you'll be sure of getting access to the fares of all airlines serving the destinations on your itinerary.

If you own a modem-equipped personal computer, you can get in touch with a rate desk on your own. Travel Plus, an on-line travel service and data base offered by the Delphi information service (telephone 800-544-4005), has access to a rate desk that will determine the best fares for multi-stop international trips. Travel Plus does, however, charge a $25 annual fee.

No-frills travel agencies – no service, just discounted tickets

No-frills travel agencies are another post-deregulation innovation. I give these agencies the no-frills tag because typically the only thing they'll do for you is write your ticket. When you contact a no-frills travel agent, you have to know where you're going and when you want to get there. You may also have to know which airline and flight you want. And you may even have to call the airline to make your own reservation!

So why in the world would you seek out this type of travel agency? Because no-frills agencies will give you a discount off the price of your ticket. Not just a low promotional fare, but an actual discount off the price the airline says the ticket costs.

Airlines pay travel agents a commission on each ticket they sell, generally around 10 percent, but sometimes less, sometimes more. No-frills travel agents rebate, or pass on to you, their commission in the form of a discount off the fare. The agent makes a profit by charging a flat fee for writing tickets. Because these agencies sell airline tickets at net, no-frills agencies may also be called net-rate travel agencies.

One of the most prominent no-frills agencies is Travel Avenue, 180 N. Des Plaines, Suite 201, Chicago, IL 60661-1012. Travel Avenue discounts domestic tickets between 5 and 16 percent, international tickets from 8 to 25 percent. They charge $10 for domestic tickets and $25 for international tickets.

Suppose you carried out a fare search and came up with a $750 fare between New York and Vienna, the lowest promotional fare available. Buy your ticket from a full-service travel agency or from the airline and you'll pay $750. But buy your ticket through Travel Avenue and you'll get a discount, say 10 percent — $75. After the $25 international ticket charge, your price comes to $700. You get a $50 savings over the lowest promotional fare just by selecting a no-frills travel agency.

Travel Avenue conducts all business over the telephone. Call them at 800-333-3335 or 312-876-1116. Know your destination and the date you want to fly. McTravel will charge your credit card the full, nondiscounted price of the ticket. But, along with your ticket, they'll mail you a check for your rebate, less the service charge. Travel Avenue pays the postage on tickets mailed first class. For an additional charge, you can pick your ticket up at an airline ticket counter or arrange next- or second-day ticket delivery to your home or office.

Drawbacks

No-frills travel agencies are difficult to find. The airlines frown on a travel agency advertising fares that undercut the airlines' prices. The key word there is *advertising*. Travel agents commonly rebate commissions to high-volume buyers, but it is done quietly. When travel agents advertise discounts to the public, some airlines put pressure on the agent to discontinue the ads.

If you want to use a no-frills agency other than Travel Avenue, turn again to the telephone book yellow pages and to the ads in newspaper travel sections. Call those agencies advertising low fares to see if they offer tickets on a net-rate basis. You might also contact one of the following firms.

Contacts

• Adam Travel Agency, 120 Blackstone St., Boston, MA 02109, telephone 617-367-7155.

• Comp-u-store, The Source, 1616 Anderson Rd., McLean, VA 22102, telephone 800-336-3366. Personal computer owners subscribing to the Source's on-line travel service called Comp-u-store can book scheduled airline flights and receive a 5 percent rebate.

• Cost Less Travel Bargain Center, 674 Broadway, Suite

201, San Francisco, CA 94113, telephone 415-397-6868. (Domestic air tickets only.)

• Pennsylvania Travel, 19 E. Central Ave., Paoli, PA 19301, telephone 800-331-0947 or 215-251-9944.

• The Smart Traveller, 3111 S.W. 27th Ave., Miami, FL 33133, telephone 305-448-3338, in Florida and Georgia 800-226-3338. (International air tickets only.)

• Travel Access. Personal computer owners subscribing to CompuServe (800-848-8199), Delphi (800-544-4005) or Genie (800-638-9636) information services can access this travel service ($39 annual surcharge) and receive a 5 percent rebate on flights booked on-line.

• Travel Brokers, 50 Broad St., Suite 1014, New York, NY 10004, telephone 800-999-8748 or 212-422-0022, fax 212-422-0099.

Legal Considerations

Even though under certain conditions the airlines take a dim view of rebating, it's perfectly legal for travel agents to rebate all or part of their commissions on domestic air fares. But rebating on international tickets and selling international tickets at a discount, even though a common practice worldwide, is illegal under U.S. law. The illegality, however, lies with the ticket seller, not the purchaser. Travelers who buy discounted international tickets are NOT in violation of the law.

International air fares are not established via a competitive marketplace, but are under the control of the International Air Transport Association — an organization whose members are the international airlines themselves. The governments involved in a flight, including the U.S. government, must approve IATA's international fares before they can take effect. And both the airlines and the governments agree to adhere to IATA's rule that tickets will not be sold for less than the official, IATA-set fare. Therefore, U.S. law prohibits an airline or a travel agency from selling an international — but not a domestic — airline ticket for less than the official, government-approved fare.

But there's a paradox here. IATA's price fixing of international fares would be illegal within the United States. The U.S. government, however, apparently feels that in the arena of international affairs it's in the country's interest to maintain the status quo. Instead, the government takes a lenient attitude toward enforcing the law. The Department of Transportation, the government agency responsible for enforcing international air-fare tariffs, has declared that its policy is not to take action against discounters of international airline tickets or travel agents who rebate commissions on international tickets as long as consumers — YOU — are not being hurt.

Ask a full-service agency for a rebate

If you're a steady customer of a full-service travel agency offering only standard, nondiscounted tickets, ask your travel agent for a rebate. At worst, he or she will say no. But you may get a yes and save about 3 to 5 percent on the cost of your tickets.

If you do most of the planning for your travels, and the agent merely provides ticketing services, point this out. Since you are a steady customer who does not take up much of the agent's time, tell the travel agent he or she is making more money on your business than on the business of someone who requires much service and planning assistance.

Your argument will carry additional weight if you are giving the travel agent any sort of volume business. It doesn't have to be a tremendously large volume. Perhaps you have a child at college who will be flying between home and school several times a year. Perhaps you and three or four family members fly a couple of times each year to visit relatives in a distant city. Perhaps you run a small business which requires you or your employees to fly every month or two. And if you have the substantial travel volume of a large corporation, you should deal only with a travel agency willing to work out a rebate agreement with you.

Consolidators — your money-saving source for deeply discounted tickets

A number of travel companies have carved a niche for themselves by catering to the traveler who wants to fly international routes for less — much less. Known as "consolidators," these firms are ticket brokers who, like no-frills agencies, sell tickets for less than an airline's lowest promotional fare. However, you'll save substantially more than with a no-frills agency. Buy your ticket through a consolidator and you can generally expect to pay about 20 to 40 percent, even as much as 50 percent, less than the airline's lowest promotional fare.

Consolidators save you more because they're not just rebating all or part of a 10 percent commission. They are selling tickets that the airlines have sold to them at substantial discounts.

I need to repeat that idea, because you need to be sure you understand it. The airlines sell tickets to consolidators at deep discounts knowing full well that consolidators will turn around and sell those tickets at attractive discounts to air travelers.

Consolidators play an essential role for the airlines. These discount outlets allow the airlines to quietly sell tickets for seats that in all probability will be empty when a flight takes off. But the airlines do not publicize their relationships with consolidators. They want the bulk of their passengers to buy tickets at official, published fares.

Because this whole airline-consolidator-consumer relationship is downplayed and very low key, it has become known as a "gray market." It's not a forbidden black market, but it's also not a market that thrives in the sunshine. It's a market for the few, for the savvy, travel-smart shopper. And that's just as the airlines want it to be.

Consolidators are not fly-by-night outfits, and the consolidator marketplace is not necessarily shady or unscrupulous. Yes, you could run into a crook, or an under-financed operation. But you can also run into crooks and under-financed operations in other businesses, including travel agencies. I know of far more airlines that have gone bankrupt than I do consolidators.

You need to look upon the consolidator marketplace as a viable and reliable source of tickets at tremendous savings. But you also need to know how it operates and understand its drawbacks. Then you can make sound, credible decisions as to when consolidators can meet your air-travel requirements.

How the consolidator marketplace works

Worldwide there is a tremendous overcapacity of airline seats. In any given year about one-third of the total available seats will remain empty. That's well over 200 million unsold seats a year. And the number of unsold seats will not diminish drastically in the future.

Most foreign airlines are government owned and are unlikely to withdraw from a market because their planes are flying with large numbers of empty seats. While making a profit is important, it is not necessarily a government's prime consideration for running an airline. National pride and a source of hard-currency revenue can keep a government-owned airline flying through red ink.

Because IATA regulates international fares, its member airlines cannot openly sell unused seats for less than IATA's official tariff. Instead, airlines worldwide override their commission structure and push commissions sky high whenever they have large numbers of empty seats to sell. These override commissions may reach as high as 50 or 60 percent. In effect, the airlines can use overrides to put unsold seats on sale, selling the deeply discounted tickets to consolidators. The consolidators mark up the tickets and sell them, still at a large discount, to a travel agency or directly to savvy travelers who are aware of this gray market.

If, for instance, an airline's yield-management computers indicate a high-season Chicago-Rome flight will have 35 empty seats when it takes off, the airline can contact its consolidators, overriding its standard commission to cut the price of the ticket. At the airline's lowest Apex fare, a round-trip ticket for one of these seats would have sold for $989. But the consolidators may pay about $396 and then sell it to the public for perhaps $613, saving you $376.

Your savings could even be astoundingly higher. If you can't meet the advance-purchase requirement for a short-notice international trip, the airline will ask for full fare. On our Chicago-Rome flight that would be $1,710. Discount tickets purchased from a consolidator, however, do not carry advance-purchase restrictions. Even on the day of the flight if seats were available, you would still pay the consolidator about $613 AND REAP A 64 PERCENT SAVINGS OF $1,097!

Another source of discount tickets involves the large blocks of seats airlines sell at deeply discounted bulk fares to wholesale tour operators. While many of these seats are assigned to a firm's tour operations, some of the companies will also act as consolidators, offering tickets at deeply discounted prices to travel agencies and the public.

Discount tickets are available on both major and lesser-known airlines for most international destinations, including Europe, Africa, South America, Asia and the South Pacific. Discount tickets, however, are subject to supply and demand and their availability will vary according to the travel season and the destination. Asian flights at times tend to have a glut of empty seats, so tickets then would be plentiful and discounts high.

But on a flight to a popular European destination during high season, the airline will be able to sell most seats at full and promotional fares. You'll find that supply of discount tickets to be extremely tight. And when they are available you may have to fly on a lesser-known airline.

Here's some examples of actual discounts once available on international tickets:

• At a time when the lowest New York-London round-trip promotional fare was selling for $468, a New York consolidator sold New York-London round trips on Air India for $349. That's $119 lower than the least expensive official fare.

• Lowest official New York-Tokyo fare: $1,229. Another New York consolidator sold New York-Tokyo round trips for $529. Savings: $700.

• New York-Bombay lowest official fare: $1,415. Discounted New York-Bombay fare: $1,090. Savings: $325.

• Chicago-Bangkok lowest official fare: $1,440. Chicago consolidator round trip to Bangkok: $899. Savings: $541.

• New York-Hong Kong lowest official fare: $1,149. Discount ticket: $800. Savings: $349.

• Boston-Copenhagen lowest official high-season fare: $875. Consolidator bulk fare: $699. Savings: $176.

• Dallas-Stockholm lowest official fare: $1,073. Consolidator bulk fare: $838. Savings: $235.

You can also get deep discounts on U.S. domestic flights

Consolidator tickets are primarily a phenomenon of international travel, growing out of IATA's prohibition against undercutting established fares. In recent years, however, discounted consolidator tickets have become available for U.S. domestic travel, particularly long-haul and transcontinental flights.

The supply of domestic consolidator tickets, however, is nowhere near as plentiful as for international travel. And the discount on domestic tickets tends to be less, so you may sometimes find it's cheaper to buy the least-expensive promotional fare rather than a domestic consolidator ticket

But if you can't meet the restrictions on a domestic ticket and would have to pay full fare, then the consolidator ticket will let you save big money. One-way domestic discount tickets are also available and will give you tremendous savings over a full-fare one-way ticket.

To check on availability and price of a domestic discount ticket, contact those consolidators who are listed in the consolidator contacts appendix at the back of this book as being active in the U.S. domestic market.

Here's how some consolidator fares on domestic tickets stacked up against nondiscounted fares.

• When Los Angeles-New York round trips were selling in a range between $435 and $643, UniTravel, a Missouri-based consolidator, was offering these unrestricted transcontinental round trips for $388.

• A California consolidator, British European Travel, has sold coast-to-coast, unrestricted discount tickets for $400 round trip.

• RMC Travel Center in New York offered transcontinental flights (New York to Los Angeles, San Francisco or San Diego and Los Angeles to Boston, Miami and Washington) for $369.

• RMC Travel has also sold New York-Dallas unrestricted discount tickets for $279 round trip, $140 one way as well as

New York-Denver or Salt Lake City tickets for $299 round trip and $150 one way.

Here's an exception to the rule that domestic consolidator tickets tend to be scarce and offer smaller discounts. A cable television show, "Travel Bargains," appears on The Travel Channel offering discounted air fares, most at about 45 percent off the lowest published fare. The one-hour show recaps discounts available on both domestic and international tickets.

Travel Bargains' domestic tickets cover most major destinations and many minor ones. Here's a sampling of some of the show's domestic discounts:

• Chicago-Albuquerque lowest promotional fare: $378. Discounted fare: $200. Savings: $178.

• Chicago-Honolulu lowest promotional fare: $728. Discounted fare: $454. Savings: $274.

• Boston-San Diego lowest promotional fare: $518. Discounted fare: $280. Savings: $238.

• San Antonio, Texas-New York lowest promotional fare: $438. Discounted fare: $20. Savings $198.

• Baltimore-Ontario, California, lowest promotional fare: $448. Discounted fare: $280. Savings: $208.

You don't have to watch the show to check on availability and prices. You can call Travel Bargains 24 hours a day, seven days a week at 800-872-8385.

Drawbacks

In exchange for your substantial discount, a consolidator ticket requires that you give up certain advantages that may be offered by standard tickets and traditional ticket outlets. Before purchasing a consolidator ticket, you have to be sure you understand and can accept the rules and restrictions that go along with the deep discounts.

When dealing with a consolidator, expect little in the way of service. Consolidators build their business on volume, not service. You'll need to know where and when you want to go.

Your ticket will bear a nondiscounted fare and will state that it is "nonrefundable." This prevents a traveler from cashing in the ticket for the fare stated on it when he or she actually paid a much lower, discounted price.

Because these tickets are nonrefundable, they may at first appear to be risky. But since they do not carry an advance purchase requirement, you can wait until your plans are absolutely firm before buying. That wait is a luxury you may not always have when purchasing a nonrefundable promotional-fare ticket 30 days in advance.

Actually, though, you may be able to get a refund, but you'll have to get it from the consolidator or the travel agency where you bought the ticket, not the airline. And if you do get a refund, chances are you will have to pay a penalty.

Your ticket will also state that it is "nonendorsable." That means your airline will not authorize you to transfer to another airline. If you miss your flight because of late connections or even if your airline cancels the flight, you'll have to wait for the next one on your airline. On an international trip that could be the next day. In an isolated location that could be next week.

You'll probably conduct your business with a consolidator over the telephone. Some will accept credit cards, others will not. Some who do accept credit cards will charge 2 or 3 percent extra for the transaction. Paying by credit card gives you a margin of safety, as it does on any purchase. If you don't get what you paid for, you can always dispute the charge with the credit card issuer. Therefore shop around. As a savvy shopper you will be calling several consolidators to check prices, also ask if you can pay by credit card.

You may not receive your ticket until a day or two before departure, or the ticket may be sent to your airport for pickup just prior to your flight. You may find that short time frame discomforting. But you can also get consolidator tickets delivered weeks in advance. Here again, shop around. And as you talk to consolidators, ask when your ticket will be delivered.

You may also find disconcerting the fact that consolidators will generally not identify the airline you will be flying until you receive your ticket. Most consolidators will only say you will be flying on a major scheduled airline — admittedly, that's pretty vague. But often the provisions of the contracts consolidators sign with the airlines prevent them from revealing the carrier involved until ticketing. The airlines are concerned that announcing their identities beforehand will undermine their fare structures.

Some discount tickets, especially those with the lowest prices, may involve roundabout routings or long layovers waiting for connections. In the New York-Tokyo example I gave above, if you paid the official $1,229 promotional fare, Japan Air Lines would have flown you to Tokyo nonstop in 14 hours. The return flight to New York would have taken 12 hours and 20 minutes.

The $529 discount ticket, however, required a flight from New York to Toronto and a two-hour layover before boarding a Canadian Airlines International flight. After a stop in Vancouver, you would arrive in Tokyo 19 hours and 30 minutes after leaving New York. Canadian Airlines International's return flight again stopped in Vancouver before arriving in Toronto 14 hours and 45 minutes after departing Tokyo. You would then have to spend the night in a Toronto hotel (included in the cost of your discount ticket) before flying to New York the next day.

When it comes to convenience, there is no comparing the Japan Air Lines and the Canadian Airlines International flights. When it comes to the $700 difference in fares, there is also no comparing the two flights. If the $700 savings is not enough to entice you to accept the inconvenient routing of the Canadian airline's flight, you could ask your travel agent or consolidator to try for a discounted ticket on the Japan Air Lines flight.

Remember, though, that when buying a discounted ticket you are buying a seat put on sale because the airline expects it to go unsold. The Japan Air Lines nonstop flight obviously would be popular with passengers. Consequently, it will have fewer sale seats. And any seats that did go on sale would not be discounted as deeply as the Canadian Airlines International flight.

The example does point out, however, that you do have options. For any destination, there can be a variety of airlines, routings and discount fares. When shopping for a discount ticket, be sure the consolidator or travel agent knows your preferences concerning:

• major versus lesser-known airline;

• non- or minimum-stop flight with direct routing versus indirect multiple-stop routing;

• absolute lowest price versus higher price with frills.

Some airlines impose additional limitations on their discounted consolidator tickets. You may not be able to select your seat until check in, and you may not be able to request a special meal. If you encounter an en route delay, the airline may not pick up the cost of your meals and lodging as they would for the other passengers. You also may not get frequent-flyer mileage for your flight. But these limitations vary from airline to airline. If any are important to you, ask the consolidator for a ticket that does not impose those particular impediments.

Apparently, however, passengers have been able to get around some of these limitations. A day or two after booking a consolidator ticket, passengers who know which airline they will be flying have called the airline's national reservation line directly and requested a special meal or a seat assignment. Passengers have also called the reservations center to ask that their frequent flyer number be added to their "PNR" — passenger name record.

Locating discount tickets

You have two options concerning where to buy discount tickets — directly from a consolidator or through a travel agency. Don't ask an airline. As I pointed out, the airlines prefer to keep the practice of discounting quiet, so only a knowledgeable few will buy these cut-rate tickets while the general public goes on paying promotional and full fares.

Buying a discount ticket through your local full-service travel agency is the easiest approach. With the agency's mark up, however, you'll pay a bit more.

Here again, though, at some agencies you may run into that persistent problem with travel agencies — discount tickets are not in their computer reservations system, so they don't handle them. An article in a newspaper serving the travel agent trade succinctly stated the viewpoint of some of these agents. The article stated that because consolidator tickets are not listed in agent computer systems, buying them is a "very tedious process" that causes travel agents "extra work and headaches." The article did not mention the concept of providing a service for customers.

Others travel agents are just not tuned in to the consolidator marketplace. They see only the gray-market aspect of consolidator tickets and shy away from selling them. They focus on the drawbacks rather than the substantial savings discounted tickets offer the air traveler.

But shop around and you'll be able to come up with a full-service travel agency that works with a reliable consolidator. Check with some of the large travel agency chains. Uniglobe agencies, for example, work with the largest consolidator in the United States — C. L. Thomson Express which sells their discounted tickets only through travel agencies. Look in your yellow pages under travel agencies for *Uniglobe.*

Consolidators themselves are not too difficult to find. Most major cities have several. Check the ads in newspaper travel sections. Look for those offering deeply discounted air fares. The ads may or may not mention the word "discount." Generally the ads will be small, merely listing very low fares for destinations worldwide.

If you can't locate a consolidator in your area, contact one of those listed in the consolidator contacts appendix.

Consolidator fares are also available to modem-equipped personal computer owners who subscribe to the Delphi information service (telephone 800-544-4005). As I mentioned earlier when telling you about rate desks, Delphi offers access to Travel Plus, an on-line data base. In addition to its rate-desk service, Travel Plus contains discounted consolidator fares. Although Travel Plus charges a $25 annual fee, it does have the advantages that you can book the fares on-line and pay for tickets with a credit card.

Precautions you can take

Consolidators are an established fact in the air travel marketplace and have proven to be a reliable source of low-cost tickets. But you can take some precautions when using a firm with whom you have not dealt before.

The best check on the past performance and reliability of a consolidator would be a reliable recommendation from someone who does business with that firm. If you do not know anyone who can recommend a consolidator, telephone the Better Business Bureau located in the consolidator's hometown. Call information for the number. The Better Business Bureau can tell you if they have received complaints about the consolidator.

When looking for a discount ticket, be aware of the cost of a promotional fare ticket to your destination. Then you will know that you are actually getting a discount fare, not just a low promotional fare. So before you start shopping, call an airline flying the route you're interested in to determine the least-expensive promotional fare. Discounted international fares generally run at least 15 to 20 percent less than the fare the airline quotes you. Remember, though, that domestic discount tickets may not offer much, if any, savings over a promotional fare.

You can also take these precautions:

• You'll want to comparison shop. The mark up on discount tickets varies, and you may find fare differences of up to several hundred dollars among consolidators.

• Pay for your ticket with a credit card if possible. Should something go wrong, you can charge back the cost when it appears on your credit card statement.

• If you must pay cash, try to find a consolidator close to you so you can pick the tickets up in person. Also look for one, if possible, who does not require full payment until the tickets are ready to be turned over to you.

• If you can't pick up the ticket in person, have it mailed to your residence or business. If you don't get what you paid for, you can ask for assistance from the Postal Inspection Service.

• Determine if the quoted or advertised price includes all extra charges such as taxes and credit card fees.

• Clarify restrictions as well as cancellation and refund policies.

Overseas consolidators

While consolidators are relatively new on the American travel scene, they have been around for decades overseas. There they are sometimes called "bucket shops," a British term that originally referred to shady stock brokers who sold worthless stock certificates by the bucket load. Although the term had disreputable beginnings, bucket shops, or consolidators, today are an established fact in international air travel. And at consolidators around the world passengers are picking up extraordinary air travel bargains. Among the major centers for consolidator tickets are: Amsterdam, Athens, Bangkok, Brussels, Frankfurt, Hong Kong, London, New Delhi, Rome and Singapore.

Most of your international air travel tickets can be purchased conveniently and at competitive prices from consolidators in the United States. But there are at least three situations when obtaining your ticket from an overseas consolidator may save you money.

1) To save on a one-way flight that fills an "open jaw." An open-jaw routing allows you to return from a city different than the destination city of your outbound ticket. Say, for example, you wanted to fly from New York to London, then on to Frankfort before returning to New York. You would probably get the cheapest fare by purchasing from a U.S. consolidator the New York-London and the Frankfort-New York legs as an open-jaw round trip. To fill the open-jaw portion, the London-Frankfort leg, you would buy a one-way ticket from a London consolidator.

2) To save on some round-the-world itineraries. If you plan to make only a few stops, a series of one-way consolidator tickets purchased as you go would probably give you a cheaper itinerary than a U.S. purchased round-the-world fare.

3) To visit widespread destinations from an overseas location. Say you wanted to visit Hong Kong and then fly on to Australia before returning to Hong Kong and then back to the

United States, you would generally find it cheaper to buy the Hong Kong-Australia round trip in Hong Kong than buying the entire itinerary in the United States. Similarly, on an itinerary such as: United States-Europe, Europe-Africa, Africa-Europe, Europe-United States, an overseas consolidator ticket for the Europe-Africa legs would probably save over buying the entire itinerary from a U.S. consolidator.

Of course, you can also use these consolidators if you are on an extended overseas stay or even if you just want to keep your itinerary open after arriving at an overseas destination.

The savings available through overseas consolidators can be substantial. When the lowest official round-trip fare between London and Cairo was $740, one London consolidator, or bucket shop, sold that round trip for $389. Savings: $351. Another London bucket shop offered London-Athens round trips for $96, that was $218 off the lowest Apex fare of $314. An Amsterdam consolidator sold $480 Amsterdam-Tel Aviv tickets for $235, saving the traveler $245. Similar bargains are available to cities throughout the world.

To obtain the best bargains through overseas consolidators, you'll have to comparison shop. Like consolidator fares in the United States, overseas consolidator fares can vary widely, depending on the airline involved, the routing, the number of stops and, of course, the markup the consolidator takes on the ticket. So you'll need to know what the official fare is, and then shop around for the lowest discount fare.

Locating consolidators in a foreign country

To find consolidators when overseas, check the local newspaper ads. Also check with your hotel clerk or concierge. And, especially, ask your fellow travelers.

For the English-speaking traveler, London is probably the best and the easiest city in which to obtain air travel bargains. London has a large concentration of consolidators, many of which are located along the city's Earls Court Road. Consequently, competition is keen. And since you speak the language, you'll be able to ask the right questions and understand the answers.

London also has an organization called the Air Travel Advisory Bureau that makes shopping for a consolidator easy. The ATAB acts as a central clearinghouse for consolidators. You can call the ATAB at 636-5000 and tell them where you want to go. They'll give you the names of several consolidators offering discount tickets to your destination.

You don't have to be in London to get information from the city's consolidators. You can telephone the ATAB by dialing 011-44-71-636-5000. Then call the consolidators which the ATAB gives you. Or, you can telephone a couple from the list below.

When telephoning London, call before 7 a.m. your local time. It will be working-hours daytime in London, but the telephone company will charge you the least-expensive night rate. Direct-dial phone rates to London are relatively low.

Consolidator contacts

You can direct dial the following consolidators by dialing the number listed.

• Bestways, 56/58 Whitcomb St., London, WC2, telephone 011-44-71-930-3985.

• Euro-Japan Holidays, 29-30 St. James St., London, SW1, telephone 011-44-71-839-2186.

• Discount Travel Centre, 216 Earls Court Rd., London, SW5, telephone 011-44-71-370-1146.

• Far East Travel Centre, 35 Piccadilly, London, W1, telephone 011-44-71-734-9318.

• Holiday Makers, 157 Praed St., London, SW, telephone 011-44-71-734-4611.

• Mundus Air Travel Ltd., 5 Peter St., London W1, telephone 011-44-71-437-2272.

• Nouvelles Frontières, 1-2 Hanover St., London W1, telephone 011-44-71-629-7772.

• Pilgrim-Air, 44 Goodge St., London, W1P, telephone 011-44-81-748-1333.

• Poundsaver Travel, 1 Hograth Place, London, SW5, telephone 011-44-71-370-6177.

• STA Travel, 74 Brompton Rd., London, SW7, telephone 011-44-71-937-9962.

• Worldwide Cheap Travel Service, 254 Earls Court Rd., London, SW5, telephone 011-44-71-373-6465.

Additional consolidator contacts

You can also contact the following overseas consolidators for price information. Just dial the number as listed. They may, however, be reluctant to work with you if they will incur additional costs to get a ticket to you in the United States. You can also use them if your travels put you in their country.

Australia

• Phil Travel, 28 George St., 6th Floor, Sydney 2000, Australia, telephone 011-66-2-232-5677, fax 011-66-2-235-3142.

Canada

• Connections Travel, 1927 W. 4th Ave., Vancouver, British Columbia V6J 1M7, Canada, 604-738-9499, fax 604-738-9228.

France

• Nouvelles Frontières, 87 Boulevard Grenelle, Paris, France, telephone 011-33-1-427-30568.

Greece

• Inter Trust Travel, 3 Kydathinaeon St. Athens, 105 57, Greece, telephone 011-30-1-323-4910, fax 011-30-1-324-1976.

• Inter Trust Travel also has a location at: 12 Sachtourit St., Piraeus 185 37, Greece, telephone 011-30-1-451-8587, fax 011-30-1-453-9161.

Germany

• Saeed Flugreisen, Mainzer Landstrasse 71-3, Frankfurt 1 6000, Germany, telephone 011-49-69-234299, fax 011-49-69-231972.

• Skytours GmbH, Basler Strasse 18, 7800 Freiburg, Germany, telephone 011-49-761-706703, fax 011-49-716-706707.

Netherlands

• Malibu Travel, Damrak 30, 1012 LJ Amsterdam, Netherlands, telephone 011-31-20-232977, fax 011-31-20-382271.

New Zealand

• Phil Travel, 112 Queen St., Auckland, New Zealand, telephone 011-64-9-336-7116, fax 011-64-9-366-7114.

Singapore

• Gasi Travel, Thongsia Bldg #01-02, 30 Bideford Rd., Singapore 0922, telephone 011-65-734-7633, fax 011-65-737-6268.

Precautions

When dealing with consolidators around the world, you can't check out the firm with the local Better Business Bureau. So you'll have to be a bit cautious. Again, the majority are dependable sources of discount airline tickets. But, being a stranger in a strange land, you would be prudent to take a few precautions to help ensure a happy outcome on oversees consolidator transactions.

• Try to use a consolidator for which you can find a recommendation — from a fellow traveler, from local hotel personnel, from local shopkeepers.

• Don't go with the first price quoted at the first consolidator you contact. Know the lowest published fare for the flight your interested in and shop around. Try to contact at least three consolidators And be sure the fare quoted includes any extra charges and surcharges.

• Have the consolidator give you the fare, additional charges if any, airline and flight information in writing.

• Verify with the airline involved that a flight actually exists for the ticket you are purchasing. Verify both segments if it's a round- trip ticket.

• You'll probably have to pay cash for your tickets. Try to put down only an initial deposit and get a receipt. Pay the balance when you pick up the tickets.

• Pick up your tickets in person. Examine them to be sure they carry an official validation stamp. The official stamp will be made with a metal die plate and will carry the name of the airline or the name of an official, bonded travel agency. A rubber stamp is not good enough. The stamp will also show a date. To comply with restrictions, the date shown may be well before the date on which you're buying the ticket. That's okay.

• Before parting with your money, call the airline to verify that you are on its passenger list for all legs on your itinerary. Have no inhibitions about calling the airline yourself, right from the consolidator's office. In fact, if you let the consolidator know right up front that, as part of the deal, you will call the airline yourself to confirm that you are on the passenger list of each flight for which you are getting a flight coupon, everything should go smoothly.

Coupon brokers — savings for bold air travelers

Some travelers who belong to one of the many airline frequent-flyer programs fly so frequently that the last thing they want to do is take another flight. They would rather sell than use their frequent-flyer awards, which are typically issued as coupons. (See Chapter 7 for information on frequent-flyer programs.) Sometimes frequent-flyer programs actually put pressure on travelers to sell their awards, since some mileage credits expire if not used within a few years

Travelers who would rather sell than fly contact a coupon broker who adds the award to the brokerage's inventory. When a buyer contacts the broker to purchase a coupon, the broker gives the coupon seller — the frequent flyer — the buyer's name. The seller then contacts the airline to have his or her frequent-flyer coupon issued in the name of the buyer. The seller of the frequent-flyer award receives cash for the coupon from the broker. The broker takes a mark up and sells the coupon to the buyer at a price usually well below the airline's official fare.

Whether you can save with a coupon broker depends on the variables

Not all air travelers will save money using a coupon broker. Savings will depend on the class of service you choose and upon your destination.

The coupon brokers offer the best savings for first- and business-class tickets. The savings on a first-class ticket can run in the thousands of dollars. Whether you can save on a coach ticket depends on your destination and whether you qualify, if you were to buy your ticket from an airline, for a promotional fare or would have to pay full fare.

For travel within the continental United States, a frequent-flyer coupon will probably cost more than an advance-purchase promotional-fare ticket. But when you don't have the flexibility to make an advance purchase, you can save dramatically with a coupon. Unlike promotional fares, coupons carry no advance-purchase requirement. And once you receive the coupon, you have a year in which to use it. If you know that within the next 12 months you'll need to make at least one short-notice trip for which you would have to pay full fare, you'll save hundreds of dollars with a frequent-flyer coupon.

The transaction involved in obtaining a frequent-flyer coupon can routinely take four or five weeks, so you need to buy ahead of time. You can then hold on to the coupon until you are ready to use it. Some brokers can speed-up the process and obtain a coupon in a day or two, usually at additional cost.

On flights to Alaska and Hawaii a coupon will generally save you money over a promotional fare. On some international flights, particularly during peak season with its higher fares, you can also save with frequent-flyer coupons. While you can normally do better with an an Apex fare to Europe from the East Coast, you would probably save with a coupon for West Coast-to-Europe flights. And on long-haul flights to South America, Asia and the South Pacific, you'll usually find coupons cheaper than the Apex fare.

How to find out if you will save with a coupon broker

Determining whether you can save by purchasing a frequent-flyer coupon is quite easy. Use the airline contacts appendix to telephone two or three carriers flying to your destination. Find out what your least-expensive fare would be.

Now contact three coupon brokers to determine the cost of a coupon good for your destination. You need to call at least three because prices between brokers can vary by several hundred dollars. Choose the brokers from the following list, or you can come up with a few on your own. You'll find coupon brokers advertising in the classified ads in *USA Today,* the *Wall Street Journal* and in the business sections of many major newspapers.

Coupon broker contacts

• Airline Coupon CO, 15706 Pomerado Rd., Suite 208, Poway CA 9206, telephone 800-354-4489 or 800-338-0099 in California.

• American Coupon Exchange, 840 Newport Center Dr., Suite 480, Newport Beach, CA 92660, telephone 714-644-4112.

• Flyin' Class, 320 W. 37th St., New York, NY 10018, telephone 212-643-0211.

• Go in Class, 230 N. Michigan Ave., Suite 2404, Chicago, IL 60601, telephone 312-236-9696.

• International Air Coupon Exchange, 2603 August Dr., Suite 580, Houston, TX 77057, telephone 800-558-0053.

• Travel Creations, 24 Perimeter Center E, Suite 2420, Atlanta, GA 30346, telephone 800-843-0737.

Drawbacks

Using a purchased frequent-flyer award has become risky business. Most airlines permit members of their frequent-flyer programs to transfer awards to family members and friends. But the airlines prohibit buying and selling the awards. Consequently, if an airline learns you've bought your ticket with a purchased coupon, or even suspects that you have, they will not let you board your flight and will confiscate your ticket. And some airlines, particularly American, Delta, Northwest, TWA and United, are taking steps to crack down on travelers using purchased frequent-flyer coupons.

Just how effective these crackdowns are, and the likelihood of an airline suspecting you are using a purchased coupon, is somewhat difficult to determine. Some insider estimates as to the number of brokered award tickets confiscated by the airlines ranges from .5 percent to 3 percent. If accurate, that's fairly low.

While the actual number of confiscations may be low, the number of challenges appears to be up. As part of their stepped-up enforcement procedures, the airlines are increasingly likely to question a passenger whose last name does not match the last name of the frequent flyer who received the award. Then it comes down to a war of wits between the passenger and the ticket agent. Brokers, however, generally give the coupon buyer the seller's name, so the buyer can say he or she received the ticket as a gift from the frequent flyer.

On the positive side, brokers say the airlines are not as tough on frequent-flyer upgrade coupons, which would let you upgrade a coach ticket to business class or business class to first class. Airline thinking here may be that you have actually paid the carrier money for a seat. The airline has received revenue from you, so they are not overly concerned if you buy a frequent-flyer coupon that just puts you in a different seating class.

While buying and selling frequent-flyer coupons violates airline rules, the practice is not illegal. But if you find intimidating the thought of a possible confrontation at the gate over how you obtained your ticket, then coupon tickets are not for you. And if you don't have the funds available to purchase a full-fare ticket to your destination should the airline confiscate yours, you have another reason to avoid award tickets.

Given the savings you can get with a discount ticket from a consolidator, I don't really see the need for you to purchase frequent-flyer coupons to reach your destination. The advantages you get with a coupon ticket are also available with a consolidator ticket, but without the serious drawbacks. Remember, the consolidator ticket has actually been sold by an airline to a ticket broker for the specific purpose of reselling it at an attractive discount to a potential passenger. The consolidator ticket represents the airline's last chance efforts to put passengers into seats it is sure will otherwise remain empty.

On the other hand, the airlines feel that brokered coupon tickets not only violate their rules, but that they put a passenger who has not contributed to the airline's revenue into a seat when that individual might otherwise become a revenue-generating passenger. Consequently, the airline's will not tolerate the practice. Hence, we have the stepped up detection and enforcement procedures.

If you decide to buy a frequent-flyer coupon anyway, you can take three steps to help protect yourself.

• First, don't brag about how you obtained your ticket, especially at the airport. Airline personnel may overhear you.

• Second, don't let the coupon broker's affiliated travel agency issue your ticket. Just get the frequent-flyer coupon itself and take it to your own travel agent or directly to the airline to have the ticket issued. Airlines know which broker-affiliated travel agencies issue coupon-purchased tickets. A ticket bearing the stamp of one of these agencies could tip-off airline personnel and lead to questioning on how you obtained your ticket.

• Third, ask your coupon broker if he or she will cover the cost of a confiscated ticket by issuing you another coupon. Most will, but get it in writing before you pay.

Restrictions

Coupon tickets come with a few restrictions. They are only valid on the airline issuing the award, so you will not be able to switch carriers. If you cancel your reservation or the airline cancels your flight, you cannot get a refund. But you will be allowed to reschedule the same itinerary during the year-long validity of the ticket.

The airlines maintain blackout periods when frequent-flyer awards may not be used for travel. They also allocate to award travel only a certain number of seats on each flight. With some airlines, extensive blackouts and a scarcity of award seats on each flight severely hampers trying to fly when you want to.

The ease with which a traveler can get an award-travel seat on a particular airline is reflected in the price of that line's coupons. Purchasing the least expensive coupons could give you an airline that has no award-travel seats when you want to fly. Ask the broker which carriers will likely have frequent-flyer seats when you plan to travel.

Banks — yes, your local banker can be a source of air-travel savings

In today's competitive banking industry, banks are ever on the look out for marketing opportunities to pull ahead of the competition. And a few have turned to travel to do it. But the banking industry offering travel services has yet to reach its full potential, because when a bank sells travel it runs afoul of the travel agency industry.

One California bank, First Interstate, offered its credit card customers a 3 percent discount on air tickets. That's 3 percent off the lowest promotional fare. However, under pressure from a travel agency consortium First Interstate discontinued its program.

But banks continue to look at discounted travel services to pull in customers. New York's Chemical Bank has started a travel program for its credit card customers that refunds from 3 to 10 percent of travel costs.

Still another New York bank, Chase Manhattan, offers its Visa and Mastercard customers a 5 percent discount on domestic air fares. The program does not offer international air discounts.

Chase Manhattan gives its credit card customers the toll-free telephone number of a travel agency that works with the bank. Customers make their reservations through the toll-free number and receive a rebate check for 5 percent of the fare after they complete their trip.

Banks look upon travel services as a profitable way to build business and customer loyalty. And discount programs such as these are on the increase. Typically, banks contract with third-party firms that specialize in marketing travel services to financial institutions.

Although specific arrangements can vary with each financial organization, the programs offered a bank's customers generally include air-travel rebates ranging from 3 to 5 percent payable after completion of the trip.

As you scour the ads promoting air-travel bargains, keep alert for any bank that advertises travel services. It could take the form of a travel club for depositors or rebates for the bank's credit card users. Regardless, check with the bank to determine exactly what they are offering. You could come upon another ticket source that will let you fly there for less.

Corporate travel departments — a possible money-saving fringe benefit

Large corporations with employees who travel frequently may maintain their own travel departments. Because of their volume of travel, the company's travel manager is often able to negotiate rebates and discounts with a travel agency or an airline.

Check with your company's travel manager to see if they have such a rebate or discount agreement. If they do, ask if employees can purchase tickets for personal travel through the travel department. If yes, you'll be obtaining your tickets at discounted fares.

Some corporations are also able to negotiate restriction waivers with an airline. Perhaps the waiver eliminates advance-purchase requirements, allowing company personnel to travel at the last minute on promotional fares. Purchasing such a ticket through your corporate travel department could keep you from paying full fare on a short-notice trip.

If your company has not considered employee purchases of personal travel through its corporate travel department, perhaps a suggestion from you for a morale-boosting, cost-free fringe benefit will get the idea going.

Corporate incentive travel — free air travel for a job well done

Some corporations use travel awards as incentives to motivate employees and to recognize a job well done. Many incentive-travel awards come in the form of packages. But one airline, USAir, offers the business community air-only incentive travel. And thus, an opportunity to go beyond flying there for less to fly there for FREE.

USAir will sell employers its "Take Flight" incentive-travel certificates in lots of 20 for travel within any one of five specific geographic zones. Cost of the certificates varies by geographic zone, class of service — coach, business class or first class — and the number of certificates purchased.

The recipient of each certificate, the rewarded employee, can exchange it within a year for one round-trip non-refundable ticket on USAir.

These tickets do carry restrictions. Travelers must make reservations either 14 or 30 days in advance, and stay at their destination over a Saturday-night.

USAir's Take Flight certificates appear to be a relatively inexpensive way to implement an incentive program or to diversify an existing one. If you are an employee in a firm without an incentive program, let the boss know about USAir's idea for boosting both morale and productivity.

Classified ads — bargains for the truly flexible

Even the firmest of travel plans can change unexpectedly. And when travelers who have purchased nonrefundable airline tickets have to change plans, they are out the cost of their ticket.

To salvage a portion of their loss, some nonrefundable ticket holders take out a classified ad in their local newspaper, offering to sell their tickets at very low prices. And as you'll see in Chapter 8, travelers using creative money-saving strategies often have unused one-way tickets left over. These passengers, too, use the classified-ad marketplace to put their left-over tickets up for sale. You can pick up some real bargains from these ads. Look for them under a classified heading such as *miscellaneous announcements*.

To use tickets offered in classified ads requires great flexibility. These tickets are for specific destinations on specific dates —

and they cannot be changed. It's unlikely you would need to fly to the same destinations on the same departure and return dates as the available advertised tickets, so these ads will be of little use to the business traveler.

The flexible leisure traveler, however, can snap up these bargains. If you've been wanting to get away and are willing to take destination potluck, you can save some real money. My local paper had an ad for two Orlando-Hartford round-trip tickets over the Christmas holidays. They were priced at "$400 or. best offer." Another ad offered an Orlando-Milwaukee round trip for just $100. Still other ads offered tickets to: Denver for $150 round trip, Pittsburgh for $100 one way, Alaska for $300 round trip and Australia for $849 round trip.

You can also use these ads to get a ticket that flies you into a city close to your desired destination, and then use alternate transportation to travel the rest of the way. If, for example, you needed to fly into Chicago, that $100 Milwaukee ticket would get you close enough so that you could rent a car or have someone drive up to Milwaukee to meet you.

You need to keep several important points in mind when buying an airline ticket through a classified ad.

• You are buying the ticket from a stranger. So verify its validity. Call the airline to confirm that the passenger named on the ticket has a seat on the flight indicated.

• Buying someone else's ticket violates airline rules, BUT...it is not illegal. Just don't let the airline know you have bought the ticket from an individual or that you are not the person named on the ticket.

• You will have to fly under the name that is printed on the ticket. If your name is Bill and the name on the ticket is Kathy, that's not a good match. Look for a ticket with a first name of the same gender or a first name that is indicated by initials.

• The name on your checked luggage should match the name on the ticket.

• DO NOT buy an international ticket through the classified ads. You will have to identify yourself before boarding an international flight. Therefore, that $849 Australian round trip advertised in my hometown paper — regardless of how attractive the fare — is not a viable means to fly to Australia for less.

• Remember that when buying through this air-ticket marketplace, the advertised price is negotiable. And the closer to the flight date, the more pressure will be on the seller to get whatever he or she can for the ticket.

Gimmicks — a source of extraordinary bargains

Airline marketing departments frequently come up with a flashy, well-advertised gimmick to boost sales. When they do, they give you a new source of bargain-priced tickets. But be cautious — not all gimmicks are bargains. You need to read the rules closely to see if the gimmick is of value to you.

Product-purchase gimmicks

The most common gimmick involves buying a nonairline product or service and receiving a discount certificate good toward the purchase of an airline ticket. Polaroid and TWA once got together to offer a product-purchase gimmick. Buyers of a low-end Polaroid camera or five packs of Polaroid film received a discount certificate good for 25 percent off any TWA round-trip fare, including fares for most international destinations.

At a discount store you could have picked up the least-expensive qualifying camera for around $25. If you applied your 25 percent discount certificate towards a $600 Apex fare, your discount would be worth $150. Subtract the $25 you paid for the camera, and you would have had a $125 bargain.

Even if you didn't want a camera, it would have paid you to buy one just to get the discount certificate. You could always give the camera as a present.

Airlines have at times teamed up with mail-order catalog firms who would, when you placed a catalog order, sell you a discount certificate for $25. This certificate was also good for 25 percent off your fare.

Giving away airline discount certificates as an incentive to buy a product is quite common, and you should watch for these money-saving opportunities. Radio Shack has rewarded its customers with airline discount coupons. Cereal boxes and detergent products have offered them. Stuffers in credit card bills have promoted discount certificates worth $100 off an American Airlines European flight. And in an immensely practical promotion, buyers of travel writer Arthur Frommer's guides have received airline discount certificates — purchase a travel guide to your destination and get a discount off your air fare.

Keep alert for these discount certificates as you read your newspaper, listen to the radio and even on your shopping trips as you walk the aisles scanning merchandise. I came across the travel guide/discount certificate promotion as I was browsing in a bookstore. At the time, I was planning to fly to San Diego. So the gimmick allowed me to buy *Frommer's San Diego* city guide AND get a hefty air-fare discount.

Not all gimmicks represent bargains

Gimmicks such as this are real bargains that can cut the cost of your air travel. Not all product-purchase gimmicks, however, are that attractive.

Chase Manhattan Bank once gave certain loan customers a coupon good for 50 percent off a British Airways New York-London flight. If you were in the market for a loan, the gimmick was a good fringe benefit. If not, it was of no value to you.

At one time General Motors gave new-car buyers two free round-trip tickets good for anywhere TWA flies. That's a nice bonus for a car buyer, but it's not a viable tool to help you fly there for less.

To save on your air fare with a product-purchase gimmick, you need to take a close look at the offer. Be sure you're getting a genuine bargain, not just a fringe benefit.

Another product-purchase gimmick which is tempting to the traveler but may or may not be of value is the free or discounted airline ticket awarded through a hotel's frequent stay program. To see if you are actually getting a bargain, you need to determine the cost and value to you of both the hotel stays and the award. If you travel frequently and normally stay at hotels in the price range of the award-giving hotel, you may have a good deal.

But you still need to look into it a little deeper. Find out if your hotel stay has to be at a particular qualifying rate. Do you have to pay full rack rate, or even higher? If you have been staying at a discounted corporate or weekend-special rate, will the increased costs negate the value of the award?

Inter-Continental hotels once offered guests staying six nights a free round-trip airline ticket to anywhere in the continental United States. The nights did not have to be consecutive. But you had to pay full rack rates and in some instances even higher.

Does this gimmick represent a bargain? Let's look into it.

The value of the award would be the fare for the flight. At the time of the offer, you could get a transcontinental round trip for around $298, which would represent the award's maximum value. Dividing the $298 fare by the six nights shows the value of each night's stay is about $50. If you could stay at an Inter-Continental hotel without increasing your normal lodging costs by more than $50 per night, you would have a bargain. How good a bargain would depend on how much of that $50 margin you have to spend. If you must spend $45 of it each night, you will wind up getting $30 off your air fare. If you spend only $10 of it, you've got a great bargain — a round trip priced at $60. And if you don't have to spend any of it, you've got a free ticket.

An old-standby gimmick

Getting back to gimmicks that save you money, here's a version of the product-purchase gimmick that has been around for several years and is still offered frequently today. Supermarket chains, banks, discount stores and retailers around the country continually conduct promotions that offer bargain-priced certificates redeemable for airline tickets.

Among the supermarkets that have used the gimmick are: Stop & Shop in New England, Shop Rite in New Jersey, Super Value in Atlanta, Acme food stores in the East, California's Lucky stores and Detroit-based Great Scott. When shoppers purchased a specific amount of groceries within a seven-day period — generally in the area of $50 to $100 — the store would sell them at a deeply discounted price a certificate redeemable for an airline ticket.

The shopper redeems the certificate at a travel agency or with a specific airline. For each certificate, the airline or travel agency issues a one-way or round-trip ticket (depending on the gimmick's rules) for any flight within the continental United States. Banks also have offered these certificates, usually to savers making a new deposit of a specified minimum amount.

You can save big with this gimmick. When the lowest round-trip Boston-Los Angeles fare was $338, one supermarket would have sold you two one-way certificates for $178. Had you redeemed them for a Boston-Los Angeles round trip, you would have saved $160. If this gimmick is offered in your area, it would pay to go out of your way to do your grocery shopping.

In another version of this gimmick, some retailers do not sell discount certificates but offer them free to shoppers making a low minimum purchase. Just buy a given amount of merchandise and you get a certificate.

One of the Phar-Mor chain's discount stores once gave away a discount certificate free to customers who made a purchase of at least $15. The certificate gave you $50 off any Continental Airlines fare priced between $200 and $350 and $75 off fares over $350.

A new gimmick

A recent marketing innovation called Air Miles is a reincarnation of the old S & H Green Stamps idea. Instead of collecting green stamps redeemable for merchandise, you collect air-travel credits to be redeemed for a round-trip ticket to your choice of destinations served by the participating airlines.

Under the program, participating retailers and services, such as supermarkets, department stores, restaurants, banks, credit card issuers and so forth, will give you a credit for one mile of air travel every time you purchase a specific dollar amount of their goods or services.

You collect the mileage credits until you have enough to fly to your destination. Then you turn them in for an airline ticket on one of the program's carriers, which can include American, United and Air Canada. The program's operators figure that, based upon typical spending patterns, an annual income of $40,000 would generate enough credits for a 2,000-mile round trip.

Air Miles is a completely new program as I go to press with this edition of *Fly There For Less*. But it looks to me as though it has the potential to take off, so watch for it in your area.

Of course, the Air Miles promotions will stress that you are getting "free" air travel. If you are a savvy consumer, though, you will realize that retailers and service providers are going to increase their prices to cover the cost of the program. Therefore you will have to comparison shop the prices of establishments providing Air Miles and those that do not to see if the program truly does represent bargain air travel to you.

Freebie coupons

I was once in a store buying merchandise that would entitle me to a discount certificate when I noticed a creative individual obtaining free certificates. After customers had gone through the check-out lines, this gentleman would discreetly ask them if they intended to use their register receipt to obtain a discount certificate. If the answer was no, he would ask them to do him a favor by going to the redemption table and turning in their register receipt so he could get the certificate. Obliging customers handed them over to him outside the store, out of range of the redemption table personnel.

Airlines have on occasion put free discount coupons into newspapers. These coupons, similar to cents-off grocery coupons, could be cut out and used to knock a specific dollar amount off the airline's fares.

United Airlines once used such coupons to give their sales a boost. Each coupon was worth $35 off a United promotional fare costing $175 or more.

At least one enterprising firm found a way to expand on the use of these coupons. Throughout the run of the promotion, the firm bought thousands of newspapers containing the coupons. The company sold the discount coupons to travel agents at $5 each or $3.50 each on quantities over 300.

Travel agents could employ the coupons in three ways:

1) Use the coupon when booking customer flights and, un-

beknownst to their customers, put the entire $35 savings into their own pockets.

2) Split the savings with the customer, perhaps giving the client a $15 or $20 discount while keeping the remainder for the agency.

3) Give their client the entire $35 savings, or the entire savings less the agency's cost, thereby gaining a tremendous amount of inexpensive goodwill.

Here's what one travel agency did for its customers when Northwest Airlines placed free discount coupons in newspapers. Omega Travel of Memphis, Tennessee, clipped out hundreds of the coupons, even sending employees down to the local newspaper office to pick up unsold copies.

The agency didn't just hold onto the coupons to hand to customers who would be coming in during the next few weeks. The agency's staff went to the trouble of also going through all its reservations for both corporate and leisure clients to find those who qualified for the coupon promotion. This is a travel agency that believes in customer service. Omega Travel obviously values all its customers and is willing to put out the effort required to save its clients money.

When you do see a freebie coupon in a newspaper, clip it out, but wait a few days before using it. The coupon locks you into the fares and schedules of the airline distributing it. But competing airlines have in the past come out and said they would accept the other airline's coupons under the same terms. You then have more air-travel and fare options from which to choose.

Free companion tickets

Still another attractive and common gimmick is the free companion ticket, or two-for-one bonus — buy one ticket and the airline will give you a second free. There are numerous variations, one of which works like this. Passengers who buy a round-trip ticket to, say, Europe would then receive a coupon entitling them to buy two tickets for the price of one to another destination.

In a more simplified version, Southwest Airlines once ran a "Friends Fly Free" promotion that did just as the name implied. When you bought a ticket, a companion could fly the same itinerary for free.

The value of a two-for-one bonus may diminish if you must buy a full-fare coach ticket to receive the free companion ticket. But not always. Southwest's Friends Fly Free promotion required purchasing a full-fare ticket. The average cost of the tickets, however, put them into the level of some advance-purchase fares but without the advance-purchase requirement. Great for a low-priced, last-minute trip.

Companion tickets requiring purchase of a full-fare ticket can also be beneficial to business travelers unable to meet advance-purchase requirements. If a company sending two people to the same destination obtains a free companion ticket, it cuts its travel costs in half.

Ticket booklets

The ticket booklet is another money-saving gimmick. With a booklet, you buy a specified number of tickets for the same routing, and the airline tosses in an extra one for free.

Continental has offered travelers booklets containing 13 flight coupons for the price of 12. Another carrier has offered 10-ticket booklets on its Boston-New York-Washington shuttle flights for the price of about nine tickets.

Because this type of gimmick requires the traveler to make

frequent flights, usually within a relatively short time, it's ideal for the frequent business traveler.

Gift certificates

Some airlines sell gift certificates good towards the purchase price of a ticket. A few words to the appropriate person at the approach of Christmas, a birthday, graduation, an anniversary, a wedding or any other gift-giving occasion and you can cut the cost of your ticket.

TWA, for example, sells gift certificates which you can use when buying any published TWA fare. The certificates come in denominations ranging from $25 to $250 and are available at TWA airport counters or through the carrier's reservations center (800-221-2000).

Some last words on gimmicks

Gimmicks continually come and go. To get the word out, airlines and retailers depend heavily upon advertising their gimmicks, so watch for them. Many are an easy way to save serious money on your air travel. But when you come upon a gimmick, be sure to determine its costs, rules and restrictions. Then calculate whether it actually does represent a savings for YOU.

A ticket auction — an innovative technique for saving air travel dollars

A San Francisco-based firm called Marketel has recently come out with an idea that calls for air travelers to submit bids on the ticket they want. Sounds gimmicky, but it may be viable.

Marketel's operation, called "Bookit!," tries to match a traveler's bid with offers from international and domestic ticket suppliers.

Bookit obtains tickets both directly from several major airlines and from sources such as consolidators and tour operators.

To enter your bid, you fill out a Bookit form that indicates your preferences and degree of flexibility. Among the areas covered on the form:

- Will you accept any class of service?

- Will you accept a stop or a connection or must the flight be nonstop?

- Will you accept any schedule or do you want to specify the latest time you can arrive at your destination?

- Will you accept a different travel day?

- Will you accept any airport serving your departure and arrival cities or do you want a specific airport?

- Will you accept a nonchangeable ticket or only one that lets you modify your return?

- Do you require that the flight earn frequent-flyer mileage on the airline accepting your bid?

You fax the completed form to Bookit, stating your specific dollar bid for the flight. Your bid can specify up to three one-way segments for a maximum of 10 travelers on the same itinerary. Bookit will charge your MasterCard or Visa $16 and circulate your bid among its suppliers.

The process takes at least three working days. To get a response within two business days, you can specify you want the firm's "premium order" which costs $25.

To increase chances of getting your bid accepted, it should be realistic. You might try slightly undercutting the route's least expensive promotional fare while stipulating fewer restrictions.

If your bid is accepted, Bookit will express ship your ticket at a $15 charge for next-workday delivery. You won't know which airline you'll be flying until you receive your ticket.

Sometimes the firm may respond with a counteroffer, perhaps a flight with a few more restrictions. You can either accept or reject the counteroffer. Should your bid not be accepted, you may resubmit a higher bid — but you'll again pay the $16 or $25 order charge.

To get a copy of Bookit's form, call 800-627-55583 or 402-398-4800. They will charge $12.95 to your credit card and fax you a copy of the form. You can then make photocopies of the form for your use when faxing bids.

With Bookit's dependence on fax machines, the operations is obviously aimed at the business traveler. But even if you're a leisure traveler without access to a fax machine, you can still get in on the action. Many print shops and pack-and-ship businesses will send and receive faxes for you at a nominal cost.

A space-available broker — big savings for the vagabond

Adventurous flexible travelers willing to take destination and airline potluck can save on flights to Western Europe. Airhitch, a firm arranging to fill last-minute unsold seats on both scheduled and charter flights, promises only to get you to Europe, not to Paris, Rome or any other specific city. The firm also makes no promises as to which airline or what type of aircraft you will fly on.

While Airhitch's space-available operation is designed mainly for students, anyone can use it. But you should be footloose and flexible. Airhitch's services are ideal for travelers who plan to use a Eurailpass for travel within Europe. Regardless of which European city you fly into, the Eurailpass will let you hop on a train at no additional cost to reach a city from which you plan to launch your rail itinerary.

After paying a $25 registration fee, which is applied to your fare, Airhitch starts the registration process for a one-way last-minute seat to Western Europe. There is no minimum registration period, but the earlier you register the better since Airhitch assigns flight priority based upon a customer's date of registration. On your registration form you list a range of consecutive days during which you would like to fly, specifying earliest, latest and preferred departure dates. Usually, your date range must be at least five days long, eight days during high season. You also list on the registration form, in order of preference, three destinations.

On the Wednesday before your date range starts, you telephone Airhitch who will have a tentative list of at least three flights for you. You tell Airhitch which you would prefer. A day or two before that flight, you again telephone Airhitch who will now know what firm flight opportunities are available for you. You then choose your exact flight.

Your seat, however, is not guaranteed, and there is always the possibility that a seat will not be available for you on your assigned flight. From Airhitch's past experience, though, that's an unlikely occurrence. More than 95 percent of travelers working with Airhitch fly on the first flight to which they are assigned. And 99 percent fly during their date range. If the worst does happen and Airhitch cannot arrange a flight during your date range, all your money will be refunded.

Is it worth the uncertainty? When New York-Paris Apex tickets cost $667 round trip, Airhitch would get you from an East Coast gateway to Europe for $160 and back again for another $160. Their $320 round trip would save you $347.

New York is the most often used East Coast gateway, but Airhitch also uses flights out of Boston, Washington, Philadelphia and Baltimore. European-bound flights from the Midwest and Southeast cost $229 one way, while West Coast departures (Los Angeles, San Francisco and Seattle) run $269 one way. The most common destinations in Western Europe include: Amsterdam, Brussels, Frankfurt, Geneva, London, Madrid, Milan, Munich, Paris, Rome, Stuttgart and Zurich.

How to make contact

Airhitch will send you a registration form and a brochure describing their operation. Contact them at:

• Airhitch, 2790 Broadway, Suite 100, New York, NY 10025, telephone 212-864-2000.

• Airhitch, 1341 Ocean Ave., Santa Monica, CA 90401, telephone 213-458-1006.

Drawbacks

Airhitch sells only one-way flights. For your return flight you have to go through a separate registration process. You can, however, accomplish this at the same time you are arranging your outbound flight. Or, you can wait until you are in Europe.

Note, though, that regardless of where or when you register, your return flight could depart from and fly into cities different than those used on your outbound flight. If you have the flexibility to take Airhitch to Europe, but need more solid flight arrangements for your return, consider buying your return ticket from a consolidator in London or Amsterdam.

Air courier travel — while not free, it's cheap

Flying as a courier may bring to mind adventure and intrigue. But you won't need your trench coat and a list of passwords. It might also raise your suspicions. But you won't be transporting drugs, running guns or smuggling diamonds.

Actually, flying as a courier is rather mundane. You'll probably be shepherding sacks of small parcels and envelopes filled with business papers and documents. But you won't even be handling the material.

In a typical flight, representatives of the courier company deliver their material to the airport and check it in as the baggage on your ticket. Then they hand you the ticket, the baggage claim check and a copy of the manifest listing the contents of the baggage.

Upon arrival, someone from the courier company will be there to meet you. You'll accompany the baggage through customs, declaring the contents to be as shown on the manifest. The courier company, however, is responsible for ensuring that the manifest accurately reflects the contents of the baggage.

Couriers have become a necessary part of today's world of big business. Getting something on someone's desk by 10 the next morning has become the norm, regardless of where in the world that desk is located. Banks, stock brokerages, insurance companies, film studios, media organizations and other firms in need of overnight delivery will contact one of the many air express or air freight companies.

These express and freight firms typically contract with an air courier company for shipment because they know their material will then fly a dependable, scheduled airline. And even more importantly, upon arrival the material will not sit in a warehouse for days awaiting customs clearance. Instead, it will be processed through customs immediately along with the rest of the passengers' baggage.

Flying as a courier will offer you both domestic and international destinations, including cities in Europe, South America,

Asia and Australia. Most courier flights fly out of New York and Los Angeles. Your return is usually arranged before departure, with your stay ranging from one to two weeks. Sometimes, though, you can leave the return date open.

Traveling as a free-lance courier has become so viable and popular that the companies no longer pay couriers. Rarely will they even give you a free flight. Instead, they buy the ticket and charge you a fee. Your reward is bargain-priced air transportation to your destination. How much you pay will depend on the travel season and the popularity of the destination. But the savings can be substantial. Discounts ranging between 50 percent and 70 percent off the cost of a promotional-fare ticket are typical. And at times discounts have shot up to 90 percent.

Here's some examples of actual courier-flight round-trip fares once available. Remember, though, fares change. Courier fares mirror supply and demand and will change as often as the fares on scheduled airlines do. And if you fly during your destination's high season, fares will be up. Conversely, fly during the off season and you'll find lower fares. The list also gives you a good idea of typical destinations to which free-lance couriers are sent.

- Chicago-Brussels: $299
- Chicago-London: $325
- Chicago-Mexico City: $200
- Chicago-Rio de Janeiro: $450
- Los Angeles-Singapore: $575
- Los Angeles-London: $600
- Miami-Caracas: $275
- Miami-Guatemala City: $150
- Miami-Quito: $200
- Miami-Rio de Janeiro: $500

- New York-Athens: $299
- New York-Buenos Aires: $399
- New York-Caracas: $175
- New York-Hong Kong: $544
- New York-Milan: $399
- New York-Rio de Janeiro: $399
- New York-San Juan: $180
- New York-Seoul: $625
- New York-Stockholm: $299
- New York-Sydney: $750
- New York-Tel Aviv: $575
- San Francisco-Hong Kong: $483

What the courier company expects from you

When you accept a courier flight, you are not just accepting a low-priced trip to a faraway destination. You will have obligations that you must meet and fulfill. Here's what the firm you are dealing with will want from you:

- To sign a contract. Among other things, the contract will indicate that you are not just purchasing an airline ticket but a courier trip.

- To pay for your trip before departure. Some companies will accept a down payment with final payment a few days before departure. Others will require full payment at once. Some companies accept credit cards, which may raise the cost of your ticket about 3 percent. Others require payment in cash, money order or certified check.

- To have a current passport.

- To get your own visa. If your courier flight takes you to a country requiring a visa, it will be your responsibility to obtain it. With some courier companies, it will also be your responsibility to be aware that your destination requires a visa. You can't depend on the courier firm to alert you. Your best bet is to obtain the U.S. State Department's "Foreign Visa Requirements" which lists both countries requiring visas for U. S. citizens and application instructions. To get the publication, send 50 cents to: Consumer Information Center, Pueblo, CO 81009.

How to make contact

You'll find courier companies in most major cities, but the bulk of the firms using couriers are based in New York, Los Angeles and Miami. Courier flights, however, depart from Chicago, Dallas, Houston and San Francisco in addition to New York, Los Angeles and Miami.

You can start by checking your telephone book. Look in the yellow pages under *Air Courier Services,* and contact those firms listed to see if they use free-lance couriers.

You may find, however, that many of the firms listed in your telephone book are merely sales offices designed to solicit and receive business for the company. The people you talk to may have not even have heard of free-lance couriers, never mind that their own company might employ such individuals.

If you have no luck with your local companies, try contacting one of the following firms which routinely use free-lance couriers. For initial contact, most firms prefer that you do not call them. Instead, write several months ahead of when you want to fly. Tell a bit about yourself and include your telephone number and a stamped, self-addressed business-size envelope. They'll send you back their courier application forms.

Contacts

• A-1 International., 6930 N.W. 12th St., Miami, FL 33126,

telephone 305-594-1184. A-1 International offers courier flights to Venezuela.

• Air Facility, 177-25 Rockaway Blvd. Jamaica, NY 11434, telephone 718-712-0630. Air Facility offers flights to South America, including such cities as Caracas, Rio and Buenos Aires.

• Courier Network, 295 Seventh Ave., New York, NY 10001, telephone 212-691-9860. Courier flights only to Tel Aviv.

• Curaçao Tours, 2725 N. Thatcher Ave., Suite 210, River Grove, IL 60171, telephone 708-453-7300. Uses couriers on flights to Mexico City and London.

• East West Express, P.O. Box 30849, JFK Station, Jamaica, NY 11430, telephone 516-561-2360 or 212-490-0279. East West has courier flights from New York to Seoul, Korea and Sydney, Australia.

• Halbart Express, 147-05 175th St., Jamaica, NY 11434, telephone 718-656-8279, fax 718-244-0559. Sends about 20 couriers a day, six days a week, to major cities in Europe.

• Line Haul Services, 7859 N.W. 15th St., Miami, FL 33126, telephone 305-477-0651. This firm uses couriers on flights to Latin America.

• Jupiter Air, 160-23 Rockaway Blvd., Jamaica, New York, 11434, telephone 718-656-6050. Jupiter Air offers courier flights only to Hong Kong.

• Micom American, JAL Cargo Terminal, North Access Road, San Francisco, CA 94128, telephone 415-872-6506, fax 415-871-4975. Micom American offers courier flights to Hong Kong and Singapore.

• Rush Courier, 81 9th St., Brooklyn, NY 11220, telephone

718-439-9043. Rush can put you on courier flights to San Juan, Puerto Rico.

• Trans-Air System, 2505B N.W. 72nd Ave., Miami, FL 33122, telephone 305-592-1771. Flights from Miami to Central America.

• World Courier, 137-42 Brewer Blvd., Jamaica, NY 11434, telephone 800-221-6600 or 718-978-9552, fax 718-276-6932. Courier flights to Europe.

Using a courier booking agent may be easier

If you plan to fly only occasionally as a courier — or even just once — the easiest way to obtain a flight would be to contact a firm that arranges couriers for these companies. Although you'll have to pay a bit more than if you dealt directly with a freight company, you'll still find the costs extremely low.

Two such firms are located in the New York City area. You'll also find one in San Francisco and another in the Los Angeles area.

One New York-based company called Now Voyager can offer you flights to destinations around the world including New York, Miami, Los Angeles, Puerto Rico, Bermuda, London, Amsterdam, Brussels, Paris, Madrid, Rome, Milan, Geneva, Frankfurt, Tel Aviv, Rio de Janeiro, Buenos Aires, Hong Kong, Singapore and Sydney.

Your cost will vary according to the season and the popularity of the destination, but here's some typical round-trip prices offered by Now Voyager in the past: New York-Brussels between $150 and $250, New York-Rio de Janeiro from $299 to $399, New York-Buenos Aires $399, New York-Hong Kong between $299 and $549 and New York-Sydney $599 round trip.

The return leg of your international flight departs one-to-two weeks after your arrival. Domestic routes are also available, with New York-Los Angeles flights as low as $50 one way.

To arrange a flight, contact Now Voyager not more than 60 days in advance by calling 212-431-1616 on a weekday. Call between 9 a.m. and 11 a.m. and you'll reach their recorded information line listing available flight dates and destinations as well as the cost and length of stay. Bookings can be made at the 212-431-1616 number between noon and 5 p.m. Eastern Standard (Daylight) Time. Have a specific destination and flight date in mind when you call.

Now Voyager charges a $50 yearly registration fee. For a brochure, write:

• Now Voyager at 74 Varick St., Mezzanine B, New York, NY 10013.

Another New York company, Courier Travel Service, specializes only in transatlantic flights to Western Europe. Should you want to fly beyond Europe, Courier Travel will arrange a flight to London where they'll put you in touch with a British courier service. The British firm can then arrange flights worldwide, but especially to destinations in Africa and Australia.

Courier Travel Service, although based in New York, offers London-bound courier flights departing from Chicago, Dallas, Houston, Los Angeles and San Francisco in addition to their New York departures.

Courier Travel does not charge you a fee. They operate in the manner of a travel agency, receiving a commission from the courier company. Call Courier Travel at 800-922-2359 or 516-791-4600 during normal business hours to determine what flights are available.

For a $25 refundable deposit, the company will put you on their telephone-notification list for last-minute courier opportunities.

Their address is:

   • Courier Travel Service, 1226 West Broadway, Hewlitt, NY 11557.

UTL Travel in San Francisco offers air courier flights to Hong Kong and Singapore. UTL charges a $20 annual registration fee. You can contact them at:

   • UTL Travel, 320 Corey Way, South San Francisco, CA 94080, telephone 415-583-5074, fax 415-583-8122.

In the Los Angeles area, Way To Go Travel arranges courier flights out of Los Angeles to Singapore and London and flights from Hong Kong to San Francisco. This firm also maintains a travel club offering its members first shot at last-minute air courier flights. Club membership also gives you discounts on other travel products including scheduled air fares.

Contact them at:

   • Way To Go Travel, 3317 Barham Blvd., Hollywood, CA 90068, telephone 213-466-1126.

Drawbacks

Flying as a courier does have disadvantages. Just how serious they are, though, depends on your travel habits and your flexibility.

If you're not used to traveling light, which does have advantages in its own right, you'll have to get in the habit — fast. Since the courier company is using your check-in baggage allotment, you're left with only carry-on baggage.

Another limitation you'll encounter — courier travel is typically one-person travel. That is, only one courier is assigned to a particular flight. If you are traveling with a companion, that traveler will have to fly out as the following day's courier to your destination. Your return courier flights will also have to be on successive days.

But you can try to get around this limitation in two ways.

1) Occasionally two couriers will be required to fly to a single destination on the same day. You can hold out and await such an opportunity. At times the two couriers will fly on the same flight, but generally separate flights are required.

2) You can contact a consolidator to see if you can purchase a discount ticket for the courier's companion. If you are arranging your courier flight through Courier Travel Service, they will obtain a discounted companion ticket for you.

If you are not completely flexible as to when you can arrive at your destination, courier flying may not be for you. While you will be flying on a regularly scheduled major airline, keep in mind that your contract is with the courier company. Occasionally — not often but it does happen — there may be insufficient cargo to justify the firm's purchasing a ticket for a courier. This would probably not be known, however, until several hours before flight time. And while the flight will take off, the only way you could then get on it would be to buy an expensive full-fare ticket.

Your stay at your destination will probably be limited. You may have to return seven days after departing. But there are exceptions. On not-too-frequent occasions you may be able to work out a stay of several weeks or longer.

Courier flying is also not for those who have a fear of flying and usually bolster their courage with an on-board drink or two. The freight firms want their couriers to maintain a professional, business-like image, which includes dressing well — in some cases that means jacket and tie for men — and refraining from in-flight drinking.

Up next, more nontraditional ticket sources

Other ticket sources spawned by deregulation include a variety of clubs and programs requiring enrollment and sometimes an enrollment fee. These clubs and programs are so prolific and diverse that they have the next chapter to themselves.

7

Discover low-fare opportunities through clubs and programs

From airline frequent-flyer plans to last-minute travel clubs, a variety of enrollment-type programs are available to travelers looking for low fares. Some clubs and programs charge a membership fee, others are free. But they'll all help you to fly there for less.

Airline frequent-flyer plans — opportunities for free and discounted air travel

One of the most successful promotions devised by airline marketing departments is the frequent-flyer program. Just about all major U.S. airlines and many foreign carriers have one. Put simply, in a typical program:

• You earn one mile of credit — sometimes more — for each mile you fly on airlines participating in your program.

• You can then trade in your accumulated mileage credits for a variety of benefits such as free flights, seating upgrades and free or discounted hotel stays and car rentals.

In reality, however, frequent-flyer plans are seldom that straight forward. A variety of rules and conditions — which differ from airline to airline — make them fairly complex.

Both business and leisure travelers should enroll

The airlines use their frequent-flyer plans to encourage brand loyalty from a particular segment of the passenger population — the business traveler. And any business traveler should enroll in one or more frequent-flyer programs.

Leisure travelers, too, should participate in these plans. Don't be put off by the term *frequent flyer.* Even if you take only one or two flights a year and feel you would never rack up enough miles to get a free flight, you still need to join the frequent-flyer program of any airline you fly. You encounter no costs to enroll, but you do receive some benefits for being a member.

The airlines offer their frequent flyers special deals that are not available to other passengers. Sometimes they announce special discounted fares for members. At other times they may promote special companion fares.

Northwest and Continental several times a year have sent their frequent flyers discount coupons. Northwest once sent its frequent flyers a coupon that allowed them to purchase a round-trip ticket to any Northwest destination in the continental United States for just $149. Continental has offered its frequent flyers a $199 round trip anywhere in the lower 48 states.

So even if you never accumulate the mileage necessary for a free flight, you can see membership is worthwhile to take advantage of these fare discounts.

Bonus miles put you closer to flying free

That free trip might not be as far from your reach as you think. Many plans offer bonus miles that can boost the not-so-frequent flyer's mileage credits. Some airlines give anywhere from 2,000 to 5,000 miles free just for enrolling in their program. And tie-ins with hotel chains and car rental firms offer more opportunities to build up mileage credits every time you use the services of these participating partners.

USAir's "Frequent Traveler" program, for example, gives a free domestic ticket for 20,000 miles. To help you reach that level, USAir will give you:

• A bonus of 2000 miles for joining.

• A minimum credit of 750 miles for flights that are under that mileage.

• Mileage credits for flights on certain regional airlines and certain international airlines, including Air France, Air New Zealand, Alitalia, British Airways, KLM, Lufthansa, Sabena and Swissair.

• A minimum 500-mile credit for a stay at a Hilton, Hyatt, Marriott, Omni, Radisson, Stouffer or Westin hotel.

• 500 miles for renting a car from Hertz or National.

• One mile for each $1 charged to USAir's affinity credit card.

Frequent-flyer programs are complex and changeable

Looking at the way you can earn bonus miles with USAir's Frequent Traveler plan, you can begin to see that these programs could become quite involved. In fact, today's frequent-flyer programs mirror today's air-fare marketplace — they are complicated and changing.

The rules governing the programs can be changed on an airline's whim. Participating partners come and go. And in today's air-travel climate, you don't even have any assurance that your airline will be around when you want to cash in your awards.

While you can keep a grasp on one program without too much difficulty, you really run into problems trying to decide which one is the best for you to join. Each airline has different rules and different ways of administering their programs. Some carriers offer minimum credit for short trips. Some do not. Among those that do, American Airlines will credit your account with 500 miles for trips that are less than 500 miles. USAir, as we've seen, will give you a 750-mile minimum. But Delta's minimum is 1,000 miles.

On the surface, it appears obvious that you should join Delta's program because you will receive more miles. HOWEVER...

• Delta requires you to accumulate 40,000 miles to earn a free trip while American and USAir only require 20,000 miles.

• But Delta gives you 5,000 bonus miles as soon as you join their program while American gives no bonus miles. USAir offers 2,000 bonus miles, but only if you fly that airline within 60 days of joining.

And when a member earns enough miles to claim an award, there is still no consistency among the carriers. Some require members to call them and then wait several weeks while the request is processed. Others automatically mail award certificates to members as soon as their mileage accumulations reach award levels.

When using a mileage award, some carriers require frequent flyers to fly off-peak. If a member wants a peak flight, it will cost more miles.

You need to take all of these differences into consideration when selecting a frequent-flyer program.

How to choose a frequent-flyer plan

I have two general rules concerning frequent-flyer programs.

1) You need to join the frequent-flyer program of every airline on which you might fly.

2) You need to concentrate your travel among as few airlines as is feasible, preferably one, two at the most.

At first glance these rules may seem to contradict each other. Actually they don't. Rule number one lets you look for discounts that will cut your air-travel costs. The money you save flying on special frequent-flyer discounts will more than offset any loss of frequent-flyer miles in your primary program.

But when you have no money-saving incentive to fly another airline, then you follow rule number two, going with your primary carrier for the frequent-flyer miles. If you seek frequent-flyer mileage on several airlines, you only dilute the miles you could accumulate in any one program. Conversely, you will maximize those miles by concentrating your travel on just one carrier.

To determine which airline should be your primary frequent-flyer carrier, you will have to compare programs among those you're likely to be flying the most. Obtain each airline's literature detailing its frequent-flyer program. Look the information over, keeping in mind the type of flying you do as well as the award destination you would select for your free ticket. Do you usually make short-distance flights that would let you take advantage of minimum-per-flight miles? Would you use your free ticket to fly within the contiguous United States? To Hawaii? To Europe? Here's what you need to compare:

• Types of awards and the mileage required to obtain them. Pay close attention to how many miles are required to earn a free round-trip ticket to destinations that interest you.

• Restrictions attached to the use of your award, such as limited seating, blackout dates or a time period after which awards expire if not used. Also verify whether you are permitted to transfer awards to relatives and friends if this would be a consideration with you.

• Opportunities for bonus miles, such as affiliation with a credit card.

• The usefulness to you of tie-ins with hotel chains, other airlines and car rental firms. An airline might have a wide selection of participating-partner hotel chains. But if you would be unlikely to stay in any of them, that wide selection is of little value to you. You would be better off with a carrier offering just one or two participating-partner hotels as long as they are chains you use in your travels.

• The amount of credit awarded for hotel, airline and car rental tie-ins. Note, especially, any restrictions attached to using the tie-ins to earn mileage credits.

If something in your literature appears ambiguous, telephone the airline to clarify it. Assume nothing. Call and ask. Put those telephone numbers in the airline contact appendix to use!

As an alternative to contacting each airline individually to obtain specifics on each of their programs, you may want to send for my *Traveler's Report* #114 HOW TO PICK THE FREQUENT-FLYER PROGRAM THAT GIVES <u>YOU</u> THE MOST FREE TRIPS. Using this report, which I continually update, you have the latest, important details of each program at your fingertips so you can easily compare benefits. The report also takes you step-by-step through a decision-making process that will help you choose a program based on the type of flying you do. To order the report, see the catalog at the back of this book.

Enrolling in and using your program

When you decide on a plan, call the airline to have them send you an enrollment form, or pick one up at an airport ticket counter. Upon joining, the airline will assign you an account number and let you know the procedures to follow to obtain credit for the miles you fly. Be sure you follow those procedures. Some airlines will disallow credit for even minor deviations from the rules.

Typically, the airline will send you a monthly statement detailing the status of your mileage account. It's a good idea, though, to save your boarding passes, used tickets and hotel and car rental receipts as proof should your airline miss crediting a flight. Unfortunately, that's not a rare occurrence.

Once you've accumulated enough mileage credits for an award, you can apply to the airline to receive your award certificate. Some airlines send the certificates (also called coupons) automatically when you reach an award level. Should you want a higher-mileage award, you can save the certificates until you have accumulated sufficient mileage. When you wish to fly, you exchange the certificates for tickets, either by mail or at an airline ticket office.

How to boost your mileage credits

You can use a variety of strategies and techniques to accumulate miles faster. Some require that you be alert to any special promotions your airline might launch. Others require that you be a savvy traveler.

Typically, periodic mailings from the airlines will keep you informed of special opportunities to earn bonus miles. On occasion, however, a competitive environment will force an airline to implement a super-fast, short-notice promotion. These promotions, which may offer double or even triple mileage, can be in full swing weeks before the airline sends its scheduled, routine correspondence to its frequent-flyer members. And if the promotion is of short duration, it may never make the carrier's mailed-out literature.

To avoid missing out on a short-notice, mileage-boosting promotion, you need to fall back on newspaper ads to help keep you informed. It would also be a good idea to telephone the airline before you fly to see if any special promotions are in effect. Once alerted to the promotion, you can then make sure your account is credited as appropriate.

If you compare notes with other frequent flyers and find some were offered special promotions while you were not, that's just the way the airlines play that game. Some promotions may be offered only to flyers living in certain areas, or only to members who have recently flown or only to members who have NOT flown recently.

Here's a run down on ways to increase your mileage:

• Take advantage of opportunities to earn bonus miles by flying a particular route. Airlines often give bonus miles to promote specific routes. American Airlines, for example, offered its frequent flyers 5,000 bonus miles for making two flights from or through its Raleigh/Durham hub during a particular seven-week period. If you were making a round-trip flight during that period, you could have picked up the extra 5,000 miles just by selecting American flights that made a stop in Raleigh/Durham.

Continental once offered double mileage to its frequent flyers making a nonstop flight between Cleveland and Los Angeles. At one time Delta Air Lines opened up its entire network of Far East routes to bonus miles by offering double mileage to frequent flyers taking Delta to any of its Far East destinations.

• Watch for bonus-mile wars. When business is slow, airlines are apt to entice air travel by offering double, even triple, frequent-flyer miles. Continental once offered its frequent flyers double miles system wide for travel during the slow fall season.

United quickly matched Continental's double mileage on those routes it shared with Continental. Anytime you learn of one airline offering bonus miles, check to see if your primary frequent-flyer carrier is matching the offer.

• Some airlines offer bonus miles for referring new members to the program, provided the new member makes a flight within a specified period after enrollment. Continental once offered its frequent flyers 2,500 bonus miles for enrolling a new member, 5,000 miles for the second individual enrolled, 7,500 for the third and 10,000 for the fourth. If you had enrolled four friends, all of whom took a Continental flight within 90 days of joining, you would have earned 25,000 bonus miles.

• Many airlines give bonus miles for flying business or first class. If your primary interest is in flying there for less, however, business or first class is not the way to go. But if you must fly in a premium class, then the additional bonus miles can be useful. In themselves, though, they in no way offset the added cost for a business- or first-class ticket.

• Be sure you know your airline's participating partners — hotels, car rental agencies and other airlines — and use them when appropriate.

• Keep alert to bonus-mile promotions offered by participating partners. Hilton hotels once offered United's and American's frequent flyers triple miles if they paid their hotel bill with a Visa card.

Thrifty Car Rental, a partner in Continental's OnePass frequent-flyer program, once ran a three-month off-season special that gave OnePass car renters an additional 500 miles. Instead of the normal 1,500 miles for a rental, the traveler would get 2,000. OnePass members could also earn an additional 1,500-mile bonus on each of three Thrifty rentals made during the three-month period.

If you were a OnePass member who had occasion to make the

three rentals, you would have received 10,500 miles total — that was more than halfway toward the miles necessary to earn a free flight. You would also accumulate miles from the Continental flights made in connection with the car rentals. Continental's 500-mile minimum would have given you at least 3,000 miles total for the three round trips. But if they were long-haul flights, you probably would have gotten your free ticket and even had a few miles left over to apply towards your next free flight.

• If a travel agent quotes a low fare on a carrier other than those whose frequent-flyer programs you belong to, ask if the fare is available on one of your frequent-flyer airlines.

• See if your program will sell you, in exchange for cash, a certain amount of frequent-flyer miles. Continental, for example, has allowed its frequent flyers to purchase a limited number of miles to reach a certain mileage plateau. Say you were 3,000 miles short of an award you wanted to take during your vacation, but were not planning to make an additional mileage-earning flight before then. You could purchase the required 3,000 miles from Continental for one cent a mile or $30.

• You can boost your mileage credits by shrewdly scheduling your flights to take advantage of minimum-mileage credit. If your airline offers minimum credits for short-distance flights, here's what to do. Select flights that will let you make a connection at an airport located as close as possible to either your departure or arrival airport. Your mileage will be calculated for each flight segment, and the shortest segment will probably earn you additional miles through the minimum credit.

I once flew Delta from Orlando to Los Angeles and received credit for 2,217 miles. On the return flight, however, I changed to another Delta flight in Atlanta — 403 miles from Orlando. Consequently, for the return trip I received credit for 2,946 miles. That broke down to 1,946 miles for the Los Angeles-to-Atlanta leg and 1,000 miles (the minimum credit) for the flight from Atlanta to Orlando. The return Los Angeles-Orlando flight via Atlanta gave me an additional 729 mileage credits.

Airline credit cards hasten mileage accumulations

As I pointed out earlier, USAir offers its frequent flyers an affinity credit card that earns bonus miles for charges made to the card. USAir is not the only carrier offering these credit cards. Most airlines do. Typically, the airlines contract with a major bank to issue a Visa card or a MasterCard in the airline's name. Whenever you use the card, the airline receives a percentage of the transaction.

The bonus miles you receive for using an affinity card are not given just for purchases related to air travel. Charges made for any purchase will earn mileage credits. Some airlines and their affinity cards offer a rate of one mile of frequent-flyer credit for each $1 charged on the card. Other cards offer one mile of credit for every $2 spent.

American Express also has a program in which its card holders can earn a mile of credit for each $1 charged to the card. Diners Club, too, has arrangements with many airlines to give frequent-flyer credit for each use of its card. The Diners Club card, however, provides fewer mileage credits than the airline affinity cards.

To obtain an airline's charge card, examine the frequent-flyer literature you receive from your carrier. It may include an application. If not, call the airline to find out which bank issues their affinity card. (You'll find the number in the airline contact appendix.) Then apply with that bank.

In addition to using airline affinity cards to boost mileage, holders of these cards may have an opportunity to get some free miles. The banks issuing the cards have sent some card holders preprinted checks to be cashed as a loan against the credit card. With some airlines, these checks when cashed will also earn you a one-mile frequent-flyer credit for each $1 of their face value.

If you use the checks for a loan, though, a hefty interest rate will probably eat up any frequent-flyer savings. Here's how to use the checks to receive frequent-flyer credit while paying little or no interest.

Suppose you receive checks that can be cashed for up to $5,000. First, call the bank and the airline to be sure the checks will earn frequent-flyer mileage. If they do, then make sure your credit card has a zero balance. Pay off any balance due if necessary. Write one of the checks for $5,000 and deposit it in your checking account. Your frequent-flyer account will then be credited with 5,000 miles for the cashed check. Now turn around and immediately send a $5,000 check from your checking account to the credit card bank to pay off the loan.

Cash for your miles

If you would rather turn your award miles into cash than take another flight, contact one of the coupon brokers listed in Chapter 6. Or pick one from the ads in *USA Today* or the *Wall Street Journal*. When selling to a broker, you can expect to get between one and two cents per mile. The more miles you have the more payment per mile you'll receive. That's because large mileage awards can be sold by the broker for high-value flights to Europe and Asia.

You need to be aware, however, that there is a risk involved in selling your frequent-flyer miles. If the airline catches you, they can kick you out of their program.

But the risk is small. Even the airlines themselves admit to the low risk level. While the airlines intensely dislike the buying and selling of frequent-flyer miles, they tend to confine their battles to the brokers, not their most loyal customers — the frequent flyers.

Drawbacks of frequent flyer plans

Frequent-flyer programs play an important role in helping you fly there for less. But these programs have a downside. They have drawbacks — some serious, some minor — that you need to be aware of. The mores serious problems include the airlines changing rules and placing severe restrictions on using free-travel awards.

It's the airlines' game, and they make — and change — the rules to suit them

One serious drawback to frequent-flyer plans is that the airlines can change rules and award levels as they see fit. The most sweeping change followed a period of intense competition during which the airlines went on a mileage-giveaway spree. During that spree they were rewarding and awarding their frequent flyers with triple mileage.

Passengers built up mileage credits so fast that airline balance sheets were about to be affected by flights carrying significant numbers of award passengers — that is, non-paying passengers. In one month 11 percent of the seats on TWA flights were filled with non-paying frequent flyers.

Realizing they had put their operations in jeopardy by giving away more potential free travel than they could profitably handle, many airlines took steps to diminish the impact. They raised award levels and tightened restrictions on use of the awards.

That tightening up on frequent-flyer awards was just the start of a continuing trend. More recently, for example, one airline raised its award level for an overseas ticket by more than 50 percent, from 60,000 to 95,000 miles. A year later, the line raised the award level to 125,000 miles!

In effect, the airlines advertise and promote their programs under one set of rules and conditions. But by the time an air traveler earns the mileage necessary to get a free trip, they have sometimes changed the rules so that the traveler no longer qualifies for the award originally sought. They have moved the goal post, and the air traveler must continue to earn mileage credits when he or she should already have received a free ticket according to the rules in effect when the traveler entered the game.

You have no recourse when an airline decides to devalue your miles by raising award levels. In earlier industry-wide mileage devaluations — the airlines call them adjustments — several state attorneys general forced the carriers to provide protection for miles earned before the devaluation. A federal court, however, overruled the state lawyers, saying federal law takes precedence over state law regarding airline advertising. The Supreme Court has backed the lower court by refusing to review the decision. That places enforcement in the hands of the U. S. Department of Transportation. Unfortunately, protection of the air-travel consumer does not appear to be high on the DOT's list of concerns.

Severe restrictions hamper using your free ticket

Blackouts and limited award-travel seats are another serious drawback to frequent flyer plans. To push award travel to off-peak flights — so award travelers are less likely to take a seat that could be filled with a cash customer — the airlines blackout extensive periods and severely limit seat availability for award travelers on each flight. Blackout dates and seat availability have such a significant impact on the value of your awards that you must look into them closely when selecting your primary airline.

Let's look at Continental Airlines' restrictions on award travel. As I write, Continental's award-travel restrictions are about the most stringent in the industry. The carrier limits domestic travel on its off-peak mileage awards to noon Monday through noon Thursday. And if you want to take a trip to Europe, your off-peak dates must be between January 11 to March 16 and October 15 to December 13. In addition to the blackouts, each off-peak flight offers only limited seating for award travelers.

Because of Continental's tight restrictions on award travel, a coupon broker will sell you a Continental frequent-flyer coupon good for an international flight below the cost of similar coupons on other airlines. The carrier's restrictions make it so difficult for travelers to get award seats on international flights that the marketplace has devalued Continental's coupons.

Although Continental may be a worst case, other carriers' restrictions on award travel will also hamper your flying when you want to. One survey showed almost a third of its respondents could not use their award to travel when they wished. They had to change dates or select a different destination so that they could use their award. Some travelers even wound up canceling a trip because they could not fly when they wanted.

Clearly, you may have problems using your mileage awards for free seats unless you are extremely flexible. Typically, you'll find it hardest to fly free over holidays, during summers and to popular destinations.

While some carriers completely blackout award travel for peak flights, others require higher credit for peak award travel. Thus, while 20,000 miles of credit gets you a free ticket on most lines, that ticket generally has to be used off-peak, conforming to blackouts and seat availability. For an unrestricted trip, most lines boost the mileage requirement to 30,000 or 40,000 miles.

More obstacles for award travelers

In addition to changing rules and tight restrictions, the airlines reward their frequent flyers with a variety of lesser drawbacks and not a few general irritants.

Some frequent-flyer plans require you to wait until between 24 and 72 hours before departure to make your reservations. This practically puts you — the frequent flyer — into the category of a standby passenger.

You'll find that award tickets generally may be used only for travel on the issuing airline. If a mechanical problem forces the carrier to cancel a flight, you will not be allowed to transfer to another airline. Instead, you will have to wait until the issuing airline's next flight. The reason here is that your airline would have to pay the other airline the cost of your ticket. But in this case, you have not paid cash for your ticket, and your carrier does not want to give away money it has not even received.

That said, however, if you plead a good case with the gate supervisor, he or she just may allow you to transfer to the other carrier. After all, it is not your fault that you can't get to your destination on time. If, on the other hand, you miss a flight through your own negligence, it's extremely unlikely your airline will allow you to transfer.

Some travelers, especially international travelers, are running into trouble getting participating-partner airlines, hotels and car rental firms to record their frequent-flyer information. Many travelers encounter blank stares by confused clerks who apparently have never heard of a frequent-flyer program or that their company is a participant in one.

The remedy here is twofold:

1) Carry with you any literature indicating the participating partners you plan to use are actually part of the airline's frequent-flyer program. It's also a good idea to bring along any literature describing bonus-mileage promotions as well as.

2) Carefully maintain your documentation, and send photocopies of any tickets, hotel bills or other receipts to your airline upon your return. Even then your account may not be promptly credited if the airline forwards your paperwork to the partner

for verification. One traveler reported that American Airlines' AAdvantage program took almost four months to credit an overseas hotel stay to his account.

Hotel-stay awards seem next to impossible to use

So many travelers have difficulty trying to book a free or discounted hotel stay earned through their frequent-flyer program that these awards are practically useless. In one survey, travelers were unable to book an award for a free hotel room 66 percent of the time. When trying to book a room with airline frequent-flyer credit, the typical response is that no award-travel rooms are available on that date...nor on that date...and that date as well.

One traveler tried some 40 times to book a room using a 50-percent-off TWA-Marriott coupon earned through the carrier's frequent-flyer program. Each time the reservation center would say no rooms were available on the TWA-Marriott coupon for that particular date. If the traveler didn't use the coupon, however, rooms were available at the going rate.

Still another hurdle to getting your frequent-flyer rewards

Some airlines play games with their flight numbers, listing a flight that requires a change of planes under a SINGLE FLIGHT NUMBER. Not only is the practice deceptive — despite its being sanctioned by the Department of Transportation — it will cost you frequent-flyer miles. Instead of picking up mileage from your departure city to the connecting city and from the connection to your destination, you'll only receive mileage from departure point to destination. And if one of those flights was a short hop, you may also be missing out on the higher minimum mileage.

Typically, you'll find the single flight numbers used when connecting at a carrier's hub, with one of the flight legs being on the carrier's affiliated commuter line.

One way to get around this practice and receive your appropriate frequent-flyer credit is to have the reservationist split the flight into two separate legs or segments. You would then receive a separately priced ticket for each segment.

As you'll see in Chapter 9, this could even result in your paying a lower fare, but it could also result in your paying a higher one. You will have to determine how ticketing your flight in two segments affects your fare. Weigh any change in cost against the benefit of increased frequent-flyer mileage to determine whether to price the ticket in two segments or grit your teeth and accept the airline's deception.

Another way around the single-flight-number deception is to take another flight — one that carries a different flight number — to or from the connecting city. You will have to spend extra waiting time at the connecting point, so you will have to weigh the inconvenience of the extra wait against the value of the additional miles.

Pay attention to details to avoid these surprises

Not only do you have to be aware of the drawbacks, you also have to delve deeply into all the rules and conditions of your program. Should you give only a cursory glance to the rules and conditions, you may get a nasty surprise should you find out after the fact about unappealing features. Here's some examples of what I'm talking about:

• Each passenger has his or her own account with the airline. You cannot pool credit among your family members or your employees — only your flight miles are credited to your account.

• Most airlines allow you to transfer your mileage awards to family members and friends. All airlines, however, prohibit selling your mileage awards.

• Some types of tickets do not qualify for frequent-flyer mileage — including senior citizen flight coupons, consolidator tickets and tickets purchased in conjunction with a package tour.

• When flying on a participating-partner airline, you cannot earn mileage credit from both carriers. You will have to choose one or the other.

• Hotel stays, on the other hand, usually earn credit both in the airline's frequent-flyer program and the hotel's frequent-stay program, if any.

• Some low-cost promotional tickets, especially those issued by some participating-partner foreign carriers, may not give frequent-flyer mileage. You need to ask. If the ticket you're considering does not, ask the cost of the next higher fare level that does. Then weigh the pros and cons of the extra dollars spent against the additional mileage credits. One of Delta's participating partners — Japan Air Lines — gives no credit at all for economy flights.

• Participating commuter airlines may not offer minimum-mileage credit. On those that do you may earn fewer miles than on the primary carrier. On TWA's commuters, for example, you earn only 500 miles instead of the 750 miles TWA gives you.

• The mileage awarded in some programs will expire if not used within a given time. American and United, for example, will delete miles not used within 36 months of their being earned. If you have enough miles for an award, including a seating-class upgrade, and are able to see ahead that you will not be using the miles before they expire, consider selling them to a coupon broker well in advance of expiration.

• To get credit for a hotel stay, you may have to fly on the sponsoring airline to the city in which the hotel is located.

Protecting your miles when your airline sells routes, merges or goes bankrupt

These are turbulent times for the airline industry, and there's a very real possibility that you could find yourself with a significant accumulation of miles on an airline that appears to be flying into financial trouble. If so, you will need to take steps to protect yourself.

Be alert to what your airline does. The larger your mileage accumulation, the closer you need to keep tabs on the carrier. Early signs of trouble can include heavy quarterly losses, withdrawing from a hub or selling off assets, including aircraft, airport gates and routes. If your local paper has a large business section, be sure to read it. Better yet, keep watch on your carrier through the pages of *USA Today* or the *Wall Street Journal.*

If things start to look particularly bleak, so much so that you would like to bail out, consider one of these two steps:

1) Cash in your miles for an award-travel ticket — not just an award coupon, actually book a flight — on a more-secure, financially stable partner airline. You may be able to stretch the time period before you have to fly on the ticket to several months, possibly even up to a year.

2) Consider insuring your mileage account. A program called "Award Guard" will insure you against loss of frequent-flyer credit. If your airline fails and you lose your mileage credits, Award Guard will obtain for you a ticket or tickets on another airline. You will, however, still have to follow the same rules that the failed airline set for using the frequent-flyer credits.

Note, though, that the insurance only applies to *complete loss* of your mileage credits. If your airline merges and you can still use the credits with the new carrier, you will not be reimbursed under the insurance. Even if the new airline does not serve the same destinations or requires more miles for a given award, you will have no claim on the insurance.

Still, at a cost of $79 a year, you may want to consider coverage just for the peace of mind it can give you if you have a large mileage account with a shaky airline. You can get the Award Guard coverage through a program called the Frequent Flyer Club. Membership costs $79 a year and includes Award Guard coverage. Contact the Frequent Flyer Club at 800-487-8893

When mulling over these options, also keep something else in mind — the airline industry has a stake in your well being as a frequent flyer. As airlines succumb to future industry shake outs, remaining carriers will have to make decisions concerning dead or dying frequent-flyer programs. They face two choices:

1) to alienate those frequent flyers in jeopardy,

2) to win the loyalty of those frequent flyers in jeopardy.

To win the loyalty of a bankrupt airline's passengers, another airline usually steps in to pick up the frequent-flyer program of the carrier that went under. One exception, however, was Braniff Airways' last bankruptcy. In a merger or buy out, where an airline picks up the assets of another, you can feel pretty confident that the airline will opt for loyalty. It's clearly in the carrier's interest to do so. Therefore, it appears you are not likely to actually loose your mileage credits entirely, which would allow you to make a claim under Award Guard. More likely, you will suffer a loss of mileage-credit value or loss of a desired destination.

Frequent-flyer variations — bargains without the complexity

Complex frequent-flyer programs impose a large administrative burden on the airlines. But competitive pressures will keep these programs going. Some airlines, however, have come up with simplified versions. These alternative frequent-flyer incentives are usually not as long lived as the frequent-flyer programs. In fact, some amount to only short-term promotions. But they still offer the reward of free or reduced-rate tickets.

Avianca Airlines, for example, has given Los Angeles- and New York-Colombia passengers making six flights a free round-trip ticket for the same route. Hawaiian Airlines has handed out a free round trip anywhere it flies after 20 inter-island flights. A flight to or from the mainland counted as five inter-island trips. And Southwest Airlines has given its frequent flyers one free round trip after 20 flights within a year.

Iberia, Spain's international airline, has used another variation. For each economy flight on Iberia, the airline has given a certificate worth $75 off a future flight. The certificates could be accumulated but had to be used within two years of issue.

And in still yet another variation, America West once offered frequent flyers a "Value Pack" coupon book. The book sold for $290 and contained 10 coupons, each valid for a nonstop segment on flights among eight specific cities in the Southwest. The coupons reduced one-way fares among those cities to as low as $29.

Anytime you foresee making several flights on a particular airline, look into its frequent-flyer opportunities. Even if the airline has a full-fledged frequent-flyer program, ask about any short-term incentives. America West's coupon book was offered in addition to the carrier's standard frequent-flyer program.

Travel agency frequent-traveler plans — a chance for double bargains

Some travel agencies have developed their own versions of the airlines' frequent-flyer plans. And by joining both an airline and a travel agency plan, you can reel in double savings.

Some travel agencies confine their programs to air travel only. Most, however, allow credit for all travel purchases, including hotels, car rentals, and travel packages. Typically, travel agency plans give clients a dollar credit based upon the cost of their travel. Clients accumulate credits and spend the dollar amount at the agency. Those interested in flying for less can use their credits to receive free or discounted flights.

One Massachusetts travel agency gives its clients a coupon worth $1 for every $50 spent. On a $1,000 trip a client receives coupons worth $20 towards future travel. A Pennsylvania travel agency, however, credits customers with $1 for every $100 spent. Thus, the Pennsylvania client purchasing $1,000 in travel receives only $10 in future travel credits.

Some travel agencies may skip the credits in favor of discounts on purchased travel. These agencies generally operate as a travel club, sometimes charging a membership fee. Once such agency is:

• Way To Go Travel, 3317 Barham Blvd., Hollywood, CA 90068, telephone 213-446-1126. The agency charges a $75 membership fee ($150 for a family membership). In exchange the traveler gets discounts on their purchases of regular air fares as well as car rentals, cruises and travel packages.

How to locate agencies offering frequent-traveler plans

To locate travel agencies offering frequent traveler plans, check your telephone book's yellow pages under *Travel Agencies*. Try calling several to ask about programs for frequent travelers. Also look for display ads in the yellow pages promoting such plans. Check too the ads in your Sunday newspaper's travel section.

Here again you'll want to comparison shop. Determine for each plan you come across just how much credit you get for the money you spend. Also consider the types of travel purchases that earn credit. If everything else is equal, you'll get more out of a plan that gives credit for all types of travel, not just air travel.

You don't have to use a travel agency in your community. If you can't find a local travel agency offering a plan, head for your library. Look in its collection of telephone books and Sunday newspapers for large cities across the country.

Also, turn to your library if you want to comparison shop with out-of-town agencies. Your telephone, a credit card and the U.S. mail will enable you to transact business with a travel agency anywhere in the country. And if you call on a Saturday, telephone rates are less expensive.

Last-minute travel clubs — bargains if you are flexible

When your local appliance store finds itself with excess inventory, it holds a sale to move the merchandise. When air-travel suppliers find themselves with excess inventory as flight day approaches — unsold package deals or charter seats — it would like to put the merchandise on sale. But if the supplier advertises sale prices, travelers who have already bought at the higher price are going to become upset. They may even turn in their tickets only to buy again at the sale price. And some travelers, knowing the seats will go on sale, would wait until just before departure to buy at the sale price.

One solution is to take the sale out of the travel industry mainstream by selling the last-minute excess inventory to travel clubs. The clubs turn around and offer the excess inventory to their members at discounted prices. Club members with the flexibility to travel on about one- to four-weeks' notice can pick up these last-minute travel bargains at savings of about 20 to 50 percent.

Trips offered by last-minute travel clubs include packages, escorted tours, cruises and to a lesser extent air-only charters and scheduled flights.

Here's a sampling of travel club opportunities that would have let you fly there for less:

• A New York-Acapulco seven-day package listing for $632, sold for $389, savings: $243.

• A Boston-Bahamas seven-night package listing for $458, sold for $219, savings: $239.

• A New York-London flight listing for $489, sold for $374, savings: $115.

• A Detroit-Frankfurt flight listing for $625, sold for $339, savings: $286.

The clubs charge an annual membership fee, which usually includes all family members. To keep members informed, most clubs use toll-free telephone numbers that play a recording of available trips and flights. Other clubs mail their members trip information.

Before joining a last-minute travel club you'll want to shop around. Obtain the promotional literature from several to compare fees and types of travel offered.

Also look into which gateway cities the clubs use. You'll want to find one using cities to which you have the least-expensive access. If you have to buy a separate airline ticket to reach your last-minute gateway city, you probably will not be able to use a promotional fare. And a full-fare ticket to the gateway would eat up any savings you obtained through the last-minute club.

Contacts

• Adventures On Call - Box 18592, BWI Airport, Maryland

21240 telephone 301-356-4080. Concentrates membership in the Baltimore-Washington, DC area. Annual fee: $49.

• Comp-u-store - The Source, 1616 Anderson Rd., McLean, VA 22102, telephone 800-336-3366. Comp-u-store offers last-minute travel opportunities to personal computer owners subscribing to the Source's on-line travel service.

• Discount Travel International - Ives Building, Suite 205, Narberth, PA 19072, telephone 215-668-7184. Annual fee: $45.

• Entertainment Hotline Travel - 2125 Butterfield Rd., Suite 109, Troy, MI 48084, telephone 800-828-0826 or 313-637-9780. Annual fee: $35.

• Last Minute Club - Offered by Travel Scan, 5 Penn Plaza, New York, NY 10001, telephone 212-695-5492. The Last Minute Club offers last-minute travel opportunities to personal computer owners subscribing to Travel Scan.

• Last Minute Travel - 132 Brookline Ave., Boston, MA 02215, telephone 800-527-8646 or 617-267-9800. Concentrates membership in the New England area. Annual fee: $35 family, $30 single.

• Moment's Notice Discount Travel - 40 East 49th St., New York, NY 10017, telephone 212-486-0503. Annual fee: $45.

• Reservation & Rebate Travel Club (R&R Travel Club) - 200 N. Martingale Rd., Schaumburg, IL 60173, telephone 800-621-5505. Annual fee: $45.

• Stand-Buys Ltd. - 311 W. Superior St., Suite 404, Chicago, IL 60610, telephone 800-255-1488, or 312-951-7589. Annual fee: $45.

• Travelers Advantage - 831 Greencrest Dr., Westerville, OH 42081, telephone 800-548-1116. Annual fee: $49.

- Up 'N Go Travel - 10 Mechanic St., Worcester MA 01608, telephone 800-888-8190. Concentrates membership in the New England area. Annual fee: $40.

- Vacations to Go - 2411 Fountain View, Houston, TX 77057, telephone 800-338-4962 or 713-974-2121. Annual fee: $45

- Worldwide Discount Travel Club - 1674 Meridian Ave., Miami Beach, FL 33139, telephone 305-534-2082. Annual fee: $50 family, $40 single.

Travel agency last-minute bargains — more savings for the flexible

Many travel agencies shy away from last-minute travel opportunities. Some travel agents, however, see last-minute travel as a sideline which will help their agencies grow while creating goodwill among their clients. A handful of travel agents offer last-minute travel bargains obtained by negotiating individual deals with travel suppliers who have excess inventory.

Travelmasters, a Chicago agency concentrating primarily on business travelers, has been successful in selling this type of last-minute travel. Travelmasters maintains a 24-hour hot line which customers can call for information on last-minute bargains. Contact Travelmasters by calling 800-323-4565. Boston-based Vacation Outlet, with agencies located in Filene's Basement stores throughout Massachusetts, has also moved into the last-minute travel market.

But a travel agency does not have to negotiate last-minute travel deals directly with suppliers, which can be risky for the agency. QuickTrips International, a Chicago firm, serves as a last-minute middleman helping to make these bargains more accessible to travel agencies. QuickTrips offers its last-minute bargains through travel agent computer reservations systems. A travel agency signing up with QuickTrips can then simply access its computer to tell you about the latest last-minute travel bargains.

The advantage of buying last-minute travel from a travel agency is that you save the annual fee charged by the last-minute clubs. To find a travel agency offering last-minute travel in your area, again check the display ads in your local yellow pages. If you can't turn up anything there, call some of your local agencies to ask if they have signed up with QuickTrips International.

Mini-vacation travel clubs — bargains for weekend travelers

If you enjoy getting away for a short vacation now and then, you may want to look into these clubs. They specialize in offering deeply discounted air fares on domestic mini-getaways that incorporate the weekend into a three- or four-day stay. International trips may run up to a week. Optional low-cost accommodations and car rentals may also be offered .

The TWA Travel Club, a program operated by Trans World Airlines, offers its members low-cost flights and tours within the United States and to the Caribbean, Europe and the Middle East.

Travel Club members receive mail notification every two weeks of trips and tours to at least six different destinations. Most are for three- and four-day weekends with flights departing either the next week or the week after that. Members can also call a toll-free hot line to get information about additional last-minute trips. And the fares TWA offers are attractive. The airline prices its club flights anywhere from 15 to 40 percent below its least-expensive promotional fares. When the carrier's transcontinental flights were selling for about $350, club members could get a transcontinental flight for $240.

The program does have some limitations. TWA is offering seats expected to be empty when a particular flight takes off.

Consequently, seating is limited and only specific flights will be offered.

Destinations available to members may be less-popular cities, and flights will tend to be off-peak departures. During holiday periods when the airline expects to fill its planes, Travel Club flights will not be available.

Departing flights are also limited to specific cities, including Atlanta, Baltimore, Boston, Chicago, Cincinnati, Kansas City, Los Angeles, New York/Newark, Philadelphia, St. Louis, San Francisco and Washington.

To solicit memberships, TWA uses promotional mailings addressed to travelers residing in the vicinity of these departure cities. A yearly membership costs $100 for a single traveler and $175 per couple, who may travel separately or together. The program also offers a $175 membership for a single traveler plus companion — different companions may take different trips.

TWA's promotional mailings, however, usually carry an introductory rate. These rates have ranged between $49.95 to $75 single and $95 to $125 per couple.

If you want to join but have not received a mail offering, call TWA at 800-872-8364. Travel agents can also enroll you in the TWA Travel Club. Be sure to ask about introductory rates.

Another weekend travel club

American Express offers travelers in several cities, including Chicago, Boston and New York, weekend domestic and longer international getaways. Called Express Weekends, the program lets you buy air only or a package combining air, lodging and sometimes a rental car. Flights tend to be priced 10 to 50 percent below promotional fares.

Express Weekends operates similar to the TWA Travel Club. Every two weeks members receive mail notification of available destinations. But instead of being confined to a particular airline, American Express trips use varied airlines, including Continental, Northwest, USAir and British Airways. The participating airlines grant frequent-flyer credit for all Express Weekends flights.

Membership in Express Weekends costs $75 annually for one person. One person plus companion can join for $135 — a different companion can go on each trip. Children under 17 are automatically included in an adult membership.

The Express Weekends program also lets additional people take a particular trip for a $35 fee in addition to the trip's cost. That's a good feature — you can round up the gang for a ski weekend or a long-distance beach party.

Members-only travel clubs — you save with rebates, but they may carry a big negative

Members-only travel clubs generally offer a full line of travel services, not just last-minute specials. While a travel agency also offers a full line of travel services, the appeal of members-only clubs is that they offer discounts on their products — including domestic and international air fares.

Travelers Advantage, for example, gives its members 5 percent cash back on all travel services, including air fares. The cash back, however, must be applied for after completion of travel. The club charges a $49 annual household membership fee. You can reach them at:

• Travelers Advantage, 831 Greencrest Dr., Westerville, OH 43081, telephone 800-548-1116.

Another members-only organization, First Travel Club, also offers a 5 percent rebate on its full line of travel services. This club charges a $59 annual household membership fee. Contact them at:

• First Travel, 955 American Lane, Schaumburg, IL 60173, telephone 312-240-2626.

Montgomery Ward department stores have developed a Y.E.S. Card club whose benefits include 5 percent rebates as well as guaranteed lowest air fares. The fee for member and spouse is $34.80 per year, but the club is only open to those 55 and over.

Watch for this unsavory business practice when you consider joining any travel club

A few of these travel clubs — and I'm not just talking about the members-only organizations, but any travel club — automatically renew your membership by charging the current dues to the credit card used when you enrolled. I dislike that practice so much that I personally would not join a club that uses it, regardless of how good the club's benefits.

Let me give you an example. The literature I received concerning Travelers Advantage included a line that offered me a "benefit" that went like this: "To ensure uninterrupted service, my membership will automatically be renewed upon expiration and the then-current membership fee charged to my credit card account."

By agreeing to a practice such as this, you allow the club to tap your credit card for the renewal fee each year. If you do not intend to renew, you must take the initiative to notify the club. They will not remind you when its time for renewal, and your membership will not automatically expire. If you forget to notify the club, they will go ahead and charge your card for the next year's membership fee. And if you still don't notify the club during the following year of your intention to quit, you'll again wind up getting a credit card charge you really don't want.

But that's not all. The club can raise its membership fee without telling you and still have the right to charge your credit card the new amount. Regardless of the size of the increase, you have obligated yourself beforehand to paying it.

Not all clubs use this practice. But if it bothers you as much as it does me, before you join a club find out if it requires you to sign up for an automatic renewal charged to your credit card. Read carefully any literature before sending in an application that asks for you credit card number. If you contact the club by telephone, have them send you their literature before giving your account number to them over the phone.

Private air-travel clubs — savings through group travel with friends

Private air-travel clubs are nonprofit organizations operating their own aircraft to fly members on trips throughout the world. The clubs are located in or near metropolitan areas but draw their members from a much larger radius.

Club members can expect to save substantially over an equivalent flight on a scheduled airline. Typically, the clubs offer an air-only price and a package price that includes hotel accommodations at the destination. One club offered a four-night Detroit-Bahamas package for $456. An equivalent package on a scheduled airline sold for $700. Another club offered a Washington, D.C.-Kennebunkport, Maine, flight for just $147 round trip.

The clubs charge a hefty one-time initiation fee that ranges from $100 to $300. They also assess yearly dues ranging from $25 to $125.

Contacts

Get in touch with any of the clubs listed below for membership information and a copy of their newsletter describing upcoming trips.

- American Trans Air, 7337 W. Washington St., Indianapolis, IN 46251, telephone 317-247-5141.

- Shillelagh Travel Club, 105 E. Annandale Rd., Suite 200A, Falls Church, VA 22046, telephone 703-241-7595.

- Ports of Call Travel Club, 2121 Valentia St., Denver, CO 80220, telephone 303-321-6767.

Bartered travel — you don't have to be a wheeler-dealer to save in this game

Airlines commonly use barter to move large blocks of unsold seats. For the most part these are large-scale transactions involving goods and services valued in the hundreds of thousands of dollars.

Advertising in particular lends itself to barter transactions. An airline might purchase $300,000 worth of advertising by giving the media corporation $300,000 worth of air-travel credits. The corporation may hold on to some of those credits, using them to meet its own travel needs. A portion may also be bartered in exchange for goods and services which the corporation needs.

But you don't have to be dealing in mega-bucks to get into the barter market. In the process of the large-scale wheeling and dealing, a bartered pie is often cut into pieces which wind up being sold and traded. Throughout the country you'll find barter exchanges and barter travel clubs trading in small — even individual-sized — pieces of the barter pie.

Barter Exchanges

You have two choices on how to move into the arena of bartered travel. If you have goods or services that you can offer, then look into a barter exchange. If not, then you'll work with the barter travel clubs described below.

But don't be too quick to write off barter exchanges, feeling you have nothing to offer. While barter exchanges are ideal for professionals and small-business owners, you may also be able to play the barter game even if you can only offer babysitting services or used household items.

Barter exchange transactions are relatively simple. You start by listing with the exchange your service or merchandise along with your asking price. When someone accepts your goods or services, you can then use your credits from the transaction to obtain any air travel or travel packages which may be listed with the exchange.

While barter exchanges can offer you discounted travel opportunities, especially for domestic air travel, you need to be sure to know the value of the air travel you are obtaining. Of course, this is easy to do by checking with the airline to learn the cost of its lowest promotional fare between the cities involved. And a travel agent can tell you the retail price of any travel package in which you are interested.

Contacts

To locate a barter exchange, check the yellow pages of your telephone directory. Look under *Barter and Trade Exchanges.* You may also try contacting the following firms:

• Lino and Associates, 6534 Central Ave., St. Petersburg, FL 33707, telephone 813-384-6700.

• Communications Development Corp, 1454 Euclid St., Santa Monica, CA 90404, telephone 213-458-0596.

If you have a business, here's a contact you can investigate.

This firm works out only business-to-business barter exchanges.

• Chicago Barter Corp., 800 E. Roosevelt Rd., Lombard, IL 60148, telephone 708-629-3450.

Drawbacks

The typical barter exchange carries a hefty one-time membership fee, anywhere from about $100 to around $600. And on top of that you'll pay an annual membership fee that can range up to $200.

The exchange will probably also charge a fee for completed transactions. So if you are interested in bartering for travel only occasionally, you'll be better off working with one of the barter travel clubs.

Barter Travel Clubs

Despite their name, when working with these clubs you do not have to engage in bartering. These travel clubs stop the bartering by purchasing the travel credits for cash. The club then sells the travel credits to its members.

While the last-minute clubs we looked at deal in travel that will expire unless it is sold by a particular date, barter travel clubs buy travel credits that have no expiration date and are valid indefinitely. This makes them extremely attractive if you are a business traveler who must make short-notice trips on which you're paying full fares.

Contacts

At least two barter travel clubs offer their members airline tickets and air-land packages. These are:

• IGT (In Good Taste) Services, 22 E. 29th St., New York, NY

10016, telephone 800-444-8872 or 212-725-9600. IGT charges annual dues of $48, but $25 of that will be credited toward future travel purchases. IGT provides discounts of about 25 percent on air fares, charters and package tours.

• Travel World Leisure Club, 225 W. 34th St., Suite 2203, New York, NY 10122, telephone 800-444-8952 or 212-239-4855. Travel World charges annual dues of $50. The club provides discounts ranging from about 25 to 40 percent on air fares, charters and package tours.

A Barter Travel Broker

A London-based company, D&H Travel, offers for sale bartered credit on a wide range of travel services, including U.S. and international air travel, car rentals, hotels and cruises. The firms sells its airline credits for about 35 to 40 percent off face value.

If you're in London, contact them at 35 Hilldrop Crescent, London N7 0HZ. Or, you can send them an international fax at 011-44-71-700-0368. D&H Travel accepts major credit cards.

8

Take advantage of circumstances to get low fares

A variety of circumstances, both within the airline industry and external to it, can offer air travelers opportunities to fly there for less. An increase in airline competition, changing economic conditions and fluctuations in international currencies can all bring about situations that will allow you to pick up air fare bargains. Here's what to look for.

New airlines — they are rare, but they offer big savings

When a new airline starts flying, it lacks that prized possession of the established airlines — a share of the market. If the new airline is going to succeed, it needs to get a share of that market, and fast. The fastest way is with deeply discounted introductory fares.

Management at an established airline can walk into the office one morning to find that a new, competing airline is drastically undercutting their fares. Such was the case when a new airline started flying out of Washington, D.C. Its initial fares were as much as 67 percent below some of its competitors.

Management at the established airlines will often respond by matching the new airline's fares. So you can look for bargains not only from the new carrier but also from the competition.

While the ads announcing the new airline's fares and those ads taken out by the competition may show similar dollar figures, investigate the restrictions. The competition may match the new airline so the ads will carry the same price, but they could also slap heavy restrictions on their fares to limit the number of passengers using them.

In recent years, airline mergers, which have substantially decreased competition, and a lack of growth in airport capacity, which means fewer gates available to a new carrier, have diminished the usefulness of this strategy.

It's unlikely you'll see a new airline taking on the major carriers. Look, instead, for new-airline opportunities among smaller, regional carriers. But even among regional carriers you can find extraordinary bargains when a new airline starts flying.

When Discovery Airways was created and started flying among the Hawaiian Islands, the airline offered free flights to all passengers flying on its first day of operation. And all of Discovery's fares for the next 30 days undercut the competition.

New routes — they offer short-duration deep discounts

New airlines aren't the only carriers offering introductory fares. Much more common are new-route introductory fares.

When an established airline expands and adds new routes, it also enters a market where it must gain a quick foothold. To introduce itself and win a fast share of the market, the airline will undercut the standard fares for that route. New-route introductory fares are usually short lived, but you do get deep discounts. Here's some examples.

• When Virgin Atlantic added Miami as a gateway for its flights to London, the airline set its round-trip fare at $598. For the first month, however, Virgin offered tickets at $398, a savings of $200.

• TWA's St. Louis-Honolulu introductory fare, which lasted only 10 days, saved travelers up to $350 on a round trip.

• When Continental extended its service to London, the airline extended travelers an introductory fare that saved them $196 on a round trip.

• Germany's national carrier, Lufthansa, offered to introduce Charlotte-Frankfurt passengers to its home country with a fare of $399 — cutting almost in half the regular $786 fare for that route.

• Southwest Airlines began flying between Phoenix, Arizona, and Ontario, California, with an introductory fare of $9. That's less than the cost of many an airport cab ride!

On occasion an airline will add a special, attention-getting twist to its introductory fares. Delta started flying between Cincinnati and London with a low introductory Apex fare of $698. But the airline also offered a companion ticket priced at just $349.

When UTA French Airlines introduced service between Newark, New Jersey, and Bordeaux, France, the airline let passengers buy two tickets for the price of one.

And in another variation, USAir highlighted a new route between Charlotte, North Carolina, and Nassau, Bahamas, with an introductory package. The four-day package, which included air fare, hotel accommodations and airport transfers, was bargain priced at just $199.

Fare wars — well-publicized opportunities to slash air-travel costs

When airline competition becomes especially fierce, a fare war will likely break out. During a fare war, the airlines follow just one criterion to establish their fares — match or beat the competition. Obviously, when the airlines set fares without regard to profitability, you can pick up some extraordinary bargains.

Highly competitive routes are prone to fare wars. During a Northeast-to-Florida fare war involving most of the major airlines, one-way Newark-Orlando tickets sank to $39! The Los Angeles-Honolulu route once saw fares slide from $358 round trip to $318, then to $298, to $278 and finally to $258 where they bottomed out. On the competitive New York-San Francisco route a fare war let fares drop to $99 one way. New York-Denver fares once fell to $69 one way.

Fare wars can erupt on any route when the competition heats up. A fare war once raged among Canadian airlines serving the British Columbian cities of Victoria and Vancouver. Fares fell as much as 60 percent. One-way Denver-Albuquerque fares once plunged to $9! Even regulated fares on North Atlantic routes can get caught up in a fare war. One summer fare war knocked transatlantic air fares $250 lower than the previous summer.

Because North Atlantic fares are regulated, the airlines do not always have as much room to maneuver. So when the North Atlantic heats up, you can also look for bonus programs such as discounts off future flights. During one North Atlantic fare war several airlines, including TWA and British Airways, gave their passengers discount coupons good for up to 30 percent off any fare on a future flight.

Transatlantic fare wars do not always provide equal bargain-fare opportunities from all gateway cities. Virgin Atlantic once kicked off a war by cutting its fares on London-bound flights originating in New York, Miami and Los Angeles. British Airways and TWA quickly matched Virgin's cheaper fares for flights to London but only from New York and Los Angeles.

If you been planning a London flight from a gateway city such as Boston, you would have been prudent to check to see if you could save money by purchasing a separate ticket to New York, one of the gateways involved in the fare war.

In future fare wars you are not likely to see the widespread slugfests of the early days of deregulation. The domestic airline mergers and bankruptcies of recent years have cut deeply into competition among the airlines. So much so that today just eight airlines control 94 percent of the U.S. air-travel market-place. Instead, watch for smaller fare wars between just two or three lines with fares matched only on a very selective basis, perhaps matched only on selected flights.

When a fare war does break out, the bargains are easy to find. Airline commercials will saturate radio stations. Large ads with destinations and fares in bold-face type will leap from your newspaper. And a spectacular fare war will even make the evening news.

Strikes — once they're settled, you can fly for less

When a strike shuts down an airline, travelers who normally fly that carrier are forced to use other airlines. After the struck carrier returns to service, it's first priority is to win back those passengers. And it will toss out some bargain fares to regain its market share.

To recover from a strike, an airline once cut all its domestic fares up to 40 percent and offered its international passengers a $200 credit towards a future round trip. After United Airlines settled a strike, the carrier slashed all its fares 50 percent.

Another airline trying to fly clear of a strike came out with low "Comeback" fares such as $79 one way between New York and Florida. The carrier's transcontinental flights were going for $139 one-way. In addition, the Comeback fares carried few restrictions, were fully refundable and required only a three-day advance purchase.

Typically, though, these bargains are short lived. Some post-strike fares have lasted between four and six weeks. The Comeback fares were raised after a month, and United's cut-rate fares lasted just a week.

These bargains are, however, easy to find. Look for the strike settlement to make the national news, possibly the airline's fare cuts as well. Regardless, the airline itself will launch an extensive promotion campaign to let the public know it's up and flying and offering bargain fares. Anytime you're flying shortly after an airline has settled a strike, be sure to include that carrier in your fare search.

Unfortunately, during the strike itself you may find fares edging up on those routes formerly flown by the struck airline. Competition will decrease and there may even be a shortage of capacity on those routes. If so, the still-flying airlines will start to raise fares.

Economic slowdowns — when the economy falls so will fares

Economic theory says prices in a competitive market will move up or down as needed to keep supply and demand equal. When the economy in the United States slows or slides into recession, demand for air travel drops. Business travel will be off as firms around the country tighten their belts. Vacation travelers will be taking fewer trips and staying closer to home.

The supply of airline seats, however, remains fairly constant. The airlines have the aircraft. They're flying their routes. Supply is up, but demand is down. And economic theory will prevail as the airlines cut prices attempting to raise air-travel demand to equal the supply of seats. A major factor in the great air fare war of 1982–83 was the recession going on at that time.

If you're insulated from a downturn in the economy, you can reap bargains. If social or business commitments send you flying in a recession, you can do it less expensively.

International currency fluctuations — they offer impressive savings for savvy air travelers

Exchange rates among international currencies do not remain stable. Each country's money is continually cycling through periods of strength and weakness. Consequently, the value of a country's currency is continually changing in relation to the value of the currencies of other countries.

You can use this relative strength and weakness of currencies to help you fly international routes for less. The savings with currency-differential ticketing, as it is known in the travel trade, can be impressive.

Most international air fares are established in the local currency of the country in which the flight originates. But there are some exceptions. In 42 countries whose currencies are unstable, fares are set in U.S. dollars. Most fares in South America, for example, are set in dollars.

If you buy a New York-London round-trip ticket, the trip originates in New York and the fare is established in dollars. If you buy a London-New York round-trip ticket, your journey starts in London and the fare is set in British pounds. But if you are in New York and buy a London-New York round trip, the fare is still established in British pounds because the first leg of the round trip originates in London. The fare in pounds will be converted to dollars based on the currency exchange rate in effect when you buy your ticket.

European round robins can offer you big savings

If you fly between the United States and Europe several times a year, you may be able to save by buying your round trips as European-originating flights, especially when the dollar is gaining strength over European currencies.

You will have to start your round robins by purchasing the least-expensive one-way ticket to Europe you can find, perhaps a discounted ticket from a consolidator. Then, either in the United States before you leave or once your one-way flight puts you in Europe, buy a round trip between Europe and the United States. Use the first ticket, the outward-bound coupon, to fly home. Have the airline or travel agent leave open the flight date on the return ticket.

When you're ready to fly to Europe again, make your reservation using the round trip's return ticket. Then, again purchase another European-originating round trip.

Round-robins have the potential to work with any foreign country whose fares are established in its local currency. European round-robins, however, allow you not only to take advantage of a strong dollar but also of the fact that IATA fares are set as much as 15 percent lower for flights between Europe and the United States when the trip originates in Europe.

At a time of an increasingly strong dollar, to fly off-season from

Los Angeles to Amsterdam and return cost $779 on Northwest Orient Airlines. But that off-season trip originating in Europe — from Amsterdam to Los Angeles and return — cost $476, a saving of $303.

Double ticketing

If you are forced to take an international flight at full fare, particularly when either the dollar or the foreign currency is especially strong in relation to the other, check to see if can fly there for less by having the airline or travel agent double ticket you. That is, write your ticket as two one-way trips instead of a round trip. (Double ticketing is also referred to as split ticketing.)

Say you're flying round trip to Hong Kong when the U.S. dollar is strong in relation to the Hong Kong dollar. You'll pay the published fare in U.S. dollars for the outbound flight. Your Hong Kong-originating one-way return trip, however, will be calculated in Hong Kong dollars. When that fare is converted to U.S. dollars at a strong-dollar exchange rate, you may pay less than you did to reach Hong Kong.

Double ticketing normally works only when you are faced with paying the full economy fare. Therefore it's a very useful strategy for the business traveler — or anyone else, actually — who cannot meet the advance-purchase requirements of a promotional fare. If you can qualify for an Apex fare, though, you'll almost always save more than with double ticketing.

Reservationists will help you save with currency-differential ticketing

There's no need to be an international monetary expert to take advantage of currency fluctuations. If you ask, the airlines and most travel agents will work with you to determine whether you can save on round robins or with double ticketing.

Currency devaluations — opportunities to save on international and foreign domestic flights

When a country devalues its currency, its money takes a sudden drop in value in relation to the currencies of other countries. And it provides an opportunity to fly there for less. When foreign-currency fares are converted to dollars for air travel originating in a country that has just devalued its currency, the fare paid in dollars will drop in price roughly equivalent to the drop in the currency's value.

In addition to the savings on international flights, you'll also save on air travel within the country. If you are buying your ticket before leaving home, you'll save when the fare is converted to dollars at the new, devalued exchange rate. If you are in the country when you buy your ticket, your dollars will buy more of the devalued currency, allowing you to spend fewer dollars to pay for the air fare.

At one time when Mexico devalued its currency, air fares within Mexico dropped by a third. (Mexican international fares did not change since they are established in dollars rather than Mexican pesos.) Travelers able to reach the U.S.-Mexican border easily and inexpensively have used Mexican devaluations to fly deep into Mexico for less.

At the time of one Mexican devaluation, the round-trip fare between Los Angeles and Mexico City was $265. But travelers using land transportation to get to Tijuana, just over the Mexican border from California, could fly round trip to Mexico City for just $147, saving $118 .— not including costs to reach Tijuana.

Currency devaluations usually make news, so they are not too difficult to hear about. The news, however, may be carried only in large-circulation newspapers and then only in the business section. The *Wall Street Journal* is a good information source for both currency fluctuations and devaluations.

Canadian fares — savings for those who can reach Canadian airports at the right time

When the U.S. dollar shows strength over the Canadian dollar, you can save on air tickets for flights originating in Canada.

If you can reach Canada without too much expense, investigate fares on flights out of Canadian cities to see if you can save money. When you need to fly from your hometown to a gateway city to catch an international flight, see if using a Canadian city as your gateway will let you fly there for less.

The savings using Canada-originating flights can be substantial. To fly round trip from Buffalo, New York, to Jamaica in the Caribbean, American Airlines once wanted $489. If you crossed the border, however, and flew from not-too-distant Toronto, American's fare dropped to $369, saving you $120. And if you flew Air Canada instead of American, your Jamaican fare would have dropped further to $338, increasing your savings to $151.

9

How to master creative money-saving strategies

The structure of today's airline industry has given rise to a variety of imaginative techniques that will help you fly there for less. The following strategies will let you turn the industry's complexity, its competitiveness and its marketing tactics to your advantage.

Negotiated fares — discounts in exchange for volume

Any business, organization or association whose employees or members purchase a substantial volume of air travel — especially full-fare travel — should investigate the possibility of negotiating discounted fares with a single airline. Big business and government agencies routinely negotiate discounts that run up to about 45 percent off the full coach fare.

Call a couple of sales representatives for different airlines (see the airline contact appendix). Let them know what you estimate your air travel needs will be over the next year. Then ask what type of discount you could get by giving all your business to that one airline. You may find some of the financially troubled, cash-hungry airlines especially responsive.

Don't just confine your negotiations to domestic routes. You'll find carriers flying international routes also receptive to negotiated volume fares, although discounts tend to be substantially lower.

One fairly common approach is to establish with an airline a charge-card account in the name of your business or organization. When you buy tickets the carrier credits the negotiated discount to the charge card. You can then use the credits for future purchases.

Competitive routes — fly these to get lower fares

The more competitive the route, the lower the fares. When several airlines compete for the passengers flying between two cities, air travelers can expect lower fares. And on some highly competitive routes, flight distance and the airline's operating costs may not even be the main considerations in determining fares. The driving force behind these fares will be gaining or keeping a competitive edge.

Among the more competitive airline routes in the United States are:

- Los Angeles - San Francisco
- Los Angeles - Honolulu

- New York - Boston

- New York-Chicago

- New York - Denver

- New York - Fort Lauderdale

- New York - Los Angeles

- New York - Miami

- New York - Orlando

- New York - San Francisco

- New York - San Juan

- New York - Washington

- New York - West Palm Beach

- San Francisco - Hawaii

Be willing to go out of your way to take advantage of competitive routes and you'll usually save money. Suppose your closest airport is San Diego's Lindbergh Field and you want to fly to New York. Instead of flying out of San Diego, consider leaving from Los Angeles. Drive your car to Los Angeles and leave it at the airport's long-term parking lot. You could also rent a car or take Amtrak. Since the Los Angeles-New York flight is on a competitive route, you may save enough to pay for your ground transportation and still have plenty left over.

When the lowest San Diego-New York round-trip promotional fare cost $389, Los Angeles-New York round-trip promotional fares were selling for $258, or $131 less.

Still another example — a business traveler wanting to fly from Fort Lauderdale, Florida, to Philadelphia could not make an advance reservation and was faced with a $270 one-way full fare. Instead, the traveler flew into New York/Newark and took Amtrak for the short trip to Philadelphia. The traveler's air fare to New York/Newark cost just $109, saving him $161.

Hubs and spokes — efficiency for airlines, potential savings for you

Picture the wheel on a pioneer's covered wagon, with the hub in the center and the spokes radiating out to the rim. That's also a picture of today's typical airline route system. Rather than flying direct or nonstop to a destination, many airlines find it more efficient to fly passengers along a spoke into one of their hubs. There, passengers deplane to board another of the same carrier's aircraft — an on-line connection — for the flight out along the spoke leading to their destination.

Of course, direct and nonstop flights are still available. But routing your flight through a hub rather than flying direct can sometimes save money. Flying Delta direct from its Atlanta hub to Chicago once cost $242. But flying USAir from Atlanta to Chicago, with an on-line connection at USAir's hub in Charlotte, North Carolina, would have cost just $194, saving you $48.

Business travelers can also save with hubs and spokes, even when forced to fly on an unrestricted full fare. Continental wanted $506 to fly one business traveler nonstop between Washington, D.C. and San Francisco on an unrestricted fare. Instead, the traveler made an on-line connection at Continental's Denver hub and her Washington-San Francisco unrestricted fare dropped to $244, saving her $262.

To fly there for less using airline hubs, you must fly through the hub — actually making a stop and changing planes. Taking a flight that originates or terminates at a hub will not necessarily give you the savings you are looking for.

In fact, originating or terminating at a hub city may cost you more. To fly USAir from New York to Dallas with an on-line connection at the airline's Charlotte hub once cost $305. At that same time, a passenger taking a Charlotte-Dallas USAir flight — thereby originating the flight at the Charlotte hub —

paid $329. That's $24 MORE than the New York-Charlotte-Dallas passenger who was flying a much greater distance!

Hubs can save you money, but fortress hubs will cost you big bucks

That Charlotte-Dallas passenger paid more to fly a shorter distance because Charlotte is a "fortress" hub. USAir is the dominant airline serving Charlotte, providing more than 80 percent of the flights into and out of that city. Competition promotes lower fares, but noncompetitive fortress hubs promote higher fares.

Let's look at how one fortress hub came about and what happened to fares at that hub. When deregulation began, TWA carried 39 percent of the passengers flying into or out of St. Louis. In 1986 TWA and Ozark Airlines merged, boosting TWA's market share of St. Louis passengers to 82 percent — St. Louis had became a TWA fortress hub. And fares to and from St. Louis rose two to three times more than the U.S. average. On flights between St. Louis and Chicago fares shot up 28 percent, between St. Louis and Denver 36 percent and St. Louis-New York 39 percent.

In addition to Charlotte and St. Louis, Cincinnati, Memphis, Minneapolis/St. Paul, Pittsburgh and Salt Lake City are also fortress hubs where one airline carries more than 80 percent of the passengers. Fares for flights into and out of these cities average 19 percent higher than other cities.

If you want to fly there for less, you'll have to avoid flights originating or terminating at these fortress hubs. You can still fly through them, but starting or terminating your journey at one will cost you plenty. If your primary airport is a fortress hub, the section that follows on "Airport selection" can give you some tips on how to avoid it.

Hub and fortress-hub cities

When planning your flight, use this list of airlines and their hub cities to help determine if you can fly there for less with hubs and spokes. Fortress hubs are so indicated.

- Anchorage - Alaska Airlines, Delta
- Atlanta (Fortress Hub) - Delta
- Baltimore - USAir
- Charlotte (Fortress Hub) - USAir.
- Chicago - American (O'Hare), United (O'Hare)
- Cincinnati (Fortress Hub) - Delta
- Cleveland - Continental, USAir
- Dallas/Fort Worth - American, Delta, Southwest
- Denver - Continental, United
- Detroit - Northwest
- Guam - Continental
- Houston - Continental, Southwest
- Honolulu - Continental, Hawaiian, United
- Indianapolis - USAir
- Las Vegas - America West
- Los Angeles - Delta, USAir
- Memphis (Fortress Hub) - Northwest
- Miami - American
- Milwaukee - Midwest Express, Northwest
- Minneapolis/St. Paul (Fortress Hub) - Northwest
- Nashville - American
- Newark - Continental
- New York - Delta (Kennedy), TWA (Kennedy)

- Orlando - Delta, United
- Philadelphia - USAir
- Phoenix - America West, Southwest
- Pittsburgh (Fortress Hub) - USAir
- Portland, OR - Alaska Airlines
- Raleigh/Durham - American
- Reno - Reno Air
- St. Louis (Fortress Hub) - TWA
- Salt Lake City (Fortress Hub) - Delta
- San Jose - American
- San Francisco - United, USAir
- San Juan - American
- Seattle - Alaska Airlines, United
- Syracuse - USAir
- Washington, D.C. - Northwest (National), United (Dulles)

Allow plenty of time for hub connections

You should be aware that the hub concept has made connecting flights prone to delays, especially during adverse weather. And problems at one hub can delay flights at other hubs throughout an airline's system. When making a hub connection, try to allow ample time between your two flights, more time than the airline typically suggests. In winter, try to avoid northern connections where flights could experience snow and ice delays. Look instead for flights connecting through Sun Belt hubs.

Connections — going out of your way can cut your costs

The hub and spoke system allows you to sometimes save on

your air fare by making a connection. But your connections do not have to be at an airline's hub for you to save money.

Off-line connections

Whenever shopping for fares, see if making an off-line connection will save you money. An off-line connection — that is, connecting two flights from different airlines — works especially well when one of the connecting airlines is a low-fare carrier. When a low-fare airline doesn't fly where you want to go, see if you can make an off-line connection to fly at least part way on a low-fare carrier.

At one time you could have flown American Airlines direct from Tulsa, Oklahoma, to New York for $176 one-way. But, if you had flown low-fare Southwest Airlines from Tulsa to Kansas City — Southwest does not fly to New York — then changed to TWA for the flight to New York, your total fare would have been just $134, saving you $42. Flying direct from Minneapolis to Miami once would have cost you $370. But an off-line connection in Chicago to a Miami flight on low-fare carrier would have dropped your total fare to $129, saving you $241.

Off-line connections do not have to involve a low-fare airline to save you money. They require only that one segment of the route carry a low-cost fare. This can, as I just pointed out, be due to a low-fare carrier flying one leg, but it can also come about because:

- a route is competitive, keeping fares down;

- carriers flying that route are engaged in a fare war;

- an airline has put a route on sale to attract passengers;

- an airline just started flying a route and is offering introductory fares.

This off-line connection strategy can also work with international flights when connecting at a U.S. gateway city. Typically, an international flight will give you a choice of two or three gateways. Check your fare using each possible gateway. You just may come up with a fare that would beat a through fare to your destination. Here's an example using a gateway city not generally thought of as a gateway.

When airlines were selling Los Angeles-Sydney tickets for $995, making an off-line connection at Honolulu would have saved you $138. United Airlines would have flown you to Honolulu for $358. At Honolulu you could have switched to an Air New Zealand Honolulu-Sydney flight that was offering a special low-priced fare to attract passengers — $499. When added together, your Los Angeles-Honolulu and Honolulu-Sydney fares would then have come to just $857.

Yes, the shortest distance between two points is a straight line. But, my traveling friend, in the air-travel bazaar the cheapest fare between two points just may be a line that zigs at an out-of-the-way city. So, always check your routings for possible money-saving off-line connections.

Separately priced segments

If the flight you book happens to include a connection — either on-line or off-line — or even a stop, ask the reservationist to see if you can save money by pricing each segment separately. Should one of the segments — either from your departure city to the intermediate stop/connection or from the intermediate point to your destination — cover a competitive route, a route on which airlines are engaged in a fare war or a route offering especially attractive promotional fares, you could come up with some big savings.

Say at one time you were flying from New York to Bozeman, Montana. When the reservationist checked the computer, it would show New York to Bozeman via Denver priced at $443.

Since you know from what I've told you in this chapter that New York to Denver is a competitive route, you would be sure to ask the reservationist to determine the fare if it were broken into two segments: New York to Denver — the competitive route — and Denver to Bozeman. The computer would then show a total fare of $195. Your savings: $248.

That separately priced segment would have saved you a bundle. But the savings are not always that dramatic. Here's some other examples of the actual savings available at one time with separately priced segments:

• If you flew from Dallas to Los Angeles with a stop in Austin your fare would have been $318. But price the Dallas-Austin and the Austin-Los Angeles segments separately and your total fare drops to $206. Savings: $112

• An Omaha-Detroit flight that makes a stop in Kansas City would have cost you $188. With the segments priced separately, your fare would have been $156. Savings: $32

• A New York-Albuquerque flight that stops in Las Vegas was priced straight through at $338. Price the segments separately, and your fare falls to $314. Savings: $24.

If you are on a direct flight that just makes a stop at the intermediate point, rather than an actual connection, you will turn that stop into a connection when the segments are priced separately. With savings of $248 or $112, the extra time the connection now adds to your trip may well be worth your while.

When your savings drop to the amount in the last example, $24, you may want to weigh any possible inconvenience caused by adding time to your trip against the potential savings.

If pricing each segment separately gives you a lower fare and you decide to go with it, you would then receive two separately priced tickets. One from your departure city to the intermediate stop. The second from the intermediate stop to your destination. You will also get two additional benefits:

1) the opportunity to make a stopover in the intermediate or connecting city;

2) the possibility to pickup additional frequent-flyer mileage credits through minimum-mileage provisions.

International connections

The rules established by the International Air Transport Association for international flights put certain connections in a different light. Instead of looking at your connections as just a potential money saver, on some international flights you have to also examine your connection to be sure it will not boost your fare.

The connecting flights you have to worry about are those for which you buy a ticket for a trip starting in another country. Let's use as an example buying a ticket in the United States for a flight from Athens to New York that makes an intermediate stop in Frankfurt.

Athens-New York flights typically cost less than Frankfurt-New York flights, even though the Athens-New York route covers a much greater distance. But IATA has established a rule to prevent Frankfurt-New York passengers from buying a cheaper Athens-New York flight that stops in Frankfurt. The rule says that when a flight makes an intermediate stop and the fare from the intermediate stop to the destination is higher than the fare from origin to destination, the higher fare must be charged.

Remember, though, the rule applies only to flights originating in a country other than the country in which the ticket is bought. If you buy the Athens-New York flight in Greece, you would pay the lower Athens-New York fare even should the flight stop in

Frankfurt. Buy that ticket outside of Greece, however, and you will pay the higher Frankfurt-New York fare.

To protect yourself from being penalized by the rule, ask your reservationist if any "higher intermediate point checks" resulted in an increase in your fare. If yes, try to get a flight that connects in a different city. If you can't avoid a high-fare intermediate city — Tokyo in particular will jack your fare up — ask if you can cut the fare by purchasing a portion of the ticket at one of your en route stops.

Airport selection — pick the right one and save

Which airport you use can greatly affect the cost of your ticket. I've shown that you want to avoid originating or terminating a flight at an airport that has become a fortress hub. Going out of your way to avoid a fortress hub will usually save you money.

If you live in the vicinity of St. Louis and it's fortress-hub airport, driving across Missouri to catch a flight out of Kansas City may not be too appealing — but it could probably save you money.

If you live in Jefferson, Missouri, however, your mid-state location would be ideal for forsaking the St. Louis airport and driving the additional distance to the Kansas City Airport.

And if you don't live in Missouri at all, you can still apply the same principle — weigh the inconvenience against the savings to determine if you should go out of your way to use a different airport.

When Eastern Airlines went out of business and its former hub at Atlanta became a fortress hub for Delta, many travelers went out of their way to save money. Shunning Atlanta, scores of passengers found the airport in Birmingham, Alabama, offered substantially lower fares. These air travelers felt it well worthwhile to endure the inconvenience of an up to two-hour shuttle bus trip, and to incur the additional cost of the ground transportation, to reach an alternate airport.

Even if your nearest airport is not a fortress hub, it still may not have sufficient competition to keep fares down. An informal survey of fares at Sacramento, California, compared with not-too-distant San Francisco showed Sacramento's fares to be about $100 higher.

You need to check the fares for all airports that are relatively convenient for you. Travelers living in southwestern Ohio, for example, are generally within driving range of four major airports — Cincinnati, Columbus, Dayton and Indianapolis. One air traveler, who had found Dayton's airport to be the most convenient, discovered that fares in Dayton tended to be higher than at the other three airports. He felt the savings involved were often sufficient to make it worthwhile to drive to one of the other three.

Multiple-airport cities

Airport selection does not always involve long distances. Some major cities such as Chicago, Dallas, Detroit, Houston, Los Angeles, New York, San Francisco and Washington are served by more than one airport.

New York City, for example, is served by three major close-in airports — La Guardia, John F. Kennedy and Newark in New Jersey. In addition, the city offers two more-distant airports — Stewart International near Newburgh and MacArthur on Long Island. If competition is keener at one of a city's multiple airports, fares will tend to be lower.

Low-fare Continental Airlines has a hub at Newark. Consequently, fares of airlines flying in and out of Newark tend to be lower than the fares those same airlines set for La Guardia and Kennedy. When one airline was charging $89 for Florida flights from La Guardia and Kennedy, the airline's fare from Newark was $79. At one time a carrier offered New York-Miami weekend fares of $159 at La Guardia, $139 at Kennedy and $99 at Newark. Picking Kennedy over La Guardia would have saved you $20. Choosing Newark would have put you $60 ahead.

You need to have your reservationist check fares for all airports from which you could possibly fly. You also have to compare fares for all airports serving your destination cities as well.

On a Memphis-Washington flight, a full coach fare to National Airport at one time cost $402. However, passengers flying into Dulles Airport, 25 miles away, could have gotten a full coach fare for $259, or $143 less. Continental once charged $50 more for its Orlando, Florida, flights going into John Wayne Airport in Orange County, California, than it did for its Orlando flights into nearby, competitive Los Angeles International Airport.

Alternative airports

Some airports have started actively promoting themselves as alternatives to nearby overcrowded airports. New York's Stewart International, a fledgling airport some 60 miles to the north, and City Airport in Detroit are two examples. One of the airlines flying out of City Airport is the low-fare carrier Southwest Airlines, so you can often come up with more attractive fares, regardless of the carrier, than those at Detroit Metropolitan Airport.

One of the more successful alternative airports is Milwaukee's Mitchell International. Mitchell has taken on Chicago's busy O'Hare, positioning itself as an airport that not only saves travelers hassles but money as well. Mitchell is served by 16 airlines, none of which dominates the marketplace, so it offers competitive fares. When the lowest Chicago-Tampa round trip out of O'Hare cost $233, the Milwaukee-Tampa round-trip fare was $188, or $45 less. When the Chicago-San Diego lowest fare was $249, the Milwaukee-San Diego lowest fare cost just $198 — a $51 saving.

Mitchell International also likes to point out that if you are leaving your car at the airport parking lot, you'll pay $12 per day at O'Hare but only $2.50 per day at Mitchell.

Competitive airports

Several airports around the country have the majority of their flights spread fairly evenly among several carriers. You'll find fares to and from these airports to be very competitive.

Among the airlines competing at San Diego's Lindbergh Field, for example, none dominates. USAir carries about 18 percent of San Diego's passengers. American flies about 14 percent, Southwest 11 percent, and America West has a 10 percent market share.

You'll also find keen competition at Los Angeles, Denver, New York (Kennedy) and Boston.

Waivers — speak up and cut the cost of your ticket

Airline rules for promotional fares can be flexible. They are not laws, but marketing strategies used to maximize revenue. When it appears that bending a rule will bring in more money than enforcing it, an airline will bend the rule.

If you can't meet the restrictions on a promotional fare and are facing a full-fare ticket, ask your travel agent to seek a waiver from the airline. Be aggressive here. You are only asking for something that is routinely done everyday. One airline, in fact, set up a "yes desk" just for the purpose of granting waiver requests.

If a particular airline won't grant a waiver, have the travel agent try another.

The same idea applies when all promotional seats on the flight you want have been sold. Ask your travel agent to see if the airline will reallocate one or more seats from a full coach fare to a promotional fare.

If the airline feels there will be unsold seats on the flight you want and that you will not be in one of those seats unless you get a lower fare, your chances of getting the waiver are good. If the airline believes it can sell the seat at full fare to someone else, you won't get the waiver.

You'll have more success if you try for waivers on less-popular flights — off-peak flights or ones that make a stop or two. You'll also have more success if the travel agent subscribes to the computer reservations system of the airline from which you want the waiver.

While you can also use this strategy dealing directly with an airline reservationist, a travel agent doing business daily with the airlines has more clout than you and is in a better position to request and receive waivers.

Talk to a supervisor

Sometimes a mid-trip change in plans can put you at an airport without a ticket. When you're standing at the airline counter trying to buy a ticket for the next available flight, you're going to be charged full fare. If an emergency has caused the change of plans, apply the techniques I've detailed in Chapter 4. If not, now's the time to try for a restriction waiver and get that full fare knocked down to a promotional fare.

Determine from the ticket agent which flights to your destination have seats available. But don't ask the ticket agent for the waiver. Seldom will he or she have the authority to grant your request. When the agent tells you which flights are available, ask to talk to a supervisor.

Ask the supervisor for a waiver on the promotional-fare restrictions. You'll need to be discreet. Keep your voice down so other passengers are not aware of what you are asking. And make it as easy as possible for the supervisor to grant the waiver. Make it clear that you are in difficult circumstances. Perhaps the restrictions impose an unusual hardship. Or the waiver may mean the difference between your flying and not flying. If you have any type of documentation to support you, show it to the supervisor. And make it clear that you'll treat any waiver confidentially.

Although this strategy is less reliable than a travel agent requesting a restriction waiver, it has worked. But it's success will depend on several variables, including the number of seats available, how convincing you are and even the disposition of the supervisor.

Nested ticketing — an alternative to paying full fare

Promotional fares usually carry the restriction that you must remain at your destination a minimum number of days, typically seven. Some promotional fares forego the minimum-stay requirement in favor of requiring you to remain at your destination over a Saturday night. If you stay only a few days, or want to be home for the weekend as many business travelers do, you won't be able to meet these restrictions and the airlines will charge you full fare.

But DO NOT pay the full fare! Use this strategy, called *nested ticketing*, to get a fare that falls between the promotional fare and the full fare.

Say you have to fly from Seattle to Orlando, Florida, on Monday the 22nd and return on Friday the 26th. Northwest airlines once charged $900 full coach for a Seattle-Orlando round trip. Northwest's least expensive round-trip promotional fare at the time was $258, but to be eligible for it you had to stay through a Saturday night. Since you must return on Friday, you won't qualify for the promotional fare.

But instead of paying full fare, buy two round-trip promotional fares. Buy the first as a Seattle-Orlando round trip for a departure on the 22nd and a return date of Monday the 29th or later. As long as you meet the Saturday-night requirement, or the seven-day stay, the return date is not important because you'll throw this portion of your ticket away. Buy the second as an Orlando-Seattle round trip with a departure date of Friday the 26th — the day you want to return to Seattle — and a return date at least seven days later. With the Orlando-Seattle ticket, you'll again meet any minimum-stay or Saturday-night restrictions. But you'll use only the first coupon for the flight on the 26th and throw away the return-flight coupon.

Instead of paying the $900 full fare, the two promotional-fare round trips would cost only $516, saving you $384.

Here's an important point. Notice that in this example we didn't buy two Seattle-Orlando round trips but one Seattle-Orlando and one Orlando-Seattle. If we had bought two Seattle-Orlando round trips, when using the second round trip we would have had to arrange the dates so that we would be flying on the second coupon — the return Orlando-Seattle coupon — while throwing away the first, or departure coupon.

The problem is that airline computer systems are so sophisticated that they would pick up that the departure coupon was not used and would then automatically cancel the return portion of the ticket. When you presented yourself at the airport gate, you would find out that your ticket is unusable.

Whenever buying a round-trip ticket for which you plan to throw away one of the coupons, you must ALWAYS arrange the dates and the departure-arrival cities so that you USE THE FIRST COUPON, the departure flight coupon, and THROW AWAY THE SECOND COUPON, the return flight coupon.

Alternatives to throwing away unused coupons

I have been telling you to throw away your unused return coupons. You do, however, have options other than tossing them out. As I pointed out in Chapter 6, a classified ad marketplace exists for unused tickets. You may want to take out your own ad in your local newspaper to sell your unused coupons for whatever you can get.

If your tickets carry only a minimal penalty for changes, you can put your throwaways to very good use. For this example let's say you can change your tickets by paying a $100 penalty. You can then change the travel dates on the two unused coupons — paying $100 each for the change — so that the new dates give you another round trip. You then have a Seattle-Orlando round-trip ticket for just $200.

Any business frequently sending travelers to the same place — travelers who will not meet stay-over restrictions — can use nested ticketing to save even more. Simply arrange travel dates so that succeeding travelers can use the coupons preceding travelers would normally throw away. Using back-to-back round trips will allow practically all your travelers to avoid stay-over requirements while allowing most to travel on lower-cost promotional fares.

Beat the stay-over restrictions by staying Saturday night

One way to beat the requirement to spend Saturday night at your destination, and still save money, is so obvious that many people fail to see it. Simply give in to the Saturday-night requirement and spend the weekend at your destination. If the alternative is to pay full fare, spending the weekend will give you a free vacation and still save you money.

Say, for example, you had to be in London on business from Monday through Friday. Catching a return flight on Friday or Saturday will not let you meet the Saturday-night rule, and you'll have to pay the full New York-London fare of $1,462. But stay the weekend and you qualify for an Apex fare of $688. The $774 you save should more than pay for the extra night or two in London. Unless you go on an all-out splurge, you'll still return home with more money than if you had purchased the full-fare ticket.

One-way trips — the airlines want full fare, but you don't have to pay it

Airlines usually require purchase of a round-trip ticket to be eligible for a promotional fare. If you want to fly one way, you'll probably have to pay full fare. And that one-way full fare will probably cost much more than a round-trip promotional fare.

Say, for example, you wanted to fly one way from Washington, D.C. to Miami. One airline's Washington-Miami one-way fare cost $259. The airline's cheapest Washington-Miami round trip, however, cost just $154. The strategy here is simple. Buy the round trip, throw away the return ticket and pocket $105.

If the one-way flight you want to make is for the return portion of your trip, remember you must schedule that flight so you will be using the first flight coupon. Suppose you had to drive cross country from Raleigh, North Carolina, to Sacramento, California. Perhaps you are accompanying someone who does not want to make the long drive alone. To get back to Raleigh, you plan on flying.

United Airlines once charged $427 for a one-way Sacramento-Raleigh flight. But a round-trip promotional fare cost just $328. Obviously, you'll buy the round-trip ticket.

You would probably want to buy the round-trip air ticket before leaving Raleigh. But don't buy a Raleigh-Sacramento round trip, planning to use only the Sacramento-Raleigh return flight coupon. As you've seen in the nested-ticketing strategy, United's computers would pick up that you have not used the Raleigh-Sacramento flight coupon and would automatically cancel the return ticket before you had a chance to use it.

Just ask your travel agent or the airline reservationist for a Sacramento-Raleigh round trip. Then you will be flying on the first flight coupon — Sacramento-Raleigh — and throwing away the second, Raleigh-Sacramento coupon.

Hidden cities — turning airline marketing strategies to your advantage

Because airline fares are driven by competition and not always based upon the distance flown, a ticket to a point beyond your destination can cost less than your own ticket.

When the fare between Los Angeles and Atlanta was $242, you could fly beyond Atlanta to Orlando, Florida, for just $159. Orlando is a popular vacation destination, so the Los Angeles-Orlando route can at times be more competitive than Los Angeles-Atlanta. Since Atlanta is a scheduled stop for the Los Angeles-Orlando flight, and since you could fly to a point beyond Atlanta at less cost, Atlanta becomes what is known in the trade as a hidden city. Here's how to save money using one and why it's called a *hidden city.*

You want to fly from Los Angeles to Atlanta. But instead of getting the $242 ticket you purchase the $159 Los Angeles-Orlando ticket on a flight that stops in Atlanta. Don't check your bags. Take carry-on luggage only. And when the plane stops in Atlanta, simply take your bags and get off the plane with an extra $83 to spend. According to your ticket, your itinerary is Los Angeles-Orlando, but your true destination — Atlanta — is hidden from your airline-ticketed itinerary.

Here's another example of a hidden-city. If you once wanted to fly from Dallas to Pittsburgh, USAir would have sold you a ticket for $270. But if you had bought your ticket to Grand Rapids instead, the flight's next stop after Pittsburgh, you would have paid only $129. When you walked off the plane in Pittsburgh, you'd have an extra $141 in your wallet.

Using the hidden-city strategy violates airline rules. The airlines want you to act as insanely as they do when they create their fare structures. So what if your Pittsburgh ticket costs $141 more than the ticket of the Grand Rapids passenger in the next seat who will fly some 900 miles farther than you. Buy the cheaper ticket to Grand Rapids and get off in Pittsburgh and the airlines cry FOUL! — YOU'RE NOT PLAYING FAIR.

Obviously, you do not want to tell an airline reservationist that you are seeking a hidden-city ticket. You can buy the ticket from an airline reservationist, just don't tell the clerk that you plan to leave the flight at a hidden city. The airlines will not help you bend their fare rules when it is not to their advantage.

Creative travel agencies are a good source of hidden cities. (Travel agents may also use the term *point-beyond ticketing.*) Many standard travel agencies, however, may decline to work with you on this strategy. If a travel agent sells you a hidden-city ticket and the airline detects it after you've taken the flight, they typically retaliate against the agent by docking the agency's account.

In view of the potential loss of funds to a travel agency should your use of a hidden-city ticket be discovered later by the airline, you should not buy your ticket at a travel agency. Of course, if the agency knows you want a hidden-city ticket and is willing to work with you, that's okay. But otherwise, purchase your hidden-city tickets through an airline reservation center.

How to find your own hidden cities

You can come up with hidden cities on your own. All airline

hubs are potential hidden cities. Use the list of hubs in this chapter to scout them out. When one of these hubs is your destination, determine fares to the hub as well as to a few cities beyond it.

If you find a fare to a point beyond the hub lower than the hub fare, you can use the hidden-city strategy. Buy your ticket to the point beyond and simply get off the plane when the flight stops at the hub — your true destination.

Occasionally, in your newspaper ad searches you'll find an airline that uses an outline map of the United States showing fares from your city to destinations around the country. Sometimes the ads skip the map and just list cities and fares. These maps and lists clearly show any hidden cities.

Continental Air Lines, for example, used such a map to show fares from Florida to points west of the Mississippi. The map showed fares of $109 to Denver and Albuquerque and $119 to Phoenix, Tucson and Salt Lake City. Several points beyond these cities, however, had lower fares: Los Angeles $79, San Diego and Las Vegas $89. If you were bound for Phoenix, for example, you could have checked with Continental for a flight that stopped in Phoenix and then flew on to San Diego or Los Angeles. With a $79 Los Angeles ticket, you could have gotten off in Phoenix and saved $30.

Another place to look for these maps and charts is in your hometown newspaper's travel section.

If you really want to dig into hidden city possibilities, start making a collection of airline timetables. You can pick them up at airport ticket counters. If they are not displayed on the various counters, ask the clerks for one.

These timetables typically detail a carrier's complete flight schedule, including connections and flight numbers. You can use the timetables to come up with flight connections to your destinations — the potential hidden cities — and to possible points beyond. Write down appropriate flights, the numbers and departure times, and then start making telephone calls to determine fares to both your destination/potential hidden city and the points beyond.

The timetable-search method involves a bit of work, but some people — like myself — enjoy that sort of digging. It's almost like searching for buried treasure, except that you'll probably have much more financial success with the hidden cities.

Drawbacks

As I pointed out above, you cannot check your baggage when using a hidden city. If you did, your bags would wind up in the ultimate destination stated on the ticket, the point beyond the hidden city. Therefore, plan on taking carry-on luggage only. And when you check in, don't tell the clerk why you're not checking your luggage. Don't say anything that would indicate you plan to depart the flight at a hidden city.

Hidden cities are useful only on one-way trips, so don't plan for a round-trip ticket. The airline's computers will pick up on the unused flight segment to the point beyond and will cancel the entire return ticket. In addition, the airline would not let you check in for your return flight from an intermediate stop — your hidden city — when your trip was supposed to start from the point beyond your hidden city.

If you need to make a round-trip, check to see if a hidden city is available for your return. Suppose, for example, you were flying from Philadelphia to Kansas City — your hidden city — with Denver as the point beyond. For your Kansas City-Philadelphia return, you would have to search for a less-expensive point beyond Philadelphia, perhaps New York, Boston or Baltimore.

European and intra-European fares — bargains are available for those in the know

Air fares between European cities have earned a reputation as being prohibitively expensive. And rightly so. The fare in the United States for a 2,400-mile flight averages about $432. A flight of that distance in Europe will cost you about $816.

Government policies designed to protect the profits of state-owned airlines are behind Europe's high fares. But the European Community has plans to increase competition among European carriers. In 1993, for example, individual governments will no longer have veto power over fares. And the airlines of EC nations will be free to fly international routes to and from the cities of all EC countries.

This liberalization of Europe's airlines will not be a complete, all-at-once deregulation along the lines of U.S. deregulation. Instead, look for a slow loosening of anti-competitive restraints on intra-European international fights. Domestic flights within European countries, however, will remain under the control of each individual country.

In the meantime, despite the high cost of European air fares there are still bargains available. Until recently, however, they were difficult to uncover and buy in the United States.

Lately, the barriers that prevented advertising and selling promotional fares in third countries (a country other than the two involved in the origin and destination of the flight) have started to weaken. U.S. travel agent computer systems now list many intra-European promotional fares. You can also obtain information on these promotional fares directly from the European airlines.

The savings can be substantial. One typical promotional fare let travelers fly round trip between London and Berlin for $125 — that's about the same as flying round trip between Washington, D.C. and Chicago.

All the barriers, however, have yet to come down, and some intra-European promotional fares are still difficult to uncover or impossible to buy in the United States.

The rules governing the availability of these fares are not always consistent. At one time, if you asked SAS — the Scandinavian airline — to sell you a London-Copenhagen promotional fare in the United States, the airline would refuse. But had you asked British Airways, they would have. When searching for a promotional fare between two European countries, be sure to obtain information from the airlines of both countries involved.

Combine these intra-European promotional fares (often called *creative fares* in Europe) with a transatlantic Apex fare and you may be able to fly to Europe for less. When the least expensive Miami-Zurich round-trip Apex fare was $786, you could have flown from Miami to Brussels, round-trip Apex, for $549. Then a Brussels-Zurich round-trip promotional fare priced at $159 would have got you to Zurich and back for a total of $708.

In addition to the $78 saved, you would have gotten a free stopover in Brussels, if you desired, since you were buying two separate tickets.

While this example used Brussels as the European intermediate city, you'll also find good buys using London. Your transatlantic fare to London will generally be less expensive than to other European cities. And London has good connections and promotional fares to the Continent.

To come up with these bargains, explore the possibilities by asking a travel agent or a helpful airline reservationist if you can cut your cost using an intra-European promotional fare.

Alternate destinations

Flying into a European city other than your actual destination can be a viable money-saving strategy. During one European peak travel season, a major airline would have charged you $753 for its least-expensive round-trip Apex ticket between New York and Zurich, Switzerland. But if you had been willing to fly into to an alternate destination, Icelandair would have put you in Zurich for $629, a $124 savings.

Icelandair, a low-fare airline, flies between cities in the United States and Luxembourg in Europe. Luxembourg is a pocket-sized country squeezed in between France, Belgium and Germany. From Luxembourg, Icelandair provides its passengers free bus transportation to Liege, Belgium; Amsterdam, Holland; and Frankfurt and Cologne in West Germany. The airline also offers bargain-fare rail travel to Paris and Zurich.

In our New York-Zurich example, Icelandair at the time would have charged you $599 round trip for the New York-Luxembourg flight and $30 round trip for the train between Luxembourg and Zurich. The rail ticket includes free airport-train station shuttle service. Keep in mind, though, you must reserve your Icelandair ground transportation when you purchase your flight ticket.

When in the market for a flight to Belgium, Holland, Germany, France or Switzerland, see if you can save money by flying Icelandair to an alternate destination then using their ground-transportation option to reach your final destination.

Flights to cities in Scandinavia — Denmark, Sweden, Norway and Finland — are consistently more expensive than to other European cities. But using an alternate destination can also help you arrive in Scandinavia with extra money in your wallet. When New York-Copenhagen 21-day Apex tickets were selling for $900, you could fly to Hamburg, West Germany, on a 21-day Apex ticket for $652. Hamburg, a European rail hub, lies about 100 miles south of Denmark. At Hamburg you can catch inexpensive rail-ferry transportation to Copenhagen and other Scandinavian cities.

Western Europe has excellent rail and bus systems. Whenever

looking into air fares to Europe, investigate to see if air transportation to an alternate destination coupled with ground transportation to your ultimate destination will save you money.

Stopovers

You can pick up a European stopover and cut the cost of your air fare at the same time by using an intra-European charter flight. As explained in Chapter 5, intra-European charters are about the cheapest form of air travel within Europe. By combining these charters with a transatlantic Apex fare — or even better, a transatlantic consolidator fare — you can save money and get a stopover.

Suppose on your trip you wanted to visit both London and Rome. While you could once obtain a high-season New York-Rome Apex fare for $889 round trip, you would not have been able to stopover in London without raising your fare. But you could have flown New York-London round trip at the time for $688. After arriving in London, you could have purchased a London-Rome charter which at the time was selling for about $175. Your total air fare including the London stopover would have cost $863, or $26 less than New York-Rome air fare alone.

Eurailpasses

When your European travel plans include purchasing a Eurailpass, you greatly increase your air travel options. Fly there for less by choosing the European city that will give you the cheapest transatlantic fare. Then plot your rail itinerary using that city as your start and stop points.

Suppose you wanted to fly to Munich, Germany, to take in Octoberfest for a couple of days and then use a Eurailpass to tour the rest of Europe. A major airline recently would have flown you between New York and Munich round trip on an Apex ticket for $806. But you could have flown into Frankfurt instead for $756. And if you flew into Paris your fare would have been only $667. Both Frankfurt and Paris offer excellent rail connections with Munich. You could have taken advantage of the lower air fares and started your rail trip in Paris or Frankfurt while including Munich as a stop on your rail itinerary.

Another example. If you had wanted to spend much of your Eurailpass travel time in Scandinavia, you might have decided upon Copenhagen as the city in which to start your rail trip. And your air fare would have been $875. But by choosing the $667 Paris air fare, your savings would have been $208, which would go a long way toward the cost of that Eurailpass.

Group fares — these little-thought-about fares can give you savings worth thinking about

If you can form a group — no, not a rock group — but a travel group, you will probably fly there for less. If you can get at least four people flying to the same destination, you may qualify as a group and get a substantial saving on air fare. In fact, as I point out below, I even found a group fare for just TWO people traveling together!

Availability of group fares varies from airline to airline. The rules governing group fares, including minimum group size, also vary. Sometimes land arrangements, hotel accommodations, car rental or ground transportation can also be included in a group fare to form a package.

If you are in business and sending several people to a meeting or convention, don't let each individual make his or own reservation without first looking into group fares. Have someone in the group contact all airlines flying to that particular destination. Tell the reservationist that you are interested in a group fare. (You will probably then be transferred to the group desk, or given the group desk's telephone number.) Determine the minimum number necessary to compose a group to your destination, and the lowest group fare available to you from each of the airlines.

If you prefer to fly a particular airline, perhaps for frequent-flyer mileage, and that airline does not come in with an acceptable group size or fare, let the group desk know what the competition will do for you. You just may get your preferred carrier's group desk to match the competing airline.

You don't have to be a business traveler to think group fares. Anytime several people intend to travel together to the same destination, you need to investigate group fares before booking promotional fares.

Here's some potential group-fare situations which may help to prime your thinking:

- Friends going on a ski trip or to a sporting event.

- Church members setting out on a retreat.

- An archeology team traveling to a dig.

- Club or association members heading for a meeting or even a getaway.

- A band playing in a distant city.

- An athletic team going to a distant game.

- Family members traveling to a reunion.

- A large family traveling anywhere.

The more travelers you come up with, the more likely you'll qualify for a group fare and the lower that fare will likely be. And if you can come up with 10 passengers in addition to yourself, many airlines will let you fly free.

Don't limit your group-fare thinking only to domestic travel.

Perhaps the local genealogy society wants to trace roots on location in a foreign country. Here's some examples of international group fares for varying group sizes:

• Houston-Sao Paulo, Brazil - least expensive round-trip Apex fare: $1,059. Fare for each traveler in a 20-member group: $748. Savings: $311.

• Philadelphia-Kingston, Jamaica - least expensive round-trip Apex fare: $435. Fare for each traveler in a 10-member group: $299. Savings: $136.

• Phoenix-Nassau, Bahamas - least expensive round-trip Apex fare: $580. Fare for each traveler in a TWO-member group: $379. Savings: $201.

• Atlanta-Ireland - package including air fare on Delta Air Lines, six nights accommodations and a rental car: $902. The package was free for a traveler who forms a group of at least 10 package-buying passengers.

Bumps — the ultimate fly-for-less strategy

I discussed in Chapter 2 how the airlines routinely overbook their flights. That discussion showed you how to avoid being bumped and the unnecessary expenses that could result. Now I'll show you how to use the airline's bumping policies to your advantage to not only fly there for less but to even FLY THERE FOR FREE!

The airlines know from experience that a certain percentage of reservation-holding passengers will not show. So for each flight, an airline may accept more reservations and sell more tickets than there are actual seats. Usually the carrier's estimates are on the mark and everything works out well. Occasionally, however, calculations are off and a flight winds up with more ticket-holding passengers than there are seats.

The airline is now in a tight situation. It stands a chance of creating much ill will among the passengers. To help resolve the dilemma to everyone's satisfaction, the Department of Transportation requires airlines to solicit volunteers to be bumped from the flight before bumping someone involuntarily.

And to entice volunteers, many airlines will offer the next available seat on a flight to the volunteer's destination PLUS A FREE ROUND-TRIP TICKET or a specific-dollar-amount voucher good for a future flight.

The volunteer bump policies of each airline differ and are not regulated. Neither are they chiseled in stone. Determine from the airline you are flying what exactly is offered to volunteers. Will your next-flight seat be confirmed or standby? If it's standby, it could take longer to reach your destination.

When an airline is seeking volunteers to be bumped, it can offer as little or as much as it thinks will be required to get the volunteers it needs. And a smart agent will start out low and then raise the incentive as needed. So don't be over anxious and jump at the airline's first offer.

You can even enter into negotiations. Let the agent know you'll volunteer for the right incentive. Perhaps, you can try to negotiate a confirmed instead of standby next-flight seat. If few passengers are volunteering, the airline would rather work with you — up to a point — than involuntarily bump a passenger.

Restrictions on using bump tickets

Rules and regulations attached to the use of free bump tickets or vouchers vary with each airline. Bump tickets used to carry few, if any, restrictions. But the airlines have recently started imposing restrictions on the use of these tickets.

Restrictions on bump tickets are not negotiable with gate personnel. They represent the policy and rules the carrier's management establishes for using, actually flying on, bump tickets. Here's some of the restrictions you could run into:

• Limited time period for making reservations. Continental, for example, limits making reservations to within seven days of departure. Northwest and United restrict making bump-ticket reservations to just 24 hours before your flight. That restriction effectively puts you into the status of a standby passenger. Delta is not much better, allowing reservations only within 48 hours. On the other hand, American, America West, Pan Am, Southwest, TWA and USAir allow you to make reservations anytime.

• Restricted transferability. Some carriers, Northwest and USAir for example, restrict use of bump tickets to the person actually bumped. You cannot transfer them to a family member or a friend, and you cannot sell them to a coupon broker. Of course, if you plan to use the ticket yourself, this restriction would have no impact on you.

• Blackout dates. If the bump ticket carries blackout dates, you will probably not be able to use it during the most popular times to fly — summer and over holidays.

Determine the restrictions attached to any bump ticket an airline may offer you, and factor those restrictions into your decision whether to be a bump volunteer. If the restrictions appear too onerous for you, try to negotiate a cash voucher which you could later apply to a less-restrictive ticket. Remember, if the airline has to bump someone involuntarily, the Department of Transportation requires the carrier give that passenger cash compensation.

Most bump tickets do not, however, carry two common restrictions tacked onto promotional-fare tickets. You can cancel your reservation with no penalty, and you won't have to stay at your destination over a Saturday night.

How to increase your chances of obtaining bump tickets

You'll need a degree of flexibility as to when you must arrive at your destination to take advantage of bumps. If you are flying to a business meeting or other appointment which would keep you from volunteering, try for the bump on your return flight when you may have more flexibility.

Some travelers trust to luck that their flight will be overbooked and they will be selected as one of the volunteers. But you can take specific steps that will increase your chances of getting a free bump ticket.

Before reaching the airport, decide if you have the flexibility to arrive at your destination several hours later than planned. If you do, decide whether you'll volunteer to be bumped.

Before boarding a flight from which you are willing to be bumped, ask the departure-gate ticket agent what the airline offers passengers who volunteer. Also find out about restrictions on using bump tickets. If the inducement and use-restrictions are satisfactory, let the agent know that you'll volunteer should the need arise. If they aren't, let the agent know what it will take to make you a volunteer.

If enough advance volunteers do not declare that they are willing to be bumped, the agent will announce the overbooking situation to the passengers on board the aircraft. The ticket agent will ask for volunteers and offer a particular inducement. If that does not bring enough volunteers forward, the agent may raise the ante. But if you volunteered at the lower inducement, that's what you'll get, even should subsequent volunteers receive an inducement of higher value.

If you have some flexibility as to when and which airline you fly, you can further increase your chances of getting bumped. Fly during the busiest air-travel times. That's when most overbooking occurs. Look for Monday morning and Thursday and Friday afternoon or evening flights. Flights at the beginning and the end of holiday periods are also more likely to be overbooked.

The airline you fly can also increase or decrease your bump chances. Most airlines bump in the area of 15 out of every 10,000 passengers. But several are well above that average: America West bumps 43 out of every 10,000, USAir 28 and Southwest Airlines 22.

At the other end, Delta Air Lines bumps only about nine out of every 10,000 passengers.

As I pointed out in Chapter 2, if you don't want to get bumped involuntarily, make sure you check-in early for those busy-time flights, especially if you have booked a high-bump airline. Typically, the last passengers to arrive are the ones selected for involuntary bumping.

I regard getting bumped as the ultimate fly-for-less strategy — you can't fly there for any less than a FREE ticket.

Conclusion

Congratulations! You've stuck with me through to the end. You can now confidently call yourself a savvy air traveler. More importantly, you have the know how to reap the rewards of your efforts to FLY THERE FOR LESS!

No longer do you have to blindly accept fare quotes from travel agents and airline reservationists. You are aware of how the air-travel bazaar works and can shop in it wisely, saving money every time you enter it.

If you've already had the opportunity to buy a ticket using some of these tips, techniques and strategies, you know first hand how significant your air fare savings can be.

If you have not yet visited the bazaar since starting this book, be assured you have equipped yourself with the knowledge that will let you fly anywhere in the world for less — substantially less. After all, as a savvy air traveler you know:

• how to give yourself flexibility and to use that flexibility to save money on your airline tickets;

• what steps to take to find the lowest fare;

• how to use little-known fares to both extend your travels and cut ticket costs;

• which types of airlines will fly you there for less;

• how to find and use not-widely-known ticket sources that will give you tremendous savings on your air travel;

• which of the many travel clubs and programs will offer you the most air-travel savings;

• how to examine situations and circumstances and use them to reduce the cost of your airline tickets;

• how to creatively apply your knowledge of the marketplace to slash the cost of your air travel worldwide.

Admittedly, you have covered a tremendous amount of material. But as you conscientiously apply the directions in this guide, you will be rewarded handsomely.

Some of the information, though, is bound to slide from your mind. You can, however, easily refresh your memory. Don't let this book sit on a shelf. Before you start hunting for an air fare, pick it up and browse through it. Look at the the detailed table of contents to remind yourself of what's included and what you can use in your current fare search. Then go to those pages and re-read them.

To organize your low-fare searches, and to help you quickly locate those portions of this book that will be most applicable to a particular hunt, let me once again recommend my *Traveler's Report* # 112-THE AIR TRAVELER'S EASY LOW-FARE FINDER.

You'll find this fill-in form to be an invaluable aid to zeroing in on that low fare. As you use the report, it reminds you of what's included in *Fly There For Less* and refers you by page number to the particular strategies that will be most helpful in your search. The catalog at the back of the book tells you how to order THE AIR TRAVELER'S EASY LOW-FARE FINDER.

A few last words

So far, I've been doing all the talking. I've revealed to you the secrets that will let you save large sums on your air travels. Now I ask for something in return — I'd like to hear from you.

I want to hear about your success in using *Fly There For Less* to slash your air-fare costs. Maybe a particular strategy has helped you make a flight you otherwise would not have been able to afford. Perhaps *Fly There For Less* has helped your business' bottom line buy reining in your air-travel costs. Or maybe you just want to share the excitement of having cut the cost of a ticket.

I also want to hear about your travel problems. The travel marketplace in general and the air-travel bazaar in particular change constantly. Are the travel industry's marketing strategies undermining your travel budget? Is the steadily rising cost of business travel adversely affecting your long-range goals? Are travel costs hampering your trip planning? Let me hear from you. Perhaps I can help.

Write to me at 160 Fiesta Drive, Kissimmee, FL 34743. I look forward to hearing from you. In the meantime, I'll continue working on the publications — books, reports and audio tapes — that will help you to both travel farther for less and put more meaning and zest into those journeys.

Appendix 1: Consolidator contacts

The following is a list of consolidators selling discounted airline tickets directly to the public. It is not a list of recommended consolidators. Therefore, just as you would with any consolidator you found on your own, check with the Better Business Bureau in the consolidator's home city. You'll also want to use the precautions listed in Chapter 6.

Arizona

- Euro-Asia, Inc., 4203 E. Indian School Rd., Suite 210, Phoenix, AZ 85018, telephone 602-955-2742. Destinations: Europe and Asia.

California

- All Unique Travel, 1030 Georgia St., Vallejo, CA 94590,

telephone 707-648-0237. Destinations: Europe, the Middle East and Hawaii.

- Bargain Air Tours, 655 Deep Valley Dr., Suite 355, Rolling Hills, CA 90274, telephone 800-347-2345, 213-377-2919 or 415-325-9944. Destinations: Europe, Asia, the Middle East, the South Pacific and the United States. Accepts credit cards.

- British European Travel, 3707 Williams Rd., Suite 100, San Jose, CA 95117, telephone 800-747-1476 or 408-984-7576, fax 408-984-5480. Destinations: Europe and United States. Accepts credit cards.

- Cenatours, 977 N. Broadway, Los Angeles, CA 90012, telephone 213-680-1288. Destinations: Hawaii, Asia and the South Pacific.

- Coast Consolidators, Inc., 2019A E. Orangethorpe, Placentia, CA 92670, telephone 714-528-3366. Destinations: Europe and the South Pacific.

- Community Travel Service, 5299 College Ave., Oakland, CA 94618, telephone 415-653-0990. Destinations: Europe and Asia.

- Cost Less Travel, Inc., 674 Broadway, Suite 201, San Francisco, CA 94133, telephone 415-397-6868. Destinations: Asia.

- Euro Asia Express, 475 El Camino Real, Millbrae, CA 94030, telephone 415-692-9966 or 800-782-9625, in California 800-782-9624. Destinations: Europe, Asia and the South Pacific. Accepts credit cards.

- Express Fun Travel, 1169 Market St., Room 809, San

Francisco, CA 94102, telephone 800-722-0872 or 415-864-8005. Destinations: Asia.

- Rebel Tours, 4455 Van Nuys Blvd., Sherman Oaks, CA 91403, telephone 818-990-2400 or 800-227-3235. Destinations: Europe. Accepts credit cards.

- Sunline Express Holidays, 607 Market St., San Francisco, CA 94105, telephone 415-541-7800 or 800-877-2711. Destinations: Africa, Europe, Asia, the Middle East, Central and South America, the Caribbean, the South Pacific and the United States. Accepts credit cards.

- Transoceanic Travel, 209 Post St., San Francisco, CA 94108, telephone 415-362-0390. Destinations: Europe and Asia.

Florida

- Getaway Travel, Inc., 1105 Ponce de Leon Blvd., Coral Gables, FL 33134, telephone 305-446-7855. Destinations: Europe, Asia, South America.

- Interworld Travel Inc., 2255 SW 32nd St., Suite 209, Miami, FL 33145, telephone 800-331-4456 or 305-443-4929. Destinations: Europe, Africa, the Caribbean, Central and South America, Asia, the Middle East, the South Pacific and the United States. Accepts credit cards.

- Travac Tours & Charters, 3501 Vine St., Kissimmee, FL 34741, telephone 800-872-8800 or 407-870-8737. Destinations: Europe.

- 25 Travel, 25 Building, 2490 Coral Way, 3rd Floor, Miami, FL 33145, telephone 800-252-5052 or 305-856-0810. Destinations: Europe, Africa, Asia, Central and South

America, the Caribbean, the the South Pacific, the United States. Accepts credit cards.

Georgia

• Sun International Travel, 6000 Dawson Blvd., Norcross, GA 30093, telephone 800-521-4161 or 404-446-3111. Destinations: Asia and Europe.

Illinois

• Hudson Holidays, 7512 W. Grand Ave., Chicago, IL 60635, telephone 800-323-6855 or 708-452-0600. Destinations: Europe, Asia, South America, the Middle East and the South Pacific.

• Japan Budget Travel, 104 S. Michigan Ave., Chicago, IL 60603, telephone 800-843-0273 or 312-236-9797. Destinations: Japan.

• McSon Travel, Inc., 36 S. State St., Chicago, IL 60603, telephone 312-346-6272 or 800-662-1421. Destinations: Europe, Asia and the South Pacific.

• Mena Travel, 2479 N. Clark St., Chicago, IL 60614, telephone 312-472-5631. Destinations: Caribbean, Central America and South America. Accepts credit cards.

• Ryan's Regent Travel, 7218 W. Touhy Ave., Chicago, IL 60648, telephone 312-774-8770. Destinations: Europe.

• Travel Avenue, 180 N. Des Plaines, Suite 201, Chicago, IL 60661-1012, telephone 800-333-3335 or 312-876-1116. Destinations: Europe, Africa, the Far East, South America and the Middle East. Accepts credit cards.

Missouri

- UniTravel Corp., 1177 N. Warson Rd., St. Louis, MO 63132, telephone 800-325-2222 or 314-569-2501. Destinations: Europe, Asia, the South Pacific and the United States. Accepts credit cards.

New York

- Able Travel and Tours, 18 E. 41st St., New York, NY 10017, telephone 212-779-8530. Destinations: Europe.

- Access International, 250 W. 57th St., Suite 511, New York, NY 10107, telephone 800-333-7280 or 212-465-0707. Destinations: Europe.

- Apex Travel, Inc., 230 Park Ave., New York, NY 10169, telephone 212-661-1606 or 800-428-8848. Destinations: the Far East.

- Consumer Wholesale Travel, 518 5th Ave., New York, NY 10036, telephone 212-391-0122 or 800-223-6862. Destinations: Europe, Africa, the Middle East, the Caribbean and the Far East.

- Council Charter, 205 E. 42nd St., New York, NY 10017, telephone 800-800-8222 or 212-661-0311. Destinations: Europe and the Caribbean.

- Go Voyages, 150 W. 80th St., Suite 90, New York, NY 10024, telephone 212-874-5040. Destinations: Europe and the South Pacific.

- Japan Budget Travel, 9 East 38th St., Room 203, New York, NY 10016, telephone 212-686-8855. Destinations: Japan.

- Maharaja Travel, 393 Fifth Ave., New York, NY 10036,

telephone 800-223-6862 or 212-213-2020, fax 212-764-3415. Destinations: Africa, Asia, Europe, the Middle East, Central America, South America and the South Pacific. Accepts credit cards.

- Nouvelles Frontières, 12 East 33rd St., New York, NY 10016, telephone 800-366-6387 or 212-779-0600. Destinations: Africa and Europe. Accepts credit cards.

- Pan Express Travel, Inc., 25 West 39th St., Suite 705, New York, NY 10018, telephone 212-719-9292. Destinations: Africa, Europe, the Caribbean and South America.

- RMC Travel Centre, 41 East 42nd St., Suite 1715, New York, NY 10017, telephone 800-344-7439, fax 212-697-6693. Destinations: Europe, Asia, the Middle East, the South Pacific and the United States. Accepts credit cards.

- TFI Tours, 34 West 32nd St., New York, NY 10001, telephone 800-825-3834 or 212-736-1140. Destinations: Europe, Asia, Africa, South America, South Pacific.

- Transpacific Delight, 97 Bowery, New York, NY 10002, telephone 212-925-8080. Destinations: Asia.

- Travac Tours & Charters, 989 Avenue of the Americas, New York, NY 10018, telephone 800-872-8800 or 212-563-3303. Destinations: Europe. Accepts credit cards.

- Up & Away Travel, 141 E. 44th St., Suite 404, New York, NY 10017, telephone 212-972-2345. Destinations: Africa, Europe, Asia, the Caribbean and the United States. Accepts credit cards.

Oregon

- STT Worldwide Travel, 10970 S.W. Beaverton Hwy., Beaverton, OR 97005, telephone 503-641-8866 or 800-348-0886, in Oregon 800-222-1778. Destinations: Africa, Asia, South America and the South Pacific. Accepts credit cards.

Pennsylvania

- Pennsylvania Travel, 19 E. Central Ave., Paoli, PA 19301, telephone 215-251-9944 or 800-331-0947. Destinations: Africa, Asia, Europe and the Middle East. Accepts credit cards.

- Travel Bargains, P. O. Box 5000, Plymouth Meeting, PA 19462, telephone 800-872-8385. Destinations: Europe, Asia, South America and the United States. Accepts credit cards.

Texas

- Airvalue, 1817 S. Broadway, Tyler, TX 75711, telephone 903-597-1181. Destinations: Europe and Asia.

- Katy Van Tours, 16526 Park Row, Houston, TX 77084, telephone 713-492-7032 or 800-528-9826. Destinations: Europe, the Middle East, Central and South America and the South Pacific. Accepts credit cards.

Virginia

- Fellowship Travel International, Inc., Box 15360, Richmond, VA 23227, telephone 804-264-0121 or 800-446-7667, in Virginia 800-446-7767. Destinations: Europe, Africa, the Middle East, Asia, Central and South America and the South Pacific and Indonesia. Accepts credit cards.

Washington

- Marco Polo Tours, 416 8th Ave. South, Seattle, WA 98104, telephone 800-831-3108 or 206-621-0700, fax 206-621-7392. Destinations: Asia. Accepts credit cards.

- Travel Team, 4518 University Way NE, Seattle, WA 98105, telephone 206-632-0520 and 25 Central Way, Kirkland, WA 98033, telephone 206-822-0521. Destinations: Europe.

Washington, DC

- European-American Travel, Inc., 1522 K Street, N.W., Suite 530, Washington, DC 20005, telephone 202-789-2255 or 800-848-6789. Destinations: Europe, Asia, the Middle East, the Caribbean, Central and South America and the South Pacific. Accepts credit cards.

Appendix 2: Airline contacts

Aer Lingus (Ireland)

- 122 East 42nd St., New York, NY 10168, telephone 212-557-1090
- Reservations: 800-333-0276 or 212-557-1110

Aerolineas Argentinas

- 9 Rockefeller Plaza., New York, NY 10020, telephone 212-698-2050
- Reservations: 800-333-0276

Aeromexico

- 13045 Northwest Fwy, Houston, TX 77040, telephone 713-744-8445

- Reservations: 800-237-6639

Aeroperú

- 8181 N.W. 36th St. Suite 5, Miami, FL 33166, telephone 305-591-9240
- Reservations: 800-777-7717

Air Afrique

- 888 Seventh Ave., New York, NY 10106, telephone 212-541-7474
- Reservations: 800-456-9192 (Reservations may also be made through Air France.)

Air Canada

- 1166 Avenue of the Americas, New York, NY 10036, telephone 212-869-8840
- Reservations: 800-776-3000 or 514-393-3333

Air China

- 185 Post St., San Francisco, CA 94108, telephone 415-392-2161
- Reservations: 415-392-2161

Air France

- 888 Seventh Ave., New York, NY 10106, telephone 212-830-4000
- Reservations: 800-237-2747 or 212-247-0100

Air India

- 345 Park Ave., New York, NY 10154, telephone 212-407-1300
- Reservations: 800-223-7776 or 212-751-6200

Air Jamaica

- 444 Madison Ave., New York, NY 10022, telephone 800-523-5585
- Reservations: 800-523-5585

Air New Zealand

- 1945 E. Grand Ave., Suite 900., El Segundo, CA 90245, telephone 310-615-1111
- Reservations: 800-262-1234

Air Niugini

- 5000 Birch St., Suite 3000, West Tower, Newport Beach, CA 92660, telephone 714-752-5440
- Reservations: 714-752-5440

Air Panama International

- 1325 NW 93rd Ct., Unit 115, Miami, FL 33172, telephone 305-594-3647
- Reservations: 800-272-6262 or 305-593-1131

Air Paraguay

- 3384 Peachtree St., Suite 576, Atlanta, GA 30326 telephone 404-233-2717
- Reservations: 800-677-7771

Air Zaire

- 1001 Bayshore Dr. Miami, FL 33131, telephone 305-372-1717
- Reservations: 800-442-5114

Alaska Airlines

- 19300 Pacific Hwy. S. Seattle, WA 98188, telephone 206-433-3200

- Customer relations: Consumer Affairs, Box 68900, Seattle, WA 98168, telephone 206-431-7286
- Reservations: 800-426-0333 or 206-433-3100

ALIA Royal Jordanian Airlines

- 535 Fifth Ave., New York, NY 10017, telephone 212-949-0060
- Reservations: 800-223-0470 or 212-949-0070

Alitalia (Italy)

- 666 Fifth Ave., New York, NY 10103, telephone 212-903-3300
- Reservations: 800-223-5730 or 212-582-8900

ALM-Antillean Airlines

- 1150 N.W. 72nd Ave., Suite 530, Miami, FL 33126, telephone 305-592-7646
- Reservations: 800-327-7230

Aloha Airlines

- P.O. Box 30028, Honolulu, HI 96820, telephone 808-836-4101
- Reservations: 800-367-5250 or 808-836-1111

America West Airlines

- 4000 E. Sky Harbor Blvd., Phoenix AZ 85034, telephone 602-693-0800
- Customer relations: Consumer Affairs, 4000 E. Sky Harbor Blvd., Phoenix, AZ 85034, telephone 800-247-5692 ext 6019 or 602-693-6019
- Reservations: 800-247-5692 or 602-894-0737

American Airlines

- P.O. Box 619616 Dallas/Fort Worth Airport, Dallas 75261-9616, telephone 817-355-1234

- Customer relations: Box 619612, Mail Drop 2400, Dallas/Fort Worth Airport, Dallas, TX 75261, telephone 817-967-2000

- Reservations: 800-433-7300 or 817-267-1151

ANA - All Nippon Airways (Japan)

- 611 W. 6th St., Suite 3100, Los Angeles, CA 90017, telephone 213-629-1500

- Reservations: 800-235-9262

Ansett Airlines of Australia

- 9841 Airport Blvd., Suite 418, Los Angles, CA 90045, telephone 213-642-7487

- Reservations: 800-366-1300

Austral Airlines (Argentina)

- 6175 N.W. 153rd St., Suite 332, Miami Lakes, FL 33014, telephone 305-477-8396

- Reservations: 800-257-0114

Australian Airlines

- 222 N. Sepulveda, Suite 1730, El Segundo, CA 90245, telephone 310-640-2040

- Reservations: 800-922-5122, 800-448-9400 in Canada

Austrian Airlines

- 608 Fifth Ave., Suite 507, New York, NY 10020, telephone 212-265-6350

- Reservations: 800-843-0002 or 212-307-6226

Avianca Airlines (Colombia)

- 6 W. 49th St., New York, NY 10020, telephone 212-399-0858

- Reservations: 800-284-2622

Aviateca (Guatemala)

- P.O. Box 20027, New Orleans, LA 70141, telephone 504-469-9421

- Reservations: 800-327-9832 or 504-522-1010

Bahamasair

- 3024 N.W. 79th Ave., Miami, FL 33122, telephone 305-593-1905

- Reservations: 800-222-4262 or 305-593-1910

Braniff International

- Reservations: 800-272-6433

British Airways

- 75-20 Astoria Blvd., Jackson Heights, NY 11370, telephone 718-397-4000

- Reservations: 800-247-9297

BWIA International Airways

- 118-35 Queens Blvd., 17th Floor, Forest Hills, NY 11375-7205, telephone 718-520-8100

- Reservations: 800-327-7401 or 305-371-2942

CAAC (People's Republic of China)

- 45 East 49th St., New York, NY 10017, telephone 212-371-9899

- Reservations: Contact Northwest Airlines which serves as North American sales agent for CAAC

Canadian Airlines International

- P.O. Box 4365, Vancouver, British Columbia, Canada, V6B 9Z9
- Reservations: 800-426-7000 or 212-581-7920

Cathay Pacific Airways

- One Embarcadero Center, Suite 747, San Francisco, CA 94111, telephone 415-982-3242
- Reservations: 800-233-2742 or 212-819-0210

Cayman Airways

- 250 Catalonia Ave., Suite 506, Coral Gables, FL 33134, telephone 305-444-7230
- Reservations: 800-422-9626 or 305-446-8696

China Airlines (Republic of China)

- 391 Sutter St., San Francisco, CA 94108, telephone 415-391-3950
- Reservations: 800-227-5118

China Eastern Airlines (Peoples Republic of China)

- 2500 Wilshire Blvd., Suite 100, Los Angeles, CA 90057, telephone 213-384-2703
- Reservations: 213-384-2703

Continental Airlines

- 2929 Allen Pkwy., Suite 500, Houston 77019, telephone 713-821-2100
- Customer relations: 3663 Sam Houston Pkwy, Suite 500, Houston, TX 77032, telephone 713-987-6500
- Reservations: 800-525-0280 (Domestic), 800-231-0856 (International), 713-821-2100

CP Air (Canadian Pacific Air Lines)

- 595 Madison Ave., Suite 2300, New York, NY 10022, telephone 212-759-1326

- Reservations: 800-426-7000, 800-552-7576 in Washington state

CSA-Czechoslovak Airlines

- 545 Fifth Ave., New York, NY 10017, telephone 212-682-7541

- Reservations: 800-223-2365 or 212-682-5833

Delta Air Lines

- Hartsfield International Airport, Atlanta, GA 30320, telephone 404-715-2600

- Customer relations: Consumer Affairs, Box 20706, Hartsfield International Airport, Atlanta, GA 30320, telephone 404-715-1450

- Reservations: 800-221-1212 (Domestic), 800-241-4141 (International), 404-765-5000

Eastwest Airlines

- Contact Ansett Australia Airlines. Ansett represents Eastwest Airlines in North America.

Ecuatoriana Airlines

- 590 Fifth Ave., 10th Floor, New York, NY 10136, telephone 212-354-1850

- Reservations: 800-328-2367, 800-626-0363 in Florida

Egyptair

- 720 Fifth Ave., New York, NY 10019, telephone 212-581-5600

- Reservations:800-334-6787 or 718-997-7700

El Al Israel Airlines

- 850 Third Ave., New York, NY 10022, telephone 212-852-0600
- Reservations: 800-223-6700 or 212-486-2600

Ethiopian Airlines

- 405 Lexington Ave., New York, NY 10174, telephone 212-867-0095
- Reservations: 800-433-9677 (West and Midwest), 800-445-2733 (East and South)

Faucett Peruvian Airlines

- 7220 N.W. 36th St., Suite 245, Miami, FL 33166, telephone 305-592-5330
- Reservations: 800-334-3356, 800-432-0468 in Florida or 305-591-0610

Finnair

- 10 East. 40th St., New York, NY 10016, telephone 212-689-9300
- Reservations: 800-950-5000 or 212-889-7070

Garuda Indonesia

- 3457 Wilshire Blvd., Los Angeles, CA 90010, telephone 213-387-0259
- Reservations: 800-342-7832

Guyana Airways

- 883 Flatbush Ave., Brooklyn, NY 11226, telephone 718-693-8000
- Reservations: 800-242-4210 or 718-693-8000

Hawaiian Airlines

- P.O. Box 30008, Honolulu, HI 96820, telephone 808-525-5511
- Reservations: 800-367-5320

Iberia Air Lines (Spain)

- 6300 Wilshire Blvd., Suite 1700, Los Angeles, CA 90048, telephone 800-772-4642
- Reservations: 800-432-1231

Icelandair

- 360 West 31st St., New York, NY 10001-2793, telephone 212-330-1470
- Reservations: 800-223-5500 or 212-967-8888

Japan Air Lines

- 655 Fifth Ave., New York, NY 10022, telephone 212-838-4400
- Reservations: 800-525-3663 or 212-838-4400

JAT Yugoslav Airlines

- 630 Fifth Ave., Suite 1960, New York, 10111-0022, telephone 212-765-4050
- Reservations: 800-752-6528 or 212-246-6401

Kenya Airways

- 424 Madison Ave., New York, NY 10017, telephone 212-832-8810
- Reservations: 800-343-2506

KLM Royal Dutch Airlines

- 565 Taxter Rd., Elmsford, NY 10523, telephone 914-784-2000

- Reservations: 800-777-5553 or 212-759-3600

Korean Air Lines

- 6101 W. Imperial Hwy., Los Angeles, CA 90045, telephone 213-417-5200

- Reservations: 800-223-1155 (Eastern United States), 800-421-8200 (Western United States)

Kuwait Airways

- 405 Park Ave., New York, NY 10022, telephone 212-319-1222

- Reservations: 800-458-9248 or 800-424-1128 or 212-308-5454

Lacsa (Costa Rica)

- 5200 NW 84th Ave., Suite 200, Miami, FL 33166, telephone 305-593-0967

- Reservations: 800-225-2272

Ladeco (Chile)

- 9500 S. Dadeland Blvd., Suite 510, Miami, FL 33156, telephone 305-670-9933

- Reservations: 800-825-2332 or 305-670-3066

LAN Chile Airlines

- 100 S. Biscayne Blvd., Miami, FL 33131, telephone 305-670-9933

- Reservations 800-735-5526

LIAT (Antigua)

- P.O. Box 819, V.C. Bird Airport, Antigua, BWI telephone 809-462-0700

- Reservations: 800-253-5011 or 212-779-2731

Lloyd Aereo Boliviano Airlines (Bolivia)

- 225 SE 1st St., Miami, FL 33131, telephone 305-374-4600
- Reservations: 800-327-7407 or 305-374-4600

LOT Polish Airlines

- 500 Fifth Ave., New York, NY 10110, telephone 212-944-8116
- Reservations: 800-223-0593 or 212-869-1074

Lufthansa (Germany)

- 1640 Hempstead Turnpike, East Meadow, NY 11554, telephone 516-296-9200
- Reservations: 800-645-3880 or 718-895-1277

Malaysia Airlines

- 5933 W. Century Blvd., Suite 506, Los Angeles, CA 90045, telephone 213-642-0849
- Reservations: 800-421-8641

Malev Hungarian Airline

- 630 Fifth Ave., Suite 1900, New York, NY 10111, telephone 212-757-6480
- Reservations: 800-223-6884 or 212-757-6446, 800-334-1284 in Canada

Mark Air

- 100 W. International Airport Rd., Anchorage, AK 99519-6769, telephone 907-243-1414
- Reservations: 800-426-6784 or 800-478-0800 in Alaska

Mexicana Airlines

- 9841 Airport Blvd., Suite 200, Los Angeles, CA 90045, telephone 213-646-9975
- Reservations: 800-531-7921 or 213-646-9500

Middle East Airlines

- 680 Fifth Ave., New York, NY 10019, telephone 212-664-7310
- Reservations: 212-664-7310

Midwest Express

- 4915 S. Howell Ave., Milwaukee, WI 53207, telephone 414-747-4652
- Customer relations: Consumer Affairs, 4915 S. Howell Ave., Milwaukee, WI 53207, telephone 800-452-2022 ext 3910 or 414-747-3910
- Reservations: 800-452-2022 or 414-747-4646

Mt. Cook Airline (New Zealand)

- 1960 Grand Ave., El Segundo, CA 90245
- Reservations: 800-468-2665

Nigeria Airways

- 15 East 51st St., New York, NY 10022, telephone 212-935-2703
- Reservations: 800-223-1070 or 212-935-2700

Northwest Airlines

- Minneapolis/St. Paul International Airport, St. Paul, MN 55111, telephone 612-726-2111
- Customer relations: Mail Stop E 5270, Minneapolis/St. Paul International Airport, St. Paul, MN 55111, telephone 612-726-2046

- Reservations: 800-225-2525 (Domestic) or 612-726-1234, 800-447-4747 (International)

Olympic Airways (Greece)

- 647 Fifth Ave., New York, NY 10022, telephone 212-735-0200

- Reservations: 800-223-1226 or 212-838-3600

Pakistan International Airlines

- 521 Fifth Ave., New York, NY 10175, telephone 212-370-9150

- Reservations: 800-221-2552 or 212-370-9155

Philippine Airlines

- 447 Sutter St., San Francisco, CA 94108, telephone 415-391-0270

- Reservations: 800-435-9725, 800-263-8187 in Canada

Polynesian Airlines

- Contact Ansett Australia Airlines. Ansett represents Polynesian Airlines in North America.

Qantas Airways

- 360 Post St., San Francisco, CA 94108, telephone 415-445-1460

- Reservations: 800-227-4500 or 415-761-8000

Reno Air

- 690 E. Plumb Lane, Reno, NV 89504, telephone 702-688-4020

- Reservations: 800-736-6247

Royal Air Maroc (Morocco)

- 55 East 59th St., New York, NY 10022, telephone 212-750-5115
- Reservations: 800-344-6726

Royal Nepal Airlines

- 265 Madison Ave., 5th Fl., New York, NY 10016, telephone 212-661-4435
- Reservations: 800-922-7622 or 212-661-4435

Sabena (Belgium)

- 720 Fifth Ave., New York, NY 10019, telephone 1-212-408-5080
- Reservations: 800-955-2000

SAS Scandinavian Airlines System

- 9 Polito, Lyndhurst, NJ 07071, telephone 201-896-3600
- Reservations: 800-221-2350

Saudi Arabian Airlines

- 747 Third Ave., 29th Floor, New York, NY 10017, telephone 212-758-4774
- Reservations: 800-472-8342 or 212-758-4727

Singapore Airlines

- 5670 Wilshire Blvd., Los Angeles, CA 90036, telephone 213-934-8833
- Reservations: 800-742-3333

South African Airways

- 900 Third Ave., New York, NY 10022-4771, telephone 212-826-0995

- Reservations: 800-772-9675

Southwest Airlines

- P.O. Box 37611, Dallas, TX 75235, telephone 214-263-1717
- Customer relations: Customer Relations, Box 36611, Dallas, TX 75235, telephone 214-904-4223
- Reservations: 800-531-5601

Surinam Airways

- 57-75 Blue Lagoon Dr., Suite 320, Miami, FL 33126, telephone 305-262-9792
- Reservations: 800-327-6864, 800-432-1230 in Florida

Swissair

- 608 Fifth Ave., New York, NY 10020, telephone 718-481-4500
- Reservations: 800-221-4750, 800-522-6902 in New York State, or 718-995-8400

TACA International Airlines (El Salvador)

- P.O. Box 20047, New Orleans International Airport, New Orleans, LA 70141, telephone 504-466-6913
- Reservations: 800-535-8780 or 504-466-6913

Tan-Sasha Airlines (Honduras)

- P.O. Box 52-2222, Miami, FL 33152, telephone 305-526-4330
- Reservations: 800-327-1225

TAP Air Portugal

- 399 Market St., Newark, NJ 07105, telephone 201-344-4490

- Reservations: 800-221-7370

Tarom-Romanian Air Transport

- 342 Madison Ave., New York, NY 10073, telephone 212-687-6013
- Reservations: 212-687-6013

Thai Airways International

- 720 Olive Way, Suite 1400, Seattle, WA 98101, telephone 206-467-9898
- Reservations; 800-426-5204 or 206-467-0600

Tower Air

- Hangar 8, JFK International Airport, Jamaica, NY 11430, telephone 718-917-4300
- Reservations: 800-221-2500 or 718-917-8500

Trans-Brazil

- Reservations: 800-272-7458

Trans World Airlines-TWA

- 100 S. Bedford Rd., Mt. Kisco, NY 10549, telephone 914-242-3000
- Customer relations: 110 S. Bedford Rd., Mount Kisco, NY 10549, telephone 914-242-3172
- Reservations: 800-221-2000 (Domestic), 800-892-4141 (International), or 212-290-2121

United Airlines

- P.O. Box 66100, Chicago, IL 60666, telephone 312-825-2525
- Customer relations: Box 66100, Chicago, IL 60666, telephone 708-952-6796

- Reservations: 800-241-6522 or 312-825-2525

USAir

- Washington National Airport, Washington, DC 20001, telephone 703-418-7000
- Customer relations: Consumer Affairs, Box 1501, Winston-Salem, NC 27102, telephone 919-661-0061
- Reservations: 800-428-4322

Varig Brazilian Airlines

- 622 Third Ave., New York, NY 10017, telephone 212-340-0200
- Reservations: 800-468-2744

Viasa Venezuelan International Airways

- 18 E. 48th St., New York, NY 10017, telephone 212-486-4360
- Reservations: 800-468-4272, 800-432-9070 in Florida

Virgin Atlantic Airways

- 96 Horton St., New York, NY 10014, telephone 212-206-6612
- Reservations: 800-862-8621 or 212-242-1330

Yemen Airways

- 318 West 102nd St., New York, NY 10025, telephone 212-286-0660
- Reservations: 800-257-1133

Zambia Airways

- 400 Madison Ave., New York, NY 10017, telephone 212-685-1112
- Reservations: 800-223-1136

Air-travel glossary

Apex fare - A type of promotional fare offered on international flights.

Basic season - A time of the year when demand for air travel is at its lowest. Also called the off-season or the off-peak season.

Blackout - A period of strong demand for air travel during which the airlines do not offer promotional fares and prevent the use of special fares.

Bucket shop - A travel agency, generally overseas, that specializes in selling discounted international air tickets.

Business class - A class of air service that offers more amenities and service than coach or economy, but less than first class. Business class costs more than coach or economy, but is less expensive than first class.

Cancelation penalty - A fee airlines charge certain promotional-fare passengers who turn in an unused ticket for a refund.

Capacity control - A system airlines use to limit the number of promotional-fare seats available on each flight.

Charter flight - A flight not operating on a recurring schedule, but flying on a specific date to a single destination, usually at a lower fare than those offered by scheduled flights.

Coach class - The least expensive class of domestic air service, offering the least amenities and service.

Consolidator - A travel firm that sells primarily international airline tickets at prices discounted below an airline's lowest promotional fare.

Currency-differential ticketing - Using the relative strength and weakness of international currencies to save on air fare.

Deregulation - The Airline Deregulation Act of 1978 ended government control of domestic airline operations, including air fares.

Direct flight - A flight on which a passenger does not have to change planes. The plane may make stops, but the passenger remains on board until arriving at his or her destination.

Double ticketing - Buying two one-way tickets for a round-trip flight. Also called split ticketing.

Easy saver - A type of promotional fare offered on domestic flights.

Economy class - The least expensive class of international air service, offering the least amenities and service.

First class - The most expensive class of service, offering the most amenities and the highest level of service.

Fortress hub - A hub airport at which there is little or no competition because one airline carries 80 percent or more of passengers using that airport.

Full fare - The most expensive type of fare. An airline's asking price for a fare that has not been put on sale.

Gateway city - The city from which the first international leg of a flight starts. Also, the city at which an international flight first arrives in a country.

Hidden city - A destination city that allows you to fly there for less by deplaning at that city while paying a fare to a more distant city. Also called point-beyond ticketing.

High season - A time of the year when demand for air travel is at its highest. Also called peak season.

Hub - An airport through which an airline funnels passengers for transfer to the airline's other flights going to the passenger's ultimate destination.

Introductory fares - Short-term, low fares used as sales incentives by a new airline. Also, short-term low fares used by established airlines to spur sales on new routes.

Leg - The portion of a flight between two scheduled stops. Also called a segment.

Low season - A time of the year when demand for air travel is at its lowest. Also called the basic season, the off-season or the off-peak season.

Matching fares - Those fares set when one airline matches the fares of another airline.

Maximum permitted mileage - A method of calculating fares that allows, as long as the passenger continues to fly in the same direction, varying the route, changing airlines and making stopovers before reaching the passenger's ultimate destination.

MaxSaver - A type of promotional fare offered on domestic flights.

Nested ticketing - Buying two round-trip promotional-fare tickets instead of one full-fare round-trip ticket to save money.

No-show - A person holding a reservation who does not show up for the flight.

Nonrefundable ticket - A still-unused ticket that cannot be turned back into the airline for a refund of the money paid for the ticket.

Off-line connection - An intermediate stop that involves changing to an aircraft of another airline.

Off-peak hours - The hours from about 9 p.m. to 7 a.m. when demand for air travel is at its lowest.

Off-peak season - A time of the year when demand for air travel is at its lowest. Also called the off-season, the low season or the basic season.

Off-season - A time of the year when demand for air travel is at its lowest. Also called the basic season, the low season or the off-peak season.

On-line connection - An intermediate stop that involves changing to another aircraft of the same airline.

Open jaw - A round trip in which you return from a city different than the destination city of the outbound flight. Or, a round trip in which you return to a city different than the original departure city.

Override - A commission, over and above the standard commission, that airlines pay to travel agents as a sales incentive.

Package - A travel arrangement that groups together and sells at a single price such components as air fare, hotel accommodations, ground transportation and possibly meals.

Peak hours - The hours from about 7 a.m. to 9 p.m. when demand for air travel is at its highest.

Peak season - A time of the year when demand for air travel is at its highest. Also called high season.

Point-beyond ticketing - A strategy that allows you to save money by deplaning at one city while paying a fare to a more distant city. The intermediate city, the passenger's actual destination, is also called a hidden city.

Prepay charge - an airline charge imposed on a ticket booked through a travel agent but issued at the airport by the airline.

Promotional fare - A fare that is priced below full fare to encourage the sale of airline seats that would otherwise remain unsold.

Published fare - an airline's official fare such as those found in an airline's or travel agent's computer reservations system. A published fare may be full or promotional, but not otherwise discounted in anyway.

Rate desk - A service that researches the lowest fares on international itineraries for travel agencies and airlines.

Rebate - A portion of a travel agent's commission given to the customer as a sales incentive.

Restrictions - Special conditions that must be met by the air traveler buying a promotional fare.

Segment - The portion of a flight between two scheduled stops. Also called a leg.

Shoulder season - A time of the year when demand for air travel is at an intermediate level. A season between the low and high seasons.

Split ticketing - Buying two one-way tickets for a round-trip flight. Also called double ticketing.

Status fare - A special fare airlines give to certain classes of passengers, such as military personnel or senior citizens.

Stopover - A break in a flight, usually 24 hours or more, in a city other than the passenger's ultimate destination.

Super saver - A type of promotional fare offered on domestic flights.

Ultra saver - A type of promotional fare offered on domestic flights.

Ultimate super saver - A type of promotional fare offered on domestic flights.

Waitlist - A listing of passengers who are waiting for a fare or a seat that is, at the moment, unavailable.

Yield management - A continuing computer-controlled process that tells an airline the optimum allocation of a flight's seats between full and promotional fares which will yield maximum revenue.

Index

Bob Martin's Travel wiser and better catalog

TeakWood Press

160 Fiesta Drive, Suite 140A
Kissimmee, Florida 34743
800-654-0403

Dear traveler:

On the pages that follow you'll find books, reports and audio tapes that will show you how to travel wiser and better — regardless of whether you travel for business or pleasure.

Some of these publications will turn you into a savvy traveler who consistently saves money — BIG MONEY. Others will show you how to get new travel experiences that will broaden your horizons. And still others develop new travel perspectives that will deepen your insight, enhance your life and give you enormous mental rewards.

Thousands of travelers have benefited from these publications. Now you can put this information to work for you. Mail your order today.

Happy traveling,

Bob Martin

Place your order NOW call toll-free 800-654-0403

Books

These money-saving books are an investment — they'll save you much, much more than their cost

Travel For Less
How to Slash Costs Without Sacrificing Quality
by Bob Martin

Today's travel marketplace operates like a bazaar, selling the same product at different prices. And if you don't know how to shop in the travel bazaar, you're spending way too much money.

Travel For Less reveals how this bazaar works and shows you step by step how to get the lowest prices shopping in it.

Whether you travel for business or pleasure, employ the tips and techniques in *Travel For Less* and you'll slash your costs every time you check into a hotel, rent a car, ride a train, exchange currency, see a show, take a tour or book a cruise. Yes, and even when you shop.

Regardless of your travel budget — be it first class or bare bones — *Travel For Less* will turn you into a savvy traveler who consistently gets maximum value for your money.

$14.95 - Available Fall 1992

Fly There For Less
How to Slash the Cost of Air Travel Worldwide
Third Edition
by Bob Martin

Bankruptcies and mergers have drastically decreased competition among the airlines. As a result, air fares are taking off. Despite rising fares, *Fly There For Less* can show you how to actually slash your air travel costs.

Whether leisure or business traveler, frequent or infrequent flyer, you can use the hundreds of concrete, easily followed tips, techniques and strategies in *Fly There For Less* to consistently save money on both domestic and international flights.

A comprehensive book, *Fly There For Less* reveals how the airlines establish and market their fares, and shows you step by step how to put this knowledge to work cutting the cost of your air travel.

You'll discover how to:

- apply basic strategies that will consistently let you save up to 25 percent on your air fare;
- avoid the unexpected, budget-busing pitfalls of today's air-travel marketplace;
- carry out low-fare searches that will get you the least-expensive fare available;
- cut the cost of flying using little-known fares
- dramatically decrease your fare by selecting the right airline. One traveler using this strategy flew from London to Nairobi, Kenya, for just $230;
- uncover little-known ticket sources that will save you as much as 60 percent off the lowest promotional fares;

Customers agree —you'll SAVE MONEY

"We're a new film company. We travel frequently, but we're on a tight budget. So *Fly There For Less,* has really been a big help to us."
— Katherine Steel, Winter Park, FL

"Fly There For Less" is great — Thanks.
— Iris Gaugahn, Riverton, NJ

"Thanks to your tips on how to get a lower air fare I was able to fly to Texas to see my husband who is in the Air Force. Without your advice I would not have been able to afford the trip. Thanks a lot."
— Sandy Pearce, St. Cloud, FL

"I just received my copy of *Fly There For Less.* I'm delighted with both the book and your fast service, so much so that I want to order another copy for my daughter."
— Jewell March, Oceanside, CA

"Thanks a million for your *Fly There For Less!!*"
— William Lund, N. Attleboro, MA

- open up low-fare opportunities with air courier travel, frequent-flyer plans, last-minute travel clubs and barter exchanges;
- reap savings by being alert to circumstances that offer air-travel bargains;
- master creative techniques such as buying two tickets instead of one to save money.

$16.95

Reviewers agree— you'll SAVE MONEY

"(Fly There For Less) is a coherent guide to ferreting out favorable fares....a handy reference for cost-conscious travelers....fascinating."
— *Travel & Leisure*

"Fly There For Less guides the air traveler through a maze of air fares....you can save some mega bucks from Martin's creative techniques and strategies."
— *Los Angeles Times*

"An exciting new travel guide called *Fly There For Less* can save you a substantial amount of money."
— **Arthur Frommer**

"Author Bob Martin helps air travelers get the lowest fares on domestic and international flights."
— *USA Today*

"An informative new handbook, *Fly There For Less,* can help the harried business traveler who doesn't have unlimited resources."
— *The Philadelphia Inquirer*

"In this easy-to-read book, Martin gives you the details so you can decide which (strategies) will work for you."
— *Seattle Post-Intelligencer*

"There is no doubt that every business traveler out there would benefit from Martin's book *Fly There For Less.*"
— *Small Business Opportunities*

"Included in this book are more strategies for saving money in the air than anyone ever thought possible. This is a great book for travelers looking for ways to avoid handing the airline industry more than they have to."
— *Going Places*

"This guide, whether you travel for business or pleasure, will give you timeless techniques and tips on how to pay the lowest possible airfare every time you fly."
— *Chattanooga News-Free Press*

"Fly There For Less details cost-cutting methods that can be used by any international traveler."
— *Toronto Sun*

"In well-ordered, logical fashion, *(Fly There For Less)* analyzes strategies for locating cheaper fares. He seems to cover all the options....A most helpful guide."
— *Booklist*

You can now have travel expert BOB MARTIN reveal his MONEY-SAVING SECRETS at your meeting or convention

For details, call Bob at 1-407-348-7330

Traveler's Reports

Get the in-depth information you need — in a capsule format

These tightly focused, concentrated four- and five-page reports each cover a specialized area of travel. You get details, facts, how-to information, step-by-step directions, names, addresses, telephone numbers — everything you need to know about your report's subject.

Prepared by travel authority Bob Martin, *Traveler's Reports* are written in a clear, concise style that makes them easy to read. And they are computer generated, so you get the latest, up-to-date data.

SAVE!!! Buy in multiples of three — any three reports for only $10

Traveling farther for less

#101 - How to cut your transportation costs by flying as an AIR COURIER

Here's everything you need to know to get in on the BIG SAVINGS available when you fly as an air courier — step-by-step directions plus complete contact information.

$4/any three reports for $10

#106 - How to SAVE BIG BUCKS shopping in the travel marketplace

If you want to cut your travel costs, get this report! Today's travel marketplace resembles a bazaar. To get maximum value for your travel dollar, you have to know the ins and outs of shopping in this bazaar. Use the tips and techniques described in this report and you'll travel farther while keeping more of your money in YOUR wallet.

$4/any three reports for $10

> "A sincere thank you. Despite the short time from the date I ordered till the date I needed the book, your prompt, priority shipment got it to my door on my husband's birthday. Thank you so much!"
> — Carol Bonnet, Scottsdale, AZ

#108 - TRAVEL FREE — Yes, there's one way you can actually do it

Organizing travel groups can be your ticket to free travel — and on some trips even PAID travel. This report gives you the easy-to-follow details.

$4/any three reports for $10

#112 - The air traveler's EASY low-fare finder — for use with *Fly There For Less, Third Edition.*

Designed to be used with *Fly There For Less: How to Slash the Cost of Air Travel Worldwide, Third Edition*, this must-have work sheet helps you organize your search for the lowest air fare. The report also directs you to specific pages in *Fly There For Less* for the detailed information you need to successfully conduct your low-fare search.

$4/any three reports for $10

> "Many thanks for your excellent service."
> — H. F. Mac Neil, Gloucester, MA

#113 - How to motivate your employees to save on travel costs

You can't control your travel costs unless your traveling employees are on your side. Get the tips and strategies that will have your business travelers SAVING YOU BUCKS by watching their travel budgets like they were spending their own money.

$4/any three reports for $10

#114 - How to pick the frequent-flyer program that gives YOU the most FREE TRIPS

At last!!! A step-by-step guide through the maze of airline frequent-flyer programs. With this report you'll zero in on the program that best matches your travel patterns and your mileage-award goals to give you the most free travel for the least miles.

$4/any three reports for $10

402 - Travel Insurance — What you need and what you need to know BEFORE buying

Today's travel marketplace is complex. And it often requires you to make substantial, up-front monetary commitments which are frequently nonrefundable. This report takes you through the types of insurance available and shows you how to determine:
1) If you really need insurance;
2) and if you do, exactly what coverage you should by.
Put this report's information to work protecting not only your travel funds, but possibly your entire nest egg as well.

$4/any three reports for $10

Geotravel—don't just visit a place, experience it!

#201 - What you need to know BEFORE you book an African safari

Get the detailed pros and cons that will make your safari a SUCCESS: where and when to go, whether to book here or there, how to choose a guide, whether or not to tent. PLUS the questions you need to ask before you book a safari. PLUS complete contact information on domestic and African-based safari operators.

$4/any three reports for $10

#202 - Trekking — How to make your organized walk a SUCCESS

This invigorating, mild form of adventure travel brings you close to nature, in the manner of yesterday's explorers. Whether you want to retrace the steps of Machú Picchú-discoverer Hiram Bingham or walk a Maori trail in New Zealand, this report will show you how to make your trek a success.

$4/any three reports for $10

#301 - Volunteering — How to travel for a cause and return richer than when you left

Give yourself an adventure and help others at the same time. Your volunteer travels can range from signing on to a research expedition to lending a hand on an archaeological dig to tagging leatherneck turtles in the Caribbean. This report details the types of projects available to you, how to select your project and how to make contact.

$4/any three reports for $10

#303 - Homestays — How to gain the ultimate cultural experience by sharing a foreign family's life and home

A homestay lets you really get to know a country and its people. In this report you'll get the facts on how your homestay will work and, of course, complete contact information. This is MUST-READING for the geotraveler. A homestay will turn your travel memories from lifeless postcard images to the faces of the friends you've made.

$4/any three reports for $10

"Thanks for the prompt delivery, it actually surprised me."
— Ray Lang, Bay City, Texas

#304 - Meet the people — Enrich your travels by getting to know the local people

Learn how to make the foreign social contacts that will add immeasurably to the quality of your travels. From organized tourist-office programs to home exchanges to turning the strangers you encounter into friends a variety of opportunities are available to add life to your travels. And they're all spelled out for you in this report.

$4/any three reports for $10

Audio Cassettes

Sixty information-packed minutes, with travel authority Bob Martin, to show you how to travel wiser and better

901 - How NOT to pay full fare on a short-notice flight

This audio tape will SAVE YOU HUNDREDS AND HUNDREDS of dollars the first time you use its tips and strategies. If a short-notice business trip, a family emergency or a sudden change in plans has you scurrying around for an airline ticket, you won't be able to meet the advance-purchase requirement of a low-cost promotional fare. And you'll be reaching deep into your bank account to finance the purchase of a full-fare ticket that can cost as much as 500 PERCENT MORE than the lowest promotional fares.

But you don't have to pay that full fare! On this tape Bob Martin reveals the details of more than a dozen alternative strategies that will let you slash the cost of a ticket for a short-notice flight. Get this tape NOW and don't get caught unprepared.

$10.95 - 60-minute audio cassette

902 - How to travel as if the planet and its human, wild and natural life mattered

You might not realize it, but YOUR travels may be contributing to the world's economic and environmental problems. But they don't have to. Whether you call it "alternative travel," "responsible travel" or "ecotourism," you can journey so as to have a positive impact on the areas you visit. And far from taking the fun out of your trips, alternative travel can add new excitement and pleasure.

Discover what alternative travel is all about — and how you can use its ideas, concepts and techniques to not only make the world a better place but to enrich your travels as well.

$10.95 - 60-minute audio cassette

> "Thank you for the way you do business."
> — Lee Nicholson, Ankeny, Iowa

903 - Geotravel — Don't just visit a place, experience it

If your travels are overly commercial, involving only passive sightseeing of lifeless monuments or pursuing mindless recreation, you're wasting your time and money.

Now you can put a new face on your travels and bring back more than just souvenirs. Bob Martin has developed the concept of "geotravel," a method of traveling that will turn your trips into stimulating, rewarding journeys of exploration and discovery.

On this tape Bob explains these geotravel concepts and shows you how to use them to raise the quality of your travels, expand your horizons and achieve personal growth. As a geotraveler you'll gain an understanding and an appreciation of the places you go, the things you see and the people you meet.

And if you're keeping an eye on your travel budget, you'll get an additional dividend — geotravel costs less and gives you more value for your dollar.

Get this tape and see how you can use geotravel techniques to put more excitement, fun and MEANING into your next trip.

$10.95 - 60-minute audio cassette

Travel Books

Additional books available from TeakWood Press

Eco-Vacations
Enjoy Yourself and Save the Earth
by Evelyn Kaye

Take an eco-vacation and you won't just visit a place, you'll even help SAVE IT! *Eco-Vacations* shows you not only how to enrich your travels but how to benefit the evironment as well. Get the details on hundreds of eco-vacations around the world—scientific research projects, wilderness treks, archaeology digs and more.

$22.50

Travel and Learn
The New Guide to Educational Travel
by Evelyn Kaye

Want to expand your horizons, stretch your mind, face new challenges — and still have a good time? Then you need *Travel and Learn.* You'll get descriptions and details for more than a thousand educational trips worldwide offered by 162 carefully selected organizations.

$23.95

Orlando and Disney World
A TravelVenture Guide

Third Edition
by Bob Martin

This book gives you information found in no other single guide. *Orlando and Disney World* saves you time and money by providing all the facts, information and inside tips needed to explore *both* Disney World and the Orlando area.

It's packed with the details that make a visit run smoothly, such as prices, times required to see attractions, restaurant menu summaries and more. The guide's 50 maps also make getting around easy.

$9.95

"The *Orlando and Disney World* guidebook is FANTASTIC! Many Thanks."
— M. Valleau, Kitchner, Ontario

"I loved your book *Orlando and Disney World*. I read it cover to cover — making notes. It gave me helpful information that I couldn't get anywhere else and allowed me to plan and organize my trip. I especially appreciated the prices — they helped with budgeting. Thank you."
— Dora Bodi, Monroe, MI

Place your order NOW — call toll-free 800-654-0403
Or complete and mail the coupon below

Please RUSH the books, tapes and/or *Traveler's Reports* I've indicated below so I may put this information to work helping me travel wiser and better.

Mail check/money order to
TeakWood Press
160 Fiesta Dr., Suite 140A
Kissimmee, FL 34743

Name _____

Address _____

City _____ State _____ Zip _____

Qty	Title	Price	Total
	Travel For Less	$14.95	
	Fly There For Less, Third Edition	$16.95	
	Eco-Vacations	$22.50	
	Travel and Learn	$23.95	
	Orlando and Disney World, Third Edition	$9.95	
	Audio cassettes (Write tape numbers here)	$10.95 each	
	Traveler's Reports (Write report numbers here)	$4 each/ 3 for $10	
	Total for books/reports/audio tapes		
	Florida residents add 7% sales tax		
	Add $3 shipping for 1st book/tape and $.75 each additional (Reports shipped free)		
	Grand total enclosed		